Official Reference Book

Official Reference Book

PRESS CLUB
of CHICAGO
OldestPressClub
, in the World ,
INCORPORATED 1879

1922

Published by Press Club
of Chicago

Announcement

THIS BOOK of the Press Club of Chicago is intended as a reference work on representative men and on representative business interests of the Chicago district. It embraces in scope accurate and comprehensive information on individual leaders of the day in finance, manufacture, commerce, politics and society. As the Chicago district has become one of the world's greatest granaries, so has it achieved wonders in industrial progress, in commercial prestige and in assuming and maintaining its position as the transportation center of the continent. The volume gives adequate space to these great financial, commercial and manufacturing interests, as well as to the individuals directing their progress.

IT IS issued not only for its future historic value, but to meet a demand for a compact reference volume.

TO THE many hundreds of members of the Press Club of Chicago, it will be a priceless souvenir as an artistic reminder of associations identified with generations of endeavor and success.

PRESS CLUB OF CHICAGO

Chicago—the Miracle City

"The Boundless Regions of the West must send their products to the East through this point. This will be the gate of Empire, this the seat of Empire."—Riene Robert Cavelier Sieur de La Salle writing of the present site of Chicago in 1682.

HISTORY OF THE PRESS CLUB OF CHICAGO

THE PRESS CLUB OF CHICAGO has become historic. Its meaning and membership are holding a growth equal at all times to that of the city and its combination of various powers has likewise become an indispensable factor for good.

The camaraderie and hospitality found within the club's precincts have drawn to it the commanding from all walks. Many of its members address world audiences and sometimes they create public opinion, but always they sway its course. Their qualities of intellect, industry, disillusion and honesty give these men at once a sympathy with and a common hold on the real affairs of life and make possible their cohesion as an organized body.

Through the vicissitudes of its forty-two-year existence and through the financial depressions of the period, the club has come unscarred. It has always emerged victor in battles with the hydra-headed monster, Debt. Internal dissension bobbed up and was just as suddenly smitten down, and the course of the club toward greater achievement has remained unaltered. Always, the spirit of the great men whose genius went into the shaping of the organization has lived.

Across the horizon of the Press Club of Chicago have flashed, at various times, great names in business and the learned professions, besides those of so many men who have earned renown as authors and journalists. Of the latter, these were and are Press Club men: Eugene Field, James Whitcomb Riley, Mark Twain, George Ade, Ben King, Stanley Waterloo, Opie Read, Bob Burdette, Henry Watterson, Charles Page Bryan, Irvin S. Cobb, Ernest McGaffey, Will Levington Comfort, John McGovern, Wilbur Nesbit, William Slavens McNutt, Richard Henry Little, Henry Irving Greene, Ring Lardner, Wallace Rice, Emerson Hough, William Lightfoot Visscher, Jack Lait and a brilliant line of others.

The Bohemian Club was the first organization of writers and men of the kindred arts in Chicago, of which there remains a trace. Patterned after the Waverly Club of New York, of which Edgar Allan Poe was a member, and intended as a protest against the priggish and puritanical conventions of that period, the club was organized in 1865.

The members inhabited two rooms in the Fourth National Bank building, at the northwest corner of Monroe and Dearborn streets, the present location of the First National Bank building. In keeping with the club's attitude toward society, the clubrooms were invested with little pomp. The club's life was brief, for it died in 1866 because of the lackadaisical attitude of its members. Elias Colbert, of the Tribune, who later became widely known for his discoveries in astronomy, was the president.

The Chicago Press Club, in reality a mutual aid and burial organization, came next, in 1867. Guy Magee, of the Republican and subsequently with the Tribune, the Inter-Ocean and the Times, was secretary and by the force of his energy, the club had a deal of vigor.

One of the functions for which the Press Club of then is noted was its banquet of December 10, 1870, given in the Briggs House, at which the honored guests were Dr. Edwards, known professionally throughout Europe as well as America; Lieutenant Governor Bross, also part owner of the Tribune; and Col. Frank A. Eastman, postmaster and editor of the Morning Post. This was the first formal dinner laid by newspaper men of Chicago.

A Press Club, whose quarters consisted of two rooms in McVicker's Theater building, was next in line of descent, and was organized in 1869, with Ferris, dramatic critic of the Times, as president. It was little more than a shadow that was lost forever during the big fire.

1

In 1872 and 1873, there was another organization of newspaper men under the name of a Press Club. It made little impression and soon was forgotten.

The next and first real club may be said to have been prefigured by the club of which Ferris was president, in that it had at first no strictly newspaper limitation in membership. It was called the Owl Club. In the sense implied by heredity, the Owl Club's continuity is attested by our own present Press Club of Chicago; for out of the Owl Club, this Press Club grew.

The admission of a vast number of opulent and free-handed members, for the most part board of trade men, set things whirling at a rate so dizzy that by the end of the next year the professional members were out of breath. Action was too swift and the air too rich for them. A desire for another try at the real thing was heightened by the next few months and this desire found its protagonist in Sam Steele, of the Chicago Times, in 1879.

To Mark Twain is commonly ascribed the origin of the Press Club of Chicago. As a matter of fact, it was Steele's suggestion that resulted in organization. When the business of considering the new club had been taken up, it was explained to Twain, and he was asked for his opinion of it. He commended it and said he could see no reason why it should not go through. That was all there was to his share of it.

The organization was effected at a meeting shortly afterward in one of the private parlors of the Tremont House. Franc Wilkie was called to the presidency, and Elwyn Barron was made secretary. Joe Dunlop was commissioned to find quarters and he obtained one room in the Morrison block at Madison and Clark streets. For more than a year, that room was the only home of the club. Later other rooms were engaged until the club had two entire floors and part of another, which it occupied for fifteen years.

The club became a corporate body on January 11, 1880. The reason for incorporating was that, income being uncertain and outgo a sure thing, individual members became uneasy lest they be held personally liable for club debts. The charter shut out that danger and somehow or other the club contrived to pay its way.

From the Morrison block, the club moved into a building in Madison street, between Clark and Dearborn streets, which had been known as the Hershey Music Hall. Its stay there was short. Then was taken the upper floor of the building at 106 West Madison street (old number), diagonally across from the Hershey location, and retained for ten years. The old house of the University Club at 26 North Dearborn street was purchased in 1907. While it was being made ready, the club occupied a floor over King's Restaurant in Fifth avenue, opposite the Daily News office. After it moved into the Dearborn street place, it stayed there until November, 1915. Then lease was taken of the upper floor of the City Hall Square building, 139 North Clark street, and from there the club moved into its present quarters on the second floor of the Ashland block.

The Press Club of Chicago is a growing power in public affairs, perhaps more than any similar organization in the northern states. One reason is in the peculiar quality of its membership. As a club, it is not the shaper of public policies. But it is distinctively the home and meeting ground of the men by whose daily work the newspapers of Chicago are brought out.

The combined industry of these men expresses every day all there is of opinion, aspiration and realization in the swiftly changing elements of this formative age. No man or party can use it for any special or personal purpose, least of all for publicity. But the responsibility and the power of the public press are carried by its individual members, each in his own position and the work that position demands; and carried with jealous conscience.

2

CHICAGO'S EARLY HISTORY

FOR GENERATIONS before the white man began his work of upbuilding the modern city, when for a thousand miles around brooded the silence of the wilderness, nature had made of Chicago a point of importance, the rendezvous of parties from far and wide bent on missions alike of war and peace.

Lying at the head of Lake Michigan, in the heart of the richest river valley on the globe, to Chicago all roads lead, even as of old they led to Rome. Into this pours the golden stream of wheat from a thousand miles of western prairie. The cornfields of Kansas and Nebraska, the livestock grown on Texas plains and those of Alberta, the forests of Wisconsin and the iron mines of Minnesota yield alike their share of tribute, with the inevitable result that here in less than a century has developed one of the chief primary markets and principal manufacturink centers of the universe.

It was inevitable that the site of Chicago should be known to Europeans from the time they first penetrated the interior of the continent.

With the momentous exploration by Louis Joliet in 1673, the recorded history of Chicago really begins. The Mississippi had been discovered by De Soto over a century before and the French had started colonizing the lower valley of the St. Lawrence. Joliet, sent out as the representative of the New France, followed the course of the Mississippi far enough to learn that it emptied into the Gulf of Mexico. Soon after Joliet came the Sieur de La Salle, bent on realizing his imperial vision of a New France stretching from the St Lawrence to the Gulf of Mexico.

While the missionaries were laying the foundations for the Church in Illinois, its commercial possibilities were being no less eagerly exploited by the traders. Of these, La Salle was for almost a decade, until his death in 1687, the leading figure; and from his Fort St. Louis, on Starved Rock, for a decade and a half longer his chief lieutenant, Tonty, continued to dominate and monopolize the trade of the region.

During the fore part of this period, the dream was first conceived of opening a waterway from the Great Lakes to the Gulf of Mexico. By cutting a canal of half a league at the Chicago portage, Joliet reported, a bark could sail from Lake Erie to the Gulf. A few years later, Joliet took sharp issue with this statement of Joliet, showing clearly the uselessness of such a canal for all practical purposes.

In later years the error of Joliet effected lodgment in the public mind and in 1836, the digging of the Michigan and Illinois canal was started, but there followed years of disappointment and it was not until 1848 when the first boat passed through the canal.

The period of French occupation of the Northwest continued for ninety years after Joliet's voyage of 1673. During these years, the prosecution of the fur trade constituted the sole economic interest of France in this region, to effect which posts were established at strategic points throughout the Northwest.

Broadly-viewed, the Revolution in the West was a twenty-year struggle, ending only with Wayne's victory over the Indians in 1794 and the evacuation by the British two years later of their posts in the Northwest. The lesson driven home by the bayonets of Wayne at the Battle of Fallen Timbers at length convinced the Tribesmen that the power of the "Long Knives," as the Americans were known, could no longer be ignored.

Fort Dearborn was Chicago for almost three decades. When the troops arrived at the mouth of the Chicago in 1803, they found here several traders, huts or cabins occupied by French-Canadians. As at all wilderness outposts, life flowed on in humdrum fashions during the years from 1803 to 1812. The outburst of war with the mother country rudely shattered this complacence. Peace with Great Britain was concluded at the close of 1814. Governmental decision resulted in the American flag flying over Chicago once more in 1816.

For several years life at the New Fort Dearborn went on much as in the

3

old days before the war. Meanwhile, far away from the wilderness stockade at the bend of the sluggish river forces were developing which were destined to remove forever the menace of Indian attack and to usher in the birth of the new Chicago. These were, in general, the persistent advance of American settlers westward, and in particular the construction of the Erie canal. The obstacle to white settlement presented by the Indian ownership and occupancy of the soil was removed by the Black Hawk War of 1832.

The spring of 1833 ushered in the first and greatest boom in the history of Chicago. Over night, as it were, the sleepy military outpost was transformed into a mushroom city, attended by all the concomitants of ugliness and vigor characteristic of such a development. By 1837, Chicago had become a community of several thousand souls and achieved the dignity of a city. About the same time, President Jackson pricked the bubble of the nation's speculative mania by the issuance of his famous specie circular and the severest financial panic of our national history ensued.

In 1807, Fulton demonstrated the practicability of steam navigation and before two decades had passed, steamboats were penetrating to the upper reaches of the Mississippi and the remotest shores of the Great Lakes. This development of steam-propelled navigation was the logical complement to the opening of the Erie Canal in promoting the settlement of the west. It remained, however, to apply steam power to transportation by land, and about the year 1830 this application was begun.

We have now reached the most important development in the history of Chicago, for it is scarcely too much to say that the modern city as we know it now is the product of the railroads. It is characteristic of Chicago's outlook and of the sources from which her economic strength is drawn, that the city's first railroad ran west rather than east, being designed not to connect her with the Atlantic, but to bring to her markets and wharves the produce of her rich hinterland.

In the lead mine region of northwestern Illinois there had begun about 1821 an era of vigorous exploitation and development, and within a few years the mining country was dotted with villages and towns. Chief among these was Galena. In the thirties, a charter had been taken out for the Galena and Chicago Union railroad, but for ten years, nothing further was done. Then William B. Ogden became president and under his administration, actual construction was begun in 1847 and a year later Chicago's first railroad extended to the Des Plaines river. Not until 1853 was Freeport reached, and the line was never built to Galena, for by that time the Illinois Central had entered the field and the Galena had arranged to use the Central's tracks from Freeport to Galena. Thus was constructed the first line of what is now the North Western system. In 1852, the Michigan Southern and the Northern Indiana ran the first train into Chicago from the east and three months later the Michigan Central entered the city.

Meanwhile Milwaukee had not abandoned the contest, and during the early fifties not one but two steel roads were being pushed westward from that city. One reached Prarie du Chien in 1857, the other entered La Crosse a year later.

The railroads completed the work which nature had begun of making Chicago the great central market of the continent. Henceforth, her growth was to be conditioned only by the growth of the country itself. In 1850, after seventeen years of development unaided by the railroads, the city had a population of 30,000; by 1860, this had more than tripled, and in the following decade, notwithstanding the Civil War, it tripled once more. Twenty years later, the population was 1,100,000 and in the Twenty years ending with 1910, this figure was almost exactly doubled.

Although the Civil War dislocated the business of Chicago, it did not greatly retard, apparently, the city's growth. What might have been in the absence of war cannot be known; but despite it the city grew from 110,000 in 1860 to 200,000 in 1866; and by 1870 another hundred thousand had been added.

Then came the Great Fire of 1871, which destroyed 17,000 buildings and left 100,000 homeless.

4

LEVY MAYER

LEVY MAYER, one of America's foremost authorities on constitutional and corporation law, was born in Richmond, Va., Oct. 23, 1860; s. of Henry D. and Clara (Goldsmith) Mayer; grad. of Chicago High Sch., 1874; took spl. studies at Yale and at law dept., Yale, 1876; Asst. librarian for Chicago Law Inst., 1876-81, and while so engaged, edited and revised MS. of Judge David Rorer's work on interstate or pvt. internat. law, and on jud. and execution sales. In active practice since 1881; sr. mem., Mayer, Meyer, Austrian & Platt. Mem. Const. Conv. of Ill.; mem. State Council of Defense, Ill.; mem. Am. Ill., and Chicago Bar Assn., Am. Econ. Assn., Western Econ. Soc., Acad. Polit. Science. Clubs: Union League, Iroquois, Press, Mid-Day, Southern, South Shore Country, Lake Shore Country (Chicago); Lawyers and Bankers (New York); Old Colony, Plymouth Country (Mass.). Homes: Chicago and Manomet, Mass. Offices: 25 Broadway, New York, and 208 S. La Salle St., Chicago.

Died - - - - - Aug. 14, 1922

JOHN STOCKER MILLER

JOHN S. MILLER, lawyer, was born in Louisville Landing, N. Y., May 24, 1847; son of Jane (McLeod) and John Miller. He received A. B. degree from St. Lawrence University, Canton, N. Y., 1869, and studied in law department, 1869-70. He married Ann Gross, Chicago, in 1887. Children: John S., Jr., Janet (Mrs. Alan C. Dixon). Admitted to New York bar in 1879; professor in mathematics and Latin and Greek in St. Lawrence University. He came to Chicago in 1874 and engaged in the practice of law, becoming a member of the firm of Herbert, Quick & Miller. Following Mr. Herbert's death, the firm became Miller & Quick. He then became associated with Senator Henry W. Leman, 1886; Merritt Starr was admitted in 1890 and later George R. Peck succeeded Mr. Leman, firm becoming Peck, Miller & Starr; at the time of Mr. Miller's death, Miller, Starr, Brown, Packard & Peckham. During his term as corporation counsel for City of Chicago, 1891-3, he argued famous Lake Front case against Illinois Central Railroad Company. Director of Chicago Morris Plan Bank. Member of American, Illinois and Chicago Bar Associations. Clubs: Chicago, Union League, Wayfarers, University, Onwentsia, Hamilton, Exmoor. Home: 1443 Astor St.

𝔇𝔦𝔢𝔡 - - - - - 𝔉𝔢𝔟. 16, 1922

HOW LAND RECORDS ESCAPED GREAT FIRE

ONE of the great deeds born of the Chicago fire that still stands out after 50 years of retrospection is the saving of the land records of three private companies, which cleared 1,000,000 land titles and prevented squatters from seizing valuable lands. By this act, the city's rehabilitation was speeded and a condition amounting almost to anarchy was warded off. A. R. Marriott, vice-president of the Chicago Title and Trust Co., tells the following story of how these records were saved:

The new Chicago that has been built in the fifty years since the Great Fire of October 8 and 9, 1871, makes the story of those strenuous days when no one knew what he owned, or could prove it if he did, seem like a "tale that is told." All public records had been destroyed—those of real estate ownership with the rest—and for days and weeks after the fire the most agitated question was how real estate titles could be acceptably and quickly proved. About 1,000,000 titles in Cook county were jeopardized.

The first issue of the Chicago Times, three weeks after the fire, featured editorially the real estate title situation and illustrated the seriousness of the "squatter" trouble.

Many proposals to insure property ownership were made, one of the chief being stated by Judge Gary that every owner of every lot in the county file a bill in chancery. The Times commended this as an adequate legal measure, but deplored the delay involved, declaring that this time was one requiring something more than law and precedent. It epitomized the suggestion of other lawyers, and then proposed the only feasible method, and the one which was adopted. That was to legalize the private title records of the three abstract firms, which were later to consolidate and form the nucleus of the present Chicago Title & Trust Company.

From a prized copy of the Times in the possession of J. P. O'Connor, of the Chicago Title & Trust Co., is quoted the following:

"We have in Chicago three firms—Shortall & Hoard, Jones & Sellers, and Chase Brothers & Company—who have saved nearly all of their papers including the indexes to every piece of property in Cook county, and actual abstracts to a large proportion of this property. We have one firm—J. H. Rees & Co.—who have saved copies of all the maps and all the plats ever made of Cook county property. There is a lapse of only one day, the Saturday before the fire—in these unofficial records, and the transactions of that day have probably been adjusted by the exchange of new papers.

"These abstract offices have had the reputation of being among the most reliable in the country. Nobody has hesitated, heretofore, to accept their copies of the records as official—why should not some equitable plan be provided, by which these copies, carefully compared and compiled, should become official, without, of course, debarring remedy in law, but providing for the security of bona fide purchasers or loaners of money on trust deeds?"

What the Times proposed was done by an act of the legislature accepting the private records of the three abstract firms. These old volumes are now to be found in the offices of the Chicago Title & Trust Company, watched over by J. P. O'Connor who helped to make them in the ante-fire days.

The story of how the records were saved is a dramatic one. In the employ of the company is one other person who has been with it since before the fire —W. F. Grimes. He was a boy of 18 when he helped to save the books on the night of the great fire. He reached the office of Shortall & Hoard, in the old

7

Larmon block, on Clark and Washington, between 12 and 1 o'clock a. m. John Shortall was there also, and half a dozen others. They watched the fire until the courthouse cupola across the street took fire. Then Mr. Shortall exclaimed: "We must have an express wagon within the next five minutes or we are utterly lost."

He took up his stand on Washington st. and a friend who was with him went to Clark st. to intercept the first wagon that came along. The first was a small one-horse express wagon on the Clark st. side. The driver was induced to come around to the Washington side, and the loading of the books began. When the wagon was full it was found that only a quarter of the essential records had been saved. But just then a two-horse truck drove up, and Joe Stockton jumped down and turned over the truck and driver to Shortall with the comment: "I think, John, this is just the thing you want."

Great volumes were transferred from the small wagon, and the remainder of the books stowed on the truck. All the while the flames were roaring and brands were flying continually upon the books, which Mr. Shortall packed, while six of the boys carried them downstairs. Then when the flames became finally so hot that further work was too dangerous, the truck worked its way down Washington to Dearborn and finally to Mr. Shortall's home on Prairie av. about 3 a. m.

CHICAGO TODAY

CHICAGO'S one great thought after the fire of 1871 was to go ahead as if nothing had happened. The attitude of the whole world helped Chicago in this determination.

Messages from merchants in the east and west with whom they had dealt poured in to Chicago business men, saying, "We know that you will need stock to replace what has been burned. Your credit is good. Order as usual." And Chicago did order. Merchants, without hesitating, ordered stocks of good and later hunted up places to sell them. Bankers agreed to resume business and the following week they resumed payment on the dollar for dollar basis. This action on the part of the Chicago banks gave the whole country confidence as to the ultimate outcome.

Refusing to take advantage of the circumstances, the Chicago Board of Trade, instead of repudiating its contracts formed before the fire, agreed as one man to keep them and did.

As soon as practicable, the work of distribution of relief supplies and funds to the 100,000 made homeless by the conflagration was taken over by the Relief and Aid Society. The churches helped in all this, gathering the frightened flocks together, furnishing shelter when they had a building left.

The Congregational Church at Washington and Ann streets became for the time the City Hall and the Methodist Episcopal Church on Wabash Avenue the post office.

With line and boundaries all but wiped out, the real estate men were nevertheless the first in the work of rehabilatation. The refuse from the razed buildings was carted away as rapidly as possible and dumped into the lagoon formerly dividing the Illinois Central tracks from the shore opposite Lake Front. As fast as the foundations of buildings were uncovered, their walls began to be rebuilt. They were made fireproof, as far as feasible. The Nixon building, the practically fireproof building downtown that had withstood the test in the big fire, became the model. Concrete was used in lining walls and covering iron work, and soon experiments with steel resulted in the "Chicago steel skeleton construction."

As for the visible governing powers of the city, they were soon housed in a building on the "reservoir lot," owned by the city, at Adams and La Salle streets, completed and occupied by 1872 and which continued to do duty until 1885. Being a mere bird cage of brick, with no ornament or convenience, it soon became known as the "Rookery."

In 1873, a reading room was opened in the City Hall and in October of the same year, Dr. W. F. Poole was appointed librarian and had a circulating department in operation the following year. The Chicago Historical Society, organized in 1854, had a lbirary, museum and art gallery at the time of the fire, and began to rebuild and re-collect soon after. The Chicago Academy of Sciences had specimens and a library of great significance. Northwestern University, founded in 1851; Chicago University, in embryonic form, organized as a Babtist college in 1855; Loyola University, chartered in 1858, all afforded opportunities for higher culture and Chicago's public schools were of notable excellence.

Chicago had enjoyed forty short "seasons" of opera before the fire. The forty-first opened in 1872 with Theodore Wachtel, a German singer in "The Postillion" and "Trovatore." The forty-second season took place at the Academy of Music and was followed with a program at McVicker's. Meanwhile, Chicagoans were not above going to minstrels and this form of entertainment vaulted to a high pinnacle.

Another evidence of culture life here in the seventies was the opening of Central Music hall in 1879. The building stood at State and Randolph streets,

9

DR. NELSON MORTIMER PERCY

NELSON MORTIMER PERCY, surgeon, was born in Dexter, Ia., Nov. 7, 1875; s. of Mary (Amidon) and Mortimer Percy; ed. in Dexter High School; attended Dexter Normal School, 1894-95; M. D. degree from Rush Medical College, 1899. Married Adaline M. Nickel, Chicago, Sept. 30, 1907. Dr. Percy, after leaving college, was attending surgeon at Augustana Hospital, Chicago; surgeon, St. Mary's Hospital, Chicago; professor of Clinical Surgery, Univ. of Ill. He served as Lieutenant Colonel, Medical Corps, U. S. A., during the war; organized Base Hospital No. 11 and went to France as its surgical director. Fellow, American Coll. of Surgeons; Am. Surgical Assn.; Internat. Surgical Soc. Mem. Am. Medical Assn.; and Ill. and Chicago Med. Socs. Clubs: University, Press, Army and Navy, Chicago Yacht. Home: 2100 Lincoln Park West. Office: 2106 Sedgwick st.

10

a site later absorbed by Marshall Field & Co. Chicago of the seventies was also devoted to the legitimate drama and the stock company at McVicker's furnished excellent support for such traveling stars as McCullough, Booth, Joe Jefferson and Maggie Mitchell.

Having got her house in order after the fire, Chicago set about devising a plan to receive visitors on a large scale. The result was the great exposition building on the Lake Front where the Art Institute stands. It first housed the Industrial Exposition, which became an annual affair for many years. Before the exposition building was removed, Edgar Lee Brown, of its management, proposed the idea of a celebration of the landing of Columbus in America. It was opened in October, 1873 and at once demonstrated Chicago's exhaustless spirit.

Out of the various private entertainments given by men grew the Chicago club, the pioneer club of the west and for many years the only social club in Chicago. The Chicago Yacht club was organized in July, 1870, the Farragut Boat club in 1872, the Chicago Cricket club in 1876, and the Bicycle club in 1879. Chicago was represented at the meeting of the National Professional Baseball Association in New York in 1871 by the "White Stockings," otherwise known as the Chicago club, which by 1876 became the champion club.

In 1875, the re-organization of the city's government was effected under the general incorporation act. In 1876, the board of public works was abolished and the single-commissioner system instituted. Such changes are not accomplished without action of organized civic bodies and chief among these were the Citizens' Association, founded in 1874, and the Commercial club, which came in 1877.

The newspapers of that period were the Journal, founded in 1844; the Tribune, founded in 1847, and the bulwark of Republicanism; the Times founded in 1854 and with Democratic leanings; the Inter Ocean, founded in 1872 by J. Y. Scammon; the News, first issued on Christmas Day, 1875.

Events touching every interest in Chicago in the eighties were the introduction of electricity in the form of light and telephone and service and the organization of the Sanitary District, with a view to purifying the city's water supply by way of the drainage canal.

The Sanitary District was organized under the acts of 1887 and 1889. Attempts to divert the course of the current in the Chicago river and its branches had been made early in the eighties and before that, by means of powerful pumping stations within the city limits. Chicago, under the new acts, was empowered to go beyond its borders, cut through the rocky stratum separating the Lakes from the Mississippi water systems and purify her own water system.

The first electric lights here were seen in 1880, a 50-light dynamo having been installed in the basement of the Y. M. C. A. building. Telephones had been talked of since 1878, when the Bell and Edison systems began to operate in Chicago, but it was in April, 1881, that the Chicago Telephone Company bought out the Bell Company of Illinois and the American District Telegraph Company, consolidating the Bell and Edison systems and giving the city a practical service.

A record in the development of commerce was made in 1880, not only throughout the Northwest but also in the direction of foreign trade. Chicago acquired two carriers, the Grand Trunk and the Wabash, St. Louis and Pacific. The Chicago & Atlantic Railway was opened in 1883, and with its connection, the New York, Lake Erie & Western, formed a direct line to the seaboard.

In addition to the enormous growth of the packing industry of Chicago, there was development along allied lines. The estimated value of wood and hides handled in Chicago in 1885 was $25,000,000, and the value of raw furs brought here about that time was between one and two million dollars annually. A notable feature of the grocery trade has been the importation of teas and coffees.

The lumber industry, already the largest in the country, in 1884 added an-

11

EDWARD J. KELLY

EDWARD J. KELLY, civil engineer, was born in Chicago in 1877; son ol Helen (Lang) and Stephen Kelly. He was educated under private tutorship and in the evening technical schools of Chicago. In 1920 he was married to Mary Edmunda Roche (deceased). Son, Edward Joseph, Jr. Mr. Kelly was remarried in 1922, his bride being Margaret E. Kirk. He entered the employ of the Sanitary District of Chicago, rising from the position of rodman to chief engineer. From 1897 to 1900 he was in the government service as engineer on the Atlantic Coast Waterway project. He was a member of the first Illinois Deep Waterway Commission under Governor Dunne and reported on practicable design of the State's deep waterway as now under construction. Mr. Kelly is a member of the South Park Commission. Member of American Society of Civil Engineers, Western Society of Engineers. Clubs: Illinois Athletic, South Shore Country, Beverly Country, Westward Ho Golf, Chicago Yacht. Home: South Shore Country Club. Office: 1102 Tower Bldg.

other district to the South branch of the river and by 1884 many firms were forced to move to South Chicago to secure space, while the North branch was already being invaded by the retail trade. The value of annual trade in lumber here is estimated at $50,000,000. By the middle of the eighties, Chicago had already become a leader in the manufacture and distribution of furniture.

Refrigerating cars came into use in Chicago in the early eighties. Pullman palace cars, Chicago's contribution to the comfort of the traveling world, began to be made in the town of Pullman—the $5,000,000 village on the outskirts of Chicago, created by George M. Pullman for centralization of his manufacturing work and in the hope of dispelling dissatisfaction of employes through advantageous surroundings.

Her position in the center of the United States, between Michigan ore beds and Pennsylvania and Illinois coal fields, made Chicago a natural center for the manufacture of railroad rails and other iron products needed in the development of the country. The year 1881 saw 202 blast furnaces and rolling mills operating in the Chicago district.

Cyrus Hall McCormick, who died here May 13, 1884, established the great business of manufacturing reapers in Chicago on a basis so firm and broad that it led eventually to the organization of the International Harvester Company.

Vast changes took place in Chicago during this period. The city passed to the age of brick, granite and brownstone. In the better districts of the city were erected palaces, usually with bulging fronts and a round tower at the corner, and the interior finished with the most massive of woodwork. Many clubhouses were also built, including the Calumet club, the Union League and the Union club.

A great deal of building in the vicinity of Jackson and La Salle streets was occasioned by the removal there of the Chamber of Commerce. The new Board of Trade building was completed in 1885.

The latter part of the eighties saw the beginning of a movement to make land east of Pine street for building purposes and out of this grew the famous Lake Shore drive. Potter Palmer was a pioneer in this movement and, contrary to all precedent, he built a castle on the new extension in what was then an uninhabited waste.

In the matter of elections, Chicago began to play a distinguished part in the eighties, becoming the city for conventions of the great national parties. Beginning with 1880, more than a score of such conventions have been held here, some of them the momentous in United States history.

Back in the seventies, the city and county had advertised for plans for a new city hall and court house and in 1885, they were ready for occupancy, having cost nearly $5,000,000.

On January 17, 1881, the Chicago City Railway Company was granted a charter to operate a line of cable cars and the following year the State street lines, running to Twenty-ninth street, was ready for use, and, with a great deal of ceremony, the first public trial took place.

West Division High school was erected in 1880, North Division in 1883 and South Division in 1884. Previous to that all three sides of the city had united in one high school. Evening schools developed rapidly. An educational event of more than passing interest to Chicago was the opening of the Chicago Manual Training school, through the insight and generosity of the Commercial Club of Chicago.

In 1886, the old University of Chicago, founded in 1858 on land contributed by Stephen A. Douglas at Cottage Grove avenue and Thirty-fourth street, had to relinquish its property because of pressing debts. Plans for a collegiate foundation were immediately instituted by T. W. Godspeed and others, with the result that John D. Rockefeller, who had been debating a choice between New York and Chicago as a site for a college to be endowed by him, chose

13

BENJAMIN HOWARD MARSHALL

BENJAMIN HOWARD MARSHALL, architect; was born in Chicago, May 5, 1874; s. Caleb H. and Celia F. (LeBaillie) Marshall; ed. Harvard Sch., Chicago. Married in Chicago, Feb. 1, 1905, Elizabeth Walton; children: Elizabeth H., Benjamin H., Jr., Dorothy. At 19 he became office boy for H. R. Wilson, architect; worked way up and at 21 was given half interest, firm becoming Wilson & Marshall, until Apr., 1902; practiced alone, 1902-5, designing $3,000,000 worth of bldgs. the first year, including Illinois, Powers, Colonial theatres (Chicago), Nixon Opera House (Pittsburgh, Pa.), etc.; in partnership with Charles E. Fox, as Marshall & Fox, since 1905; architects of the Blackstone Hotel, Blackstone Theatre, Steger Bldg., Burlington Bldg. (Chicago), Northwestern Mutual Life Insurance Bldg. (Milwaukee), Forrest Theatre (Phila.), Maxine Elliott's Theatre (N. Y.), Drake Hotel (Chgo.), etc. Episcopalian. Clubs: Chicago, Old Elm, Exmoor Country, South Shore Country, Onwentsia, Seaview Golf, Shore Acres. Home: 49 Cedar st. Office: 700 Lincoln Parkway.

Chicago and subscribed $600,000 to that end. Chicago contributed the remainder and by 1891 William Rainey Harper was chosen president and the great enterprise was launched on an unprecedented scale, with such foresight as to make the University of Chicago known throughout the world today.

, Hull House—Chicago's famous settlement house, from which some of the greatest sociological plans have sprung in the past thirty years—was founded in 1889 by Miss Jane Addams and Miss Ellen Gates Starr in a long-neglected family mansion on South Halsted street.

An annual art exhibition was given all through the eighties in the Exposition building on the lake front. The first Chicago May festival was given in 1882, with Theodore Thomas as director of music and W. L. Tomlins in charge of the choral work. The first opera festival occurred in 1885.

With the dawn of the last decade of the nineteenth century, there occurred in Chicago an event once more bringing Chicago to the attention of the world. In 1889, a "World's Exposition Company" was founded with a capital of $5,000,-000, and in 1890 Senator Shelby M. Cullom, of Illinois, introduced a bill in Washington providing for the holding of the "World's Columbian Exposition of the Arts and Industries," but neglected to say where it should be held. New York, St. Louis and Washington immediately entered into competition with Chicago. By reason of the action already taken and backed up with funds, Chicago received the award.

A national commission was appointed, with Thomas W. Palmer as president. Acting as professional adviser, Daniel H. Burnham, Chicago's master magicia.i architect, was appointed chief of the construction. Burnham's problem involved a site far from the center of town—Jackson Park—but reached by seven railroads. Out of orderliness and art sprang beauty such as had never been seen before on American soil.

The year following the fair, the South Park Commission proposed the improvement of the lake front from Jackson Park to Lincoln Park. A plan for connection between the two parks was. drawn and presented at a meeting of the West and South Park commissioners and later at a dinner given by the Commercial club. The lake front plan was also endorsed by the Merchants' club in 1902. Early in 1906, the Merchants' club arranged for the preparation of a complete plan for the development of Chicago by Daniel H. Burnham and Edward H. Bennett. In 1907, the Commercial club and the Merchants' club coalesced to form one club, the Commercial club, and the Chicago Plan has proceeded under its auspices, with the aid of every other civic agency.

The Chicago Women's Club was organized in 1876 by Mrs. Caroline M. Brown and this important advance of organized women into the cultural life of the city had been preceded in 1873 by the Fortnightly club. The Friday club, composed of younger women of tastes similar to those of the Fortnightly, extended the fields of cultural interest which the women of Chicago were more and more exploiting.

There was a steady progress of that great engineering enterprise, the Drainage canal, and much building during this time. The Field Museum was incorporated in 1893. The Art Institute, incorporated in 1879, came into its own in an adequate building on the lake front at Adams street in 1893 and the Chicago Academy of Sciences, through the generosity of Matthew Laflin, received title to a new building at Lincoln Park and Center street. The same year saw the cornerstone of the new public library laid and the Newberry library, the largest general reference library in the west, opened at Dearborn and Walton Place.

In 1899, the Chicago city council created the special park commission and provided for a study of needs of the city in the matter of parks and recreation grounds. In the same year, the Illinois juvenile court came into being.

Technical and industrial education in Chicago was much forwarded by

15

several events in the nineties, including the opening of the Armour Institute of Technology, the incorporation of the John Crerar Library as a free library and the organization of Lewis Institute. Sociological studies and welfare service were advanced by the organization of Chicago Commons in 1894, and the incorporation of the settlements of the Northwestern University and the University of Chicago.

Chicago, in 1903, celebrated the centennial of her foundation under the name of Fort Dearborn. An important event in 1904 was the organization of the Chicago Association of Commerce. A list of the things done in a single year, 1919, by this organization follows:

Organized the Mississippi Valley association.

Obtained enactment of the convention hall bill by the Illinois General Assembly.

Fathered the movement resulting in the organization of the Illinois Chamber of Commerce.

Organized Chicago Crime Commission.

Obtained federal legislation establishing a $1,500,000 harbor at the Great Lakes Training school and obtained passage of the Illinois Waterway bill.

Sponsored movement for improvement of St. Lawrence river, the success of which will make Chicago an ocean port.

The small parks and playgrounds movement, well under way in 1910, developed enormously. In 1920, there were 194 small parks and playgrounds maintained by city and park authorities. Prior to 1910, the bathing facilities were limited. In 1920, there were twelve public bathing beaches, the largest of which is the Clarendon, accommodating 23,000 bathers a day.

Special schools opened in the new century were the Francis Parker school, founded on principles of advanced education held by Dr Parker, and the Chicago School of Domestic Science. The college of education at the University of Chicago is one of the most highly specialized schools in the world.

Benefits of the Art Institute today are taken advantage of by more than 5,000 students in a year and by 1,100,000 visitors to the Institute's museum. The building and dedication in 1904 of the permanent home of the Chicago Orchestra was one of the most notable events in the musical world of America. Grand Opera has likewise come here to make its home. For several years, the Chicago Opera company has been the recipient of support from the public, aided by the munificence of its guarantors, chief of whom was Harold F. McCormick.

The new century brought to Chicago a number of new theaters, including the Columbus in 1901, the Iroquois and the Garrick in 1903, the Colonial in 1904, the New Olympic in 1904, the New theater in 1906, the Apollo in 1921 and the Harris and Selwyn in 1922. Today the moving picture houses of Chicago number 450.

Meeting requirements as a center of population and patriotism in the Spanish-Amrican war of 1899, as in the prolonged struggle of the Civil War, Chicago and Illinois mightily took up the huge responsibilities of the world war and Illinois gave 351,153 men to the army and navy during this conflict, furnishing one man for every twelve in the army and more men to both army and navy than any other state excepting New York and Pennsylvania, both of which have larger populations. The state's own division was the 33d, and this was the only distinctively Illinois organization that saw service in France.

About seven per cent of the war loan subscriptions of the nation came from Illinois, which has but five and one-fourth per cent of the population of the United States. The state's total contributions to various funds for war aid and relief organizations were more than $45,000,000.

16

DR. ELMORE SLOAN PETTYJOHN

DR. E. S. PETTYJOHN, physician and surgeon, was born in Ripley O., July 9, 1855; s. of Elizabeth Ann (Wallace) and Collard Fitch Pettyjohn. Ed. in Ill. pub. schs., Indiana Normal Sch.; grad., Rush Med. Coll., 1882; post-graduate courses in Chicago Seminary of Sciences, 1898; Ph. B. and special courses in Berlin in 1900 and 1901. Married Ada E. Lozier, Mt. Vernon, Ia., June 25, 1885. Children: Hogarth, Elmore S., Jr., Mrs. Macgregor Adams Bancroft. Asst. med. supt. at Ill. Eastern Hosp. for Insane, 1882-5; med. supt. of Alma Sanatorium, 1893-1901; prof. at Harvey Med. Coll., 1902-06; prof. at Post-Grad. Med. Sch., 1904-08; neurologist at Ill. Gen. Hosp., since 1921. Mem. A.M.A., Mich., Kansas, Ill., State and Chicago Med. Socs.; Nat. Frat. Cong. of Am.; Am. Assn. for Advancement of Science. Author: "Rheumatism, Pathology and Treatment," "Med. Directors' Manual," etc., etc. Med. dir. for Security Ben. Assn. for eight years. Mem. Alma, Mich., Lodge, A. F. & A. M. and O. E. S. of Evanston. Well known as traveler and lecturer on Finland and Russia in Daily News course. Appointed by Governor of Michigan as commissioner to visit hospitals for insane in France, Austria and Germany. A. M. A. Delegate to 13th International Congress, Paris. Delegate to National Fraternal Congress. Rep. 6,000,000 members (6th Int. Congress) on tuberculosis, 1908. Club: Press. Home: Evanston. Office: 59 E. Madison st.

DR. ABE FRANK NEMIRO

ABE FRANK NEMIRO, physician and surgeon, was born in Russia, Oct. 25th, 1885; s. of Rose (Bistritski) and Frank Nemiro; ed. in pub. schs. of New York; Brown Coll. Prep. 1903, graduated from Medical Department Univ. of Louisville, 1907. Married Beatrice Baum, Philadelphia, June 4, 1911. Chief house phys. for Multhonomah Co. Hosp., Portland, Ore. Took post-grad. courses in New York and Ill. Med. Schs. Ass't. prof. in venereal diseases at Chicago Coll. of Med. and Surgery, 1916-20; associate in surgery, Coll. of Phys., Chicago Coll. of Med. and Surgery, 1916-20; supervision of Municipal Venereal Clinic, 1918-19; clinical dir. for U. S. Pub. Health Clinics, 1919-21; attending phys. at Jefferson Pk. Hosp., Mem. of Am. Med. Assn., Am. Pub. Health Assn., Chicago Med. Soc., Ill. State Med. Soc., Oregon State Med. Assn. Clubs: Lincoln. Elks, Press. Home: 631 S. Ashland Blvd. Office: 59 E. Madison St.

EDWIN F. MEYER

EDWIN FRANK MEYER, capitalist and philanthropist, was born in Chicago, Dec. 30, 1865; son of Sarah (Frank) and Max A. Meyer. He was educated in grammar and high schools and in Yale University, where he received the degree of bachelor of philosophy in 1886. Mr. Meyer is unmarried. He is president of Malt Maid Co. and vice-president of Winslow Boiler & Engineering Company, and head of the syndicate that is now erecting a $10,-000,000.00 office building at Jackson and Michigan boulevards. Mr. Meyer is a trustee of the Michael Reese hospital. Republican. Jewish religion. Clubs: Illinois Athletic, Press, Standard, North Shore, Chicago Automobile, Saddle and Sirloin. Home: 45 E. Oak st.

18

THE WRIGLEY BUILDING

THE Wrigley building, situated on the plaza at the north end of the new Michigan Boulevard bridge, is Chicago's tallest building. The main part of the building is 210 feet high and on top of the 16 stories is a 188-foot tower, around which revolves a giant searchlight, which serves as the beacon light of the northside district of Chicago. The height of the entire structure is 398 feet. It covers an area of 11,496 square feet and cost approximately $3,500,000 to build.

JESSE GRANT CHAPLINE

JESSE GRANT CHAPLINE, president of La Salle Extension University, was born in Waverly, Mo., Jan. 13, 1870; son of Sallie Ann and William Purnell Chapline. Ed. in Pub. Schs. and in St. Louis Coll. He married Anne J. Johnson, May 12, 1909, Chicago. Children: Marjorie Anne and Dorthy Jane. Mr. Chapline is founder of La Salle Extension University. Under his leadership this institution has developed as the largest school in the world devoted to higher business training, having a total enrollment of over 350,000. He is widely known for his writings on sales and business subjects. He is also director of Commercial Research Assn. He was former manager, John Wanamaker Century Club, Philadelphia. Former Pres. Associated Publishing Co. Honorary mem., Soc. of Applied Psychology; mem. Associated Advertising Clubs, Assn. of National Advertisers, Chicago Assn. of Commerce, Chicago Art Institute. Clubs: South Shore Country, Colonial. Office: Michigan Ave. and 41st St. Home: 7158 Luella Ave.

CHICAGO AS AN EDUCATIONAL CENTER

UPON the intelligent sympathy of the people hangs the success of a school system. Chicago has been much benefited by this circumstance and the present indications are for the continuance and extension of this co-operation, which, it is believed, will receive great impetus when the Committee on Education of the Chicago Association of Commerce will submit to the public the result of a long study of the American problem of education in the related elements of city, state and nation.

Fifty-one new activities have been undertaken by the Chicago school system since 1846. Music came in 1847 and German in 1865; the problem of crippled children became recognized in 1900, and then, too, were baths and the blind thought of; in 1909 vacation schools and the industrial arts were new activities; in 1911 vocational guidance obtained attention and in 1916 the teaching of commerce and administration; in 1917 Americanization recognized the alien and also out of war work came in the same year the cadet corps and school gardens. Chicago's necessities and Europe's example set continuation schools going in 1918, and in 1919 and 1920, respectively, the physical welfare movement begat summer camps and athletic directors.

The annual increase in cost of operating the Chicago school system is $2,-000,000 and the current budget is more than $30,000,000. Chicago has more pupils per teacher, and there are 9,700 classroom teachers, than any city of comparable size with the exception of Philadelphia.

Three elementary schools were completed at the beginning of 1922 at a cost of $500,000 each, and construction has been ordered on eighteen other elementary schools. Construction has also been ordered on two high schools, at approximately $1,250,000 each. Additions to four high schools have been ordered. It is expert opinion that Chicago in the near future should have at least twenty-five more buildings for elementary schools and four more buildings for high schools.

Northwestern University in 1921 installed as its president, Dr. Walter Dill Scott, who at once strengthened official purpose and general interest in development of new and great university projects, not as a part of the campus at Evanston, but near the edge of the expanding business district of Chicago. The university has bought nine acres of land on the lake shore, four blocks north of the Municipal Pier, where they expect to place the institution's medical school, law school, dental school, school of commerce and school of journalism. It is hoped to erect on this site buildings to accommodate as many as 10,000 students, although the total registration in the university in 1921 was only 8,500.

Although youngest of the great American universities, the University of Chicago in thirty years of remarkable growth has received within its doors 87,000 students and its annual enrollment is 11,000. Its library numbers 1,000,000 books, many of them tomes of priceless value, and its assets are $50,000,000.

Distinguishing a five-year program outlined by the university's veteran president, Harry Pratt Judson, in 1920, are increases of salary to faculty members, a step first taken in 1919, and development of the graduate schools for investigation of the basic principles of pure science involved in important problems of society and its industries.

Within these graduate schools will be organized a series of institutes, the first being that of physics and chemistry, with necessary buildings and equipment, requiring building funds or an endowment. The second institute will be that of plant agriculture, and here will be trained men in the fundamental science of agriculture, and it will be notably advanced work. Here again many thousands of dollars will be required.

The fourth institute will be that of the science of education and will call for liberal endowment. Indeed, in establishment of these institutions, there will be necessary new endowments amounting to $3,000,000, while for the buildings will be required $1,250,000. To meet the growing needs of the great library and the need of classrooms, and to provide an adequate administration building and residence halls for both men and women, there will be required not less than $1,750,000. The total financial requirements of the university within a five-year period are $10,000,000.

A new feature of university development with co-operation of all interests is to be the appointment of university commissions, fourteen in all, one from each of the main groups of university interests. On each commission will be two alumni, a university trustee, two faculty members and two or more citizens. The duty of each commission will be to study the work of its particular school or group of interests and to make the board of trustees suggestions for improvements.

The university has been active in the Near East in the field of archaeology. It is desired to establish a field school for geology. The department of geography hopes to organize research expeditions and the department of zoology plans a museum, while botany needs an experimental garden, laboratory and greenhouses.

By the invention of Professor Michelson, of the university, a twenty-foot interferometer operating in connection with the 100-inch telescope at Mount Wilson, California, there was measured the diameter of the giant star, Betelgeuze, which is learned to have a diameter of nearly 300,000,000 miles, or 300 times that of the sun. Such is astronomical research by gifted scientists well equipped, while one of the world's most remarkable astronomical equipments is the property of the University of Chicago in the Yerkes observatory at Geneva Lake, Wisconsin, where a 40-inch telescope is in operation.

LA SALLE EXTENSION UNIVERSITY

L A SALLE EXTENSION UNIVERSITY is the largest higher business training institution in the world—with assets of over $7,000,000, with more than 350,000 enrolled members, with an educational, administrative, and service staff of more than 1,500 people.

LaSalle's field is vocational training, that is, training men practically for such work as certified public accounting, executive accounting, traffic management, salesmanship, business correspondence, and executive positions.

LaSalle training is primarily for adults. The average age of students is nearly thirty years and ranges from eighteen to seventy-two. Among these are rich and poor, college graduates and those who have obtained most of their education in the school of hard knocks, presidents of large corporations and ambitious men in the ranks.

PLAN FOR NEW ADMINISTRATION BUILDING
LA SALLE EXTENSION UNIVERSITY

LaSalle training is by the Problem Method. The student gains strength and experience in working problems. He learns by doing. Thru the medium of the mails, the University is taken to the student at his home. He learns while he earns. He is held accountable for every part of the lesson—he recites on every lesson. Each student is a class by himself; there is no holding back—no crowding.

Among other services LaSalle maintains a research and consulting service for students and business men, by reason of which it is often referred to as "a clearing-house for business information;" a placement service providing free employment service to students and firms alike; a lecture bureau furnishing speakers for Chambers of Commerce, Rotary Clubs, business meetings, etc.

The executive staff consists of J. G. Chapline, president; Morris L. Greeley, vice-president; L. G. Elliott, treasurer; William Bethke, secretary. Directors are J. G. Chapline, L. G. Elliott, William Bethke, Morris L. Greeley, Irving R. Allen, Arnold B. Hall, William A. Colledge, H. E. Farquharson, Arthur B. Hall.

23

ARTHUR CHARLES LUEDER

ARTHUR CHARLES LUEDER, postmaster of Chicago, was born in Elmhurst, Ill., March 12, 1876; son of Juliane (Brumund) and John Lueder; ed. in parochial sch. and Elmhurst Coll. Received L. B. degree from Chicago Law Sch. Married Martha R. Mueller, Apr. 6, 1904, in Chicago. Children: Roland Gerhard, Ruth Helene. Mr. Lueder was in employ of real estate firm of Madlung & Eidmann for 12 years beginning in 1890, after which he entered real estate and loan business on his own account. Served in Spanish War with First Ill. Volunteer Infty. Appointed postmaster of Chicago by Pres. Harding, Aug. 24, 1921. Secy. of Chicago Real Estate Bd.; secy.-treas. and director of Cook County Real Estate Bd.; secy. of Secretaries Assn. of Nat'l. Assn. of Real Estate Bd. Mem. of Oriental Consistory, Mystic Shrine, Chicago Assn. of Comm., Woodmen, Chicago Turners, Soc. of Santiago De Cuba, Nat'l. Union, Chicago Historical Soc., North Am. Union, Elks, Loyal Order of Moose, Royal League. Clubs: Hamilton, Ridgemoor, Country, Lincoln, German. Office: Federal Bldg. and 40 N. Dearborn St. Home: 3832 Rokeby St.

CHICAGO CHURCHES

ONE of the towers of strength of Chicago is its churches and it is to be hoped their mission and virtues are conserved through a distinct program of development.

In the twenty centuries of the Roman Catholic church, the story of the growth of this faith in Chicago and Illinois forms an important chapter. The church has kept pace with the great growth of the city since the day when Father Jacques Marquette, the Jesuit priest, and two companions pushed their way into the Chicago river.

The first resident priest came in 1833 in the person of Father St. Cyr and ten years later Chicago was selected as the see of a new diocese embracing all Illinois and Bishop William Quarter became Chicago's first Roman Catholic bishop. The institutional work before the fire laid the foundations for the present great activities of the church. In 1844, the University of St. Mary of the Lake was established.

Losses suffered by the Catholic church in the great fire were estimated at $1,000,000 and many of its churches, asylums, parish schools and colleges were enveloped in flames. Among the great builders that arose after the conflagration was the Rt. Rev. Thomas Foley, whose work led to the early restoration of fine academies, colleges, schools and church edifices. More than fifty years have passed and today the Catholic population here numbers 1,200,000 and there are 227 churches and 643 diocesan priests.

The great educational plan of Archbishop Mundelein, which is rapidly unfolding, centers about the University of St. Mary of the Lake, the seat of which has been erected on a 1,000 acre tract on the shore of St. Mary Lake at Area, near Area, about forty miles from the heart of the loop. The university departments of Loyola and De Paul and of the new college for women—Rosary college—are to be a part of the great university.

In Chicago are to be found the churches of all races and creeds, the Christian church predominating, although the presence of Jewish synagogues marks that age-old faith. The two best-known Jewish temples are Sinai, whose eminent leader, Dr. Emil G. Hirsch, has celebrated his forty-second anniversary as rabbi, and Temple Sholem, whose leader, Dr. Abram Hirschberg is to celebrate his silver jubilee.

A twenty-one story building on the same site is being built to supplant the old First Methodist church building at Clark and Washington streets, having the distinction of being the only church in the loop.

Probably the most notable church edifice in Chicago, from an architectural standpoint, is the First Presbyterian, and the most beautiful chapel or church of the Roman communion is the Quigley Memorial preparatory seminary.

Lutheranism was founded in Chicago as long as seventy-five years ago, the pioneer community being that of the First St. Paul's Evangelical Lutheran church on the north side.

Of the inter-denominational churches, of which Chicago has not a few, a representative organization is the Moody Bible Institute. Chicago has sixteen Christian Science churches, two recently having been dedicated and free from debt. There are three Greek Catholic churches, the population to which they minister numbering about 25,000. There is also a Russian Orthodox church.

MICHAEL J. FAHERTY

MICHAEL J. FAHERTY, realtor, was born in Ireland, 1859; s. Patrick Charles and Bridget (Fahey) Faherty; came to U. S. in 1863; ed. in pub. schs., East Windsor, Conn. Married Mary O'Rielly of Hagardville, Conn. (now deceased); married 2d, Hannah O'Malley, of Milwaukee. Children: Roger, Edward, Phillip, Charles. Settled in Chicago, 1880; machinist by trade and followed same until 1885; in real estate business since 1885. Pres. Bd. of Local Improvements, by appmt. of Mayor Thompson, since Apr. 26, 1915. Republican. Mem. Knights of Columbus, Catholic Order of Foresters, Columbian Knights, Friends of Irish Freedom, Irish Fellowship Club. Home: 2735 Pine Grove av. Office: 207 City Hall.

WORKS IN RELIGION, EDUCATION, CITIZENSHIP AND UNIFICATION IN CHICAGO BY THE CATHOLIC CHURCH

OFFICIAL records show that in the territory of Chicago and vicinity, which comprises the archdiocese of Chicago of the Roman Catholic church, there are more than 1,150,000 persons enrolled as the Catholic population and that they include native-born Americans of many generations as well as American citizens descended from those who came to this country from all parts of the world.

Official records also show that the roll of honor of the men who volunteered, who served, who fought and who died under the stars and stripes during the world war, included members of every one of the 344 Roman Catholic churches under the jurisdiction of Archbishop George W. Mundelein. Both in war and in time of peace, in every one of these churches from the pulpit and from the altar, come uniform lessons of loyalty and patriotism to the United States, of devotion and support to the ideals and principles of our country and of unselfish service, sacrifice and devotion to it both in time of war and in time of peace.

During the war, under the leadership of Archbishop Mundelein, the Catholic people did their full duty in service, loyalty and sacrifice, in giving and supporting the army and navy, in standing by the government in every way, in generous and unstinted support of all war activities and agencies, of government loans, of the Red Cross and other relief works. With letters, addresses and sermons of Archbishop Mundelein as their keynotes, the entire priesthood of the archdiocese presented with their congregations one solid, harmonious and loyal American family which never wavered in its service and devotion to the government of the United States.

In time of peace, the clergy and laity of the Catholic church continuously seek to serve and do their full duty as citizens of the United States. They strive by their works, deeds and utterances to live up to and maintain the ideals, principles and government of this country and to help in its progress and advancement.

No matter from what part of the world their fathers or they themselves have come, no matter what their original mother tongue has been, no matter what their race, color or condition of life has been or is, the people who attend the various churches which are under the direction of Archbishop Mundelein are given the same lesson for the good of citizenship. In the magnificent church edifices, which, by their generosity, the Catholic people constructed as an outward expression of their inward religious faith and in emulation of their forefathers who constructed magnificent churches in the lands from whence they came, are daily taught the lessons, ideals and principles which are fundamental to the permanency of our national institutions. The purity and sanctity of the home and of the marriage life is emphasized as a necessity for the future as well as the present. The unity, sanctity and indissolubility of the marriage tie and the sanctity of human life as soon as the body is animated by the vital spark until the time when it is extinguished by death, are invariably and uniformly expounded as fundamental to real happiness and progress. In those churches comfort is given to all by instructing them to bear ills of life with Christian philosophy, and at all times

27

is the lesson taught that honest toil is ennobling and that all people are children of God and should do unto others as they would have them do to themselves.

Believing that the education of the heart, mind and body is the right of every child as well as duty of citizenship, the Catholic church established and maintains an extensive system of educational institutions.

At their own expense, the Catholic citizens, who also faithfully pay their taxes to support all public institutions, are maintaining two hundred and eighty-one parochial schools, in which one hundred and forty-two thousand children are given not only the regular educational course required by the municipal, state and government authorities, but who are also daily given lessons in religion, love of God and respect for law and order. This vast army of children is being educated at the expense of their kin and co-religionists who expend millions therefor every year. This great work of education is made possible by the service rendered for life by nuns who join religious teaching orders and devote their entire life and time to the cause of properly bringing up and educating boys and girls.

In addition to the parochial schools there are maintained twenty-two high schools with 2,172 students, twenty-five academies for girls with 5,375 students, twelve colleges and academies for boys with 7,291 students, one preparatory seminary with 466 students, five seminaries for religious orders with 206 students.

Under the great educational plan of Archbishop Mundelein, the various colleges and universities conducted by the Catholic religious teaching orders in Chicago and vicinity are all co-ordinated. The center and keystone of all the higher educational institutions is now the St. Mary of the Lake University, located on the shores of a beautiful lake in a magnificent park at Area, near Libertyville, Ill., not far from Chicago. This university, built by Archbishop Mundelein, is in charge of the best trained Catholic educators available in this country and in Europe and is recognized as one of the largest and most important factors in Catholic education in this country.

In all of the churches and in all of the schools, Archbishop Mundelein put into effect the system of making people of all elements constitute one harmonious family. Children of peoples of various nationalities are all given the same lessons to make them good, loyal and upright Americans and good religious citizens. In the common as well as in the higher educational institutions, from the primary grade through the colleges, university and seminary which brings forth the priests, all students are educated primarily to make them good Christian men and women, good children of America ready to serve and sacrifice for their country and its flag. The hatreds of the old world which their forefathers had because of strifes are wiped out and into the American life these students are taught to bring those ideals and principles which go to preserve Christian morality, real advancement and freedom of our nation.

For God and for country, is the slogan of Archbishop Mundelein, of his auxiliary bishop, the Right Rev. Edward F. Hoban, and of every one of his priests, nuns, teachers and laity. In the schools and churches it is constantly preaching, moulding the people into a solid phalanx which stands for religion, for morality, for law, order and government. The teachings strengthen these people to all times combat irreligion, immorality and lawlessness and to always be ready and ever serve and work to protect, preserve and uphold the American government and its institutions.

FRANCIS J. HOULIHAN

FRANCIS J. HOULIHAN, prominent lawyer, was born in Ogdensburg, N. Y., July 20, 1865; son of Mary (O'Gorman) and Francis R. Houlihan. He was educated in Ogdensburg Academy and Northwestern University. Mr. Houlihan came to Chicago in 1890 and on April 28, 1897, he married Mary J. Conway. Children: Robert A. (killed while serving with U. S. Army in France), Mary T. Eileen, Francis J., Jr. Mr. Houlihan first served with the law firm of Byam, Weinschenk & Hirschl. He was a member of the firms of O'Hara & Houlihan; Rosenthal, Kurz & Hirschl and is now affiliated with Rosenthal, Kurz & Houlihan. He has handled important cases among which, West Pullman Car Works, Graham & Sons Bank and Edward W. Morrison. Member National Guard, New York. Republican. Member Knights of Columbus. Member American, Illinois and Chicago Bar Associations. Home: 229 N. Austin blvd. Office: 208 S. La Salle street.

JOSEPH WILLIAM McCARTHY

JOSEPH WILLIAM McCARTHY, architect, was born in Jersey City, N. J., June 22, 1884; s. of John W. and Nora (O'Leary) McCarthy; ed. in parochial schs. New York and Chicago. Married Mary Lynch, of Chicago, July 15, 1908; daughter, Miriam L. Began active career in 1901 with D. H. Burnham & Co., architects, continuing until 1909; later in employ of J. E. O. Pridmore; practiced alone since 1911; designer of St. Mary's-of-the-Lake University, Area, Ill., Corpus Christi Church and numerous parochial schools and churches in Chicago. Mem. A. I. A. and Ill. Soc. Architects. Mem. Knights of Columbus. Mediaevalists. Home: 665 Sheridan Rd. Office: 139 N. Clark St.

CHARLES H. WACKER

CHARLES HENRY WACKER, real estate, was born in Chicago, 1856; s. of Catherine (Hummel) and Frederick Wacker; ed. in Chicago pub. schs., Lake Forest, Ill., Acad., and at Stuttgart, Germany. In 1887, married Ottilie M. Glade (died 1904). Married Ella G. Todtmann, Chicago, 1919. Children: Frederick G., Charles H., Jr., Rosalie. In 1880, he joined father in malting firm of F. Wacker & Son, later the Wacker & Birk Brewing & Malting Co., of which he was president, 1884-1901; also president of McAvoy Brewing Co. several years; Pres. Chgo. Heights Land Assn., Chgo. Heights Gas Co., Chgo. Heights Terminal & Transfer R. R.; dir. Corn Exchange Nat. Bank, Calumet & Chgo. Canal & Dock Co.; ex-pres. United Charities; chmn. Chgo. Plan Comm., 1909; mem. Cook Co. Forest Preserve Comm.; dir. Chgo. Zoological Gardens; gov. mem. Chgo. Art Inst.; mem. execut. comm., Chgo. chapter Red Cross; dir. of Columbian Expo. & Mem. Ill. State Council of Defense and fulfilled many other patriotic duties in the war. Mem. Ill. Chapter, A. I. A.; Fellow Am. Geog. Soc.; Am. Hist. Soc.; dir. Am. Social Science Assn.; Chgo. Real Estate Board, Cook County Real Estate Board, Ill. Mfrs. Assn.; pres. Chgo. Singverein, dir. Civic Music Assn., treas. Murphy Memorial Assn. Mem. Chgo. Assn. of Comm. Clubs: Chgo. Commercial, Union League, Univ., Press, Germania, Chgo. Athletic, Iroquois, Arts, Bankers, City, Cliff Dwellers, German, Mid-Day, Onwentsia, Lake Geneva Country, Lake Geneva Yacht. Home: 33 Bellevue Place, City. Office: 134 S. La Salle St.

THE CHICAGO PLAN

CHICAGO—"the biggest young city in the world"—owes much of its growth, its beauty and its recreational facilities to the Chicago Plan Commission.

The Commission, headed by Charles H. Wacker, chairman, and Frank I. Bennett, vice-chairman, was created in 1909 by the city council, with a membership of 328, appointed by Mayor Fred A. Busse with the council's approval. It followed the presentation to the city of the Chicago Plan by the Commercial club.

The Plan was conceived in 1908-9 by Daniel H. Burnham and Edward H. Bennett, working in co-operation with other architects and city builders. Their primary aim was to unify Chicago.

"Make no little plans," urged Burnham. "Make big plans, aim high in work and hope, remembering that a noble, logical diagram once recorded will never die, but long after we are gone will be a living th.ng, asserting itself with ever growing intensity. Let your watchword be 'order' and your beacon 'beauty.'"

That his inspiring words have been kept in the foreground of the city's consciousness is now patent. The Chicago plan has outgrown a mere unification program. It has given the city long stretches of boulevards and thoroughfares, expediting traffic and relieving congestion. It has given Chicago public parks and buildings which will draw sightseers from every part of the globe. It has given also great pleasure grounds, bathing beaches and lagoons to provide for the recreation of millions.

The Chicago Plan Commission's outstanding accomplishments came during the administration of Mayor William Hale Thompson. Foremost among these is the opening of the North Michigan Boulevard Extension by Mayor Thompson in 1920. This has increased the value of property fronting the boulevard on the north side approximately $100,000,000. Today the boulevard stretches over 45 miles along the lake shore and it is the intention of Mayor Thompson to improve it and utilize all its possibilities until it is second to no world thoroughfare in architectural beauty, metropolitan interest and scenic beauty.

Chicago Plan Accomplishments
(As of May 1, 1922. Listed alphabetically)

Ashland Avenue—Not open at four places; varies in width from 42 to 100 ft. To be opened as a through north-and-south traffic artery 100 ft. wide between Pratt Blvd. and 95th St. Recommended by Plan Commission Dec., 1918, as through street from city limits to city limits. Majority protest filed, May, 1921, on sections between Rogers Av. and Pratt Blvd. Five million eight hundred thousand dollar bond issue approved, Nov., 1919. City Council ordinances covering various sections passed June, 1920-Jan., 1921. Petitions and assessment rolls filed in court by Board of Local Improvements, but case not yet brought to trial. One of the three through north-and-south traffic arteries on the west side.

Bridges—Technical staff of Plan Commission co-operates with city in developing design and architectural work of all new bridges, including bridge houses, lighting standards, etc.

Canal Street—Widening from 80 to 100 ft. accomplished. Twenty-ft. strip on east side given by railroads, and cost of widening borne by them as part

GEORGE F. HARDING

GEORGE FRANKLIN HARDING, Comptroller City of Chicago, and one of its leading real estate operators, was born in Chicago Aug. 16, 1868, son of Adelaide (Mathews) and George F. Harding. His grandfather was Gen. Abner C. Harding of the Civil War and his great grandfather was Gen. Abner Clarke of Revolutionary War fame. He was educated in the Moseley Public School, graduated Phillips Exeter Academy, 1888, and from the Harvard Law School in 1892. Was a member of the Harvard Football Varsity for four years—went to England on the All-American Team in 1891 and held the Inter-Collegiate light-weight championship, 1890-91. Married Ellen Davis, 1896 (now deceased); Catherine Fay, 1914 (now deceased); one daughter, Mary Milsom Harding. Alderman of second ward, Chicago, for six terms; State Senator, Illinois, for two terms; president Chicago Real Estate Loan & Trust Co. Clubs: Chicago Athletic, South Shore Country, Chicago Yacht, Illinois Athletic, Hamilton, and Olympia Fields Country. Home: 4853 Lake Park Avenue. Office address: 3101 Cottage Grove Avenue, Chicago.

of the West Side Union Station ordinances. Western boundary of traffic quadrangle around heart of city.

Cicero Avenue—Negotiations pending for widening from 66 to 100 ft. between Pershing Rd. and Archer Ave. The new 100-ft. wide bridge to be constructed by the Sanitary District across the drainage canal at Cicero Ave. at the suggestion of Plan Commission was so designed that it will save the city $2,000,000 in the cost of approaches, and will be adequate for the combined traffic of Cicero Ave. and Pershing Rd., after the widening and extension of those streets.

Crawford Avenue—Technical staff of Plan Commission co-operating with Sanitary District in design of new Crawford Ave. bridge across drainage canal.

Clinton Street—Widening from 40 to 80 ft. (by taking 20 ft. on each side) between Harrison St. and Roosevelt Rd. Recommended by Plan Commission, May, 1921; City Council ordinance passed July, 1921; court petition filed by Board of Local Improvements Aug., 1921. Part of West Side Warehouse District development.

Desplaines Street—Widening from 60 to 80 ft. (by taking 20 ft. on east side) between Harrison St. and Roosevelt Rd. Recommended by Plan Commission May, 1921; City Council ordinance passed July, 1921; court petition filed by Board of Local Improvements Aug., 1921. Part of West Side Warehouse District development.

Field Museum—Opened May 3, 1921. Part of Lake Front development.

Forest Preserves—Out of a total available area of approximately 35,000 acres, the Board of Forest Preserve Commissioners of Cook Co. have already acquired 21,516 acres. These tracts practically encircle the city from Lake Michigan on the north back again to the lake on the south, extending for approximately eleven miles along the Desplaines River on the west. The total cost of acquiring these preserves has been between eight and ten million dollars. During 1921, an association was formed with John T. McCutcheon at its head, to develop a zoo on land near Riverside given to the Forest Preserve Board for that purpose by Mrs. Edith Rockefeller McCormick.

Good Roads—The road building program of the Cook Co. Board of Commissioners continues. During 1921, according to President Daniel Ryan, 48.81 miles of new pavement were laid at a cost of approximately $1,800,000.

Harbors—During 1921 the Illinois State Legislature passed two acts having to do with harbor development at Chicago. One empowered the Sanitary District to create and operate the proposed Lake Calumet Industrial Harbor. The other provided for joint action with the State of Indiana in the establishment of the proposed Illiana Transfer Harbor on the shore of Lake Michigan near the Indiana state line.

Illinois Central Terminal—Recommended by Plan Commission Feb., 1912, as part of the lake front development. City Council ordinance passed July, 1919, fixing a permanent boundary between the railroad and the South Park Board property. This ordinance provides for the construction of the proposed new depot and the electrification of the tracks; includes provision for track depression; and imposes restrictions as to the use by the railroad of the newly acquired right-of-way. The ordinance also designates certain land to be exchanged in order to permit the extension of Grant Park to Roosevelt Rd. and the extension of Roosevelt Rd. east of Michigan Av. to the lake shore, etc. Under the terms of the ordinance, the suburban service is to be electrified within seven years; the freight service north of Roosevelt Rd. within ten years; the freight service south of that point within fifteen years, and the through passenger service within twenty years after the date of the passage of the ordinance. Estimated total cost of electrification, $88,000,000. In April, 1922, the stockholders and directors of the Illinois

33

P. J. CARR

P. J. CARR, Cook County Treasurer; was born in Chicago, Sept. 4, 1880; s. James and Bridget (Bolger) Carr; ed. grammar schs.; and De LaSalle Inst., Chicago; married Agnes McAuley, Chicago, Aug. 9, 1905; daughter, Margaret Isabelle. Newsboy for 9 yrs.; sidewalk inspector, City of Chicago, about 6 yrs.; elected Alderman from 5th ward, 1911, and re-elected 1913; elected mem. bd. of trustees, Sanitary Dist. of Chicago, Dec. 1914, term of 6 yrs.; pres. P. J. Carr & Co., real estate; Chairman, Board of Directors, Consolidated Co., stone, gravel, etc. Democrat. Member: Royal Arcanum, K. of C., Hibernians, Elks, Chicago Lodge No. 4. Clubs: Chicago Yacht, Lincoln, Chicago Sharpshooters' Assn., South Shore Country, Ill. Athletic. Home 3519 S. Western av. Office: 212 County Bldg.

Central Railroad Company voted a stock issue of $50,000,000 to start the terminal and electrification work.

Indiana Avenue—Widening from 66 to 100 ft. (by taking 34 ft. from the east side of the street) between Roosevelt Rd. and 22d St., recommended by the Plan Commission, Oct., 1921. City Council ordinance passed April, 1922. Part of general south side lake front development.

Jefferson Street—Widening from 40 to 80 ft. (by taking a 20-ft. strip on both sides) from Harrison St. to Roosevelt Rd., recommended by Plan Commission, May, 1921. City Council ordinance passed July, 1921; court petition filed by Board of Local Improvements, Aug., 1921; part of west side warehouse district development.

Lake Front—1,138 acres of new parks including recreational facilities, extending for five miles from Grant Park to Jackson Park. A 600-ft. wide lagoon will extend the entire distance. The land between the lagoon and the Illinois Central right-of-way will vary in width from approximately 350 to 700 ft., and the land between the lagoon and the lake will vary from 800 to 2,500 ft. The plans include a commercial harbor reservation between 16th and 47th Sts., as decreed by the United States War Department; a yacht harbor between 16th St. and the Municipal Pier at Grand Ave.; two motor boat race courses; and the extension of Grant Park 314 ft. eastward. The plan also includes the Field Museum (completed) and the construction of a stadium immediately adjoining the museum on the south. The plan further includes the widening of South Park Ave. from 66 to 198 ft. between 35th and 23d Sts., in order to extend Grand Blvd. north through the new park to Randolph St., where it will eventually connect with Lake Shore Drive at the foot of the Municipal Pier. A diagonal street 120 ft. wide is to be constructed between 22nd St. at Calumet Av. and South Park Av. at 23d St.; and 23d St. is to be widened across the Illinois Central right-of-way to bring Grand Blvd. into the new park. Eight direct east-and-west street car lines will give ready access to the new park from every section of the city for a single car fare.

Recommended by Plan Commission, Feb., 1912. City Council ordinance passed July, 1919; accepted by the South Park Commissioners and the Illinois Central Railroad, and the necessary permit secured from the War Department of the United States. This ordinance fixes the permanent boundary between the railroad and the park property. For its provisions with reference to the Illinois Central Terminal, see under heading "Illinois Central Terminal." Twenty million dollar bond issue passed Feb., 1919.

The lake front park development comes within the jurisdiction of, and is being carried out by the South Park Commissioners.

Michigan Avenue—Widening from 66 to 130 ft. between Randolph St. and the Chicago River, and to 141 ft. from the river north to Chicago Ave. accomplished. Cost, $16,000,000. Has increased property values $100,000,000 and facilitated traffic 200 per cent. Three bond issues—total $8,800,000—passed 1914, 1918, 1919.

Two-level construction—upper level for light traffic, lower for heavy traffic—double-decked bascule bridge, 235 ft. long, 90 ft. wide, carries heaviest traffic of any bridge in the world—100 per cent greater than famous London Bridge. Plazas approximately 225 ft. square on the upper and lower levels at both the north and south approaches. Sculptural embellishment of bridge houses has been made possible by the gift of $100,000 jointly from William Wrigley, Jr., and the Ferguson Fund trustees.

Recommended by Plan Commission, July, 1911; city ordinance passed March, 1914; case brought to trial Feb., 1916; ended March, 1918; first building torn down April, 1918. Improvement constructed by Board of Local Improvements. Street opened May, 1920. Eastern boundary of traffic quadrangle around heart of city.

Ogden Avenue—Opening at a width of 108 ft. northeast from its present terminus at Union Park for 2.7 miles to Lincoln Park at Clark and Center Sts.

DANIEL J. SCHUYLER, JR.

DANIEL J. SCHUYLER, JR., attorney, was born in Chicago, Sept. 28, 1874; s. of Daniel J. and Mary (Byford) Schuyler; ed. Harvard Prep. Sch.; LL.B. Degree from N'Western Univ. 1896; married Sybil Moorhouse of Chicago, Feb. 27, 1906. Children: William Moorhouse, Daniel Merrick. Adm. to Ill. Bar, 1896; formerly mem., Schuyler, Ettelson & Weinfeld, now Schuyler & Weinfeld. Represented Ill. Central R. R. in negotiations with S. Park Comm. and City of Chicago in Lake Front imp. plan involving $130,000,000.00 and brought negotiations to successful conclusion. Mem. Am., Ill., and Chicago Bar Assns. Republican. Mem. Phi Delta Phi. Clubs: Union League, University, Indian Hill. Home: 3741 Grand Blvd. Office: 39 S. La Salle St.

Accessibility to and from all parts of the city; Adequate surrounding street area; Advantage of fronting upon two-level portion of Canal St., affording truck access from Clinton St. to the lower floor, and from Canal St. to the main floor; Location between the Northwestern and Union Stations, where 62 per cent of the mail of Chicago is handled, resulting in a saving to the government in haulage, equipment, and operation; Shortest and most direct connection by wagon or tube with the present post office; Maximum convenience and economy in postal operation and in dispatch of the mail service.

Final government action not yet taken.

Railway Terminals—See "Illinois Central Terminal" and "Union Station."

River Straightening—Union Station ordinance, passed by the City Council, March, 1914, contains a provision binding the railroad companies to cooperate in the straightening of the Chicago River between Polk and 16th Sts.

Robey Street—Not open in nine places, and varies in width from 30 to 100 ft. at 19 places. To be opened as a through street 86 ft. wide between Montrose Av. and 87th St.; Beverly Av. between Robey and 87th Sts. and Ashland Av. and 95th St. to be widened to 80 ft. as an extension of the Robey St. improvement. Recommended by Plan Commission, Dec., 1918. $9,200,000 bond issue authorized Nov., 1919; City Council ordinance covering sections between Roosevelt Rd. and 23d St. and 47th and 51st Sts. passed Jan. and Feb., 1921; and court petitions have been filed by the Board of Local Improvements on sections between Harrison St. and Roosevelt Rd. and Garfield Blvd. and 87th St. One of the three through north-and-south traffic arteries on the west side.

Roosevelt Road—Widening from 66 to 108 ft. between Ashland Av. and Canal St., and to 118 ft. between Wabash Av. and Michigan Av. accomplished; construction of 118-foot wide viaduct between Canal St. and Wabash Av., including new bridge across Chicago River, less than one-third completed. Cost approximately $8,000,000. Two bond issues total $2,950,000, passed 1912 and 1919. Recommended by Plan Commission Jan., 1910. City Council ordinance passed during administration of Mayor Fred A. Busse, April, 1911; court trial began Nov., 1914, during administration of Mayor Carter H. Harrison; and ended June, 1916, during the administration of Mayor William Hale Thompson. Street widened by Board of Local Improvements, Michael J. Faherty, President; work began August, 1916, and ended December, 1917. Southern boundary of traffic quadrangle around heart of city.

South Water Street—Widening from 80 to 135 ft. between Michigan Av. and Market St. by taking all land between the Chicago River and north line of South Water and River Sts. Two-level construction—upper street 110 ft. wide, at new bridge height established by the United States Government. Lower surface, at present dock level, 135 ft. wide, the extra 25 ft. providing a dock a mile long. The upper level meets all north-and-south streets, including the upper level of Michigan Av. and the normal street grade at Lake and Market Sts. Ample communication is provided between the lower level and the normal street grade. Estimated cost, $20,000,000; annual saving, $12,000,000. Recommended by Plan Commission November, 1917; City Council ordinance for widening passed December, 1919; construction ordinance not yet complete. $3,800,000 bond issue passed November, 1919; court petition filed by Board of Local Improvements, but case not yet brought to trial. Northern boundary to traffic quadrangle around heart of city.

Stadium—To be constructed by South Park Commissioners immediately south of the Field Museum as a part of the general lake front development.

Taylor Street—Widening from 60 to 80 ft. (by taking 20 ft. from south side of street) between Canal and Halsted Sts. Recommended by Plan Commission May, 1921; City Council ordinance passed July, 1921; court petition filed by Board of Local Improvements Aug., 1921. Part of west side warehouse district development.

Recommended by Plan Commission Dec., 1916; City Council ordinance passed February, 1919; court petition filed by Board of Local Improvements, March, 1919; $5,400,000 bond issue passed Nov., 1919; construction started April 8, 1922.

Polk Street—Widening from 40 to 80 ft. (by taking a 40-ft. strip on the south side) between Canal and Halsted Sts., recommended by Plan Commission May, 1914. City Council ordinance passed July, 1919; court petition filed by Board of Local Improvements Aug., 1921; part of west side warehouse district development.

Post Office—Chicago Plan Commission, Jan., 1915, recommended the two-block site fronting on Canal Street between Madison and Adams Sts., for a post office, because of the inadequacy of the present facilities, and for the following reasons:

Twenty-second Street—Widening to 120 ft. (by taking 54 ft. of property on the south side) between Calumet and Michigan Avs., and the creation of a new diagonal street 120 ft. wide between 22nd St. and Calumet Av. and 23d St. and South Park Av. Recommended by Plan Commission, Oct., 1921; City Council ordinance passed April, 1922. Part of general south side lake front development.

Union Station—Negotiations begun in Aug., 1912; ended March, 1914, with passage of city ordinance; estimated cost of railroad development, $75,000,-000. Sixteen Chicago Plan improvements were agreed to by the railroad companies, and will be constructed at an expense to them of approximately $6,000,000, in addition to which, the companies paid the city $1,500,000 in cash for vacated thoroughfares—a total of $7,500,000. These plan projects include the construction of a connection between Canal St. and Orleans St., connecting the north and west sides of the city via a two-level Kinzie St. bridge; widening Canal St. from 80 to 100 ft. between Washington St. and Roosevelt Rd.; grading Canal St. to as uniform a level as possible; opening Monroe, 14th and 16th Sts. as east-and-west thoroughfares; present and future widening of all east-and-west viaducts from Lake St. to Roosevelt Rd., inclusive; and provision for a viaduct on Congress St. when the city opens that thoroughfare from Franklin St. to the river.

West Side Railway Terminals—See "Union Station."

West Side Warehouse District—See "Clinton, Desplaines, Jefferson, Polk and Taylor Sts."

Western Avenue—Varies in width from 50 to 330 ft. at 18 places. To be made a minimum width of 100 ft. from city limits to city limits. Recommended by Plan Commission Feb., 1918. $2,400,000 bond issue passed Nov., 1919. City ordinances covering entire improvement in various sections passed July-Dec., 1919; court petitions filed by Board of Local Improvements during 1920 and 1922. One of the three through north-and-south traffic arteries on the west side.

Zoning—Chairman Charles H. Wacker of the Chicago Plan Commission is secretary of the Chicago Zoning Commission, and Consultant E. H. Bennett of the Plan Commission is Zoning Director.

JOHN A. MULDOON

JOHN A. MULDOON, one of the leading truck operators of the middle west, was born in Chicago in 1878; son of Anasthasia and John Muldoon. He was educated in public schools of the city. In 1900 he married Matha Thompson, by whom he had a son, John A., Jr. Mr. Muldoon married a second time in 1917, taking for his wife Josephine Cashin. Children: Paul John, Josephine Helen, Andrew. Mr. Muldoon has been identified with the wholesale drug business for many years. He now represents the Fuller-Morrison Co., the largest wholesale druggists in the West. He is one of the founders of the Motor Transportation Company, 1201 W. Lake street, which was incorporated in 1903. In addition to long-distance hauling, the company maintains a large garage and repair shop, which is noted for the excellency of its work. Mr. Muldoon resides at 4320 Hazel avenue. His office is at 1201 W. Lake street.

JOHN F. SIKYTA

JOHN F. SIKYTA, secretary to Postmaster A. C. Leuder, was born in Chicago, in 1871; s. of Mary (Turecek) and Mathias Sikyta. He was ed. in grammar schs. and business colleges of Chicago. In 1899, he married Millie Sindelar, in Chicago. Children: Robert, John, Edith and Mildred. Mr. Sikyta entered postal service January 1, 1890. His ability soon became recognized and he was advanced from one position to another until he was made secretary to Postmaster Leuder. Mr. Sikyta is generally recognized as one of the leading authorities on postal affairs in the country. Home: 1914 S. Avers Av. Office: Chicago Post Office.

HENRY AUGUSTUS BLAIR

HENRY AUGUSTUS BLAIR, financier, was born in Michigan City, Indiana, July 6, 1852; son of Chauncey Buckley and Caroline O. (DeGraff) Blair; educated at Williston Sem., Easthampton, Mass.; married Grace E. Pearce, of Chicago, February 19, 1878; children: Natalie, Anita. After leaving school in 1871 entered the Merchants' National Bank of Chicago, of which his father was founder and with which he continued, becoming vice president, until 1902, when the bank consolidated with the Corn Exchange National Bank; became receiver North Chicago Street Ry. and West Chicago Street Ry., 1904, and continued as such until the reorganization of the properties into the Chicago Rys. Co., of which he has been president since November 3, 1913; chairman of board and president of Chicago Surface lines; vice president, Illinois Trust & Savings Bank; director Elgin National Watch Company, Commonwealth Edison Company, Public Service Company of Northern Illinois, etc. Republican. Clubs: Chicago, Union League, Caxton, Chicago Golf, Midlothian, South Shore Country, Shore Acres, Onwentsia, Saddle and Cycle. Recreation: golf. Home: 2735 Prairie Avenue; (summer) Jefferson, N. H. Office: 105 S. La Salle St., Chicago.

CHICAGO'S PUBLIC UTILITIES

FIFTY YEARS AGO, a Chicago millionaire rose from his bed, lighted the gas jet (one of the few in the neighborhood), dressed and shaved by its flickering, uncertain light, and made his way downstairs by the dimly lighted stairway. At breakfast he and his wife talked about the high cost of cord wood and coal; gas for cooking and heating and electricity for light and power were unknown then.

Breakfast finished, he climbed into his horse-drawn rig and was "jogged" down to the office at five miles an hour. Laboriously he climbed several flights of stairs, there were no high speed elevators making skyscrapers possible), penned some business letters, got into his buggy and drove around to keep some business appointments. The day then gone, he went home, tired from his labors, but only to repeat the same monotonous routine on each succeeding day.

"I haven't heard from daughter for three weeks and I'm worried about her," said his wife during the evening meal. "She hasn't answered the last letter I wrote her. Let's drive out and see her tonight."

"Oh, it's four miles out there, the horse is tired, and we will be so late getting back. Let's wait until next week," replied her husband.

So the journey was postponed and mother wrote her daughter another letter instead.

Members of the same family, residents of the same city, yet practically strangers! That was the plight of Chicagoans of 50 years ago.

All the Millionaire's Money Could Not Buy the Workingman's Comforts of Today

Today the whole manner of living has changed. Distance has been annihilated. The telephone and electric cars place the whole world just beyond our threshold. Electricity and gas, whether in our waking or sleeping hours, are now ready at our instant touch of a button or lever to be our willing, obedient servants.

All the money of the millionaire of 50 years ago could not buy these most commonplace comforts, conveniences and luxuries of the ordinary workingman of today.

These services did not exist.

A wonderful transformation—a miracle—has happened in the last half century, that has placed all men and women, rich or poor, on the same level in relation to the fundamental conveniences of life.

Today the worker in the factory or mill, in the construction gang, or the clerk in the store or office, arises from his bed, presses a button which causes his room to be flooded with light as bright as day. Breakfast is cooked over an instantaneous gas fire—clean, dependable and always ready.

An electric car whisks him to work at 20 miles an hour. If he works in a factory, he finds an untiring electric machine ready to relieve him of great physical labors in his work. An electric fan throws a cooling breeze. If he

41

BRITTON I. BUDD

BRITTON I. BUDD, railway president, was educated in the public schools of Chicago and Shattuck School, Faribault, Minn. Married Katharine Kreigh, of Chicago, January 1, 1900. Began as member of a railway surveying corps in 1895; entered service of Metropolitan West Side Elevated Railway Company and served in various capacities, becoming president April 10, 1910; also president Northwestern Elevated Railroad Company, South Side Elevated Railroad Company, and chief executive for receiver of Chicago & Oak Park Elevated Railroad Company; president of Chicago North Shore and Milwaukee Railroad. Director of Middle West Utilities Company, Northwest Utilities Company, Ironwood & Bessemer Company, Utilities Securities Company, Eastern Wisconsin Electric Company, Auditorium Association. Clubs: Union League, Exmoor Country, Industrial. Member Western Society of Engineers. Home: Highland Park, Illinois. Office: 1234 Edison Building, Chicago.

works in an office there are electric lights to turn dark corners into daylight; a telephone that connects with home, around the corner or to New York and San Francisco. His work ended, he speeds home again on the dependable electric car, and during the evening meal learns that his wife also has spent a pleasant day.

Mr. Workingman's wife says to her husband at the evening meal:

"I talked to Betty, Jane and Mary over the telephone today. This was my big day, but with my electric washing machine, my electric iron and my vacuum cleaner I can accomplish so much without being tired. I called up the store for my groceries, and the doctor gave me a prescription over the wire for baby, so I didn't have to go there. Let's take a car and run down and see the Smiths tonight. Call them on the telephone and let them know we're coming."

Although the Smiths live 10 miles away, they are able to visit them and spend several hours before bed time, because transportation has cut down the barrier of distance and opened all of Chicago and its suburbs to all the people.

What a Transformation! It's a "Half Century Miracle"

Great genii have brought about this wonderful transformation. They have made possible the modern Chicago. Without them, the city could not function commercially, industrially, socially, or even exist as it is today. These public servants serving the poor and rich alike are represented by the wonder workers of modern times—the public utilities; the electric, gas, street and elevated railways and telephone companies.

They did not spring into existence overnight, nor do they grow and give service by magic. They are the fruits of tremendous effort by men of vision, of fighting spirit, of great inventive ideas and unparalleled constructive ability. They are the products of uncountable sums of money which hundreds of thousands of workers saved from their earnings, so that they might purchase securities and become part owners of these public utility companies, having faith in this investment and confidence that they would receive a fair rate of interest for the use of their money.

With this money, vast plants have been built and pipes, wires and tracks laid by great armies of men, so that all the people, whether they had invested in these great enterprises or not, would receive the same degree of service.

The Housewife's Servant: Business Man's Partner

These efficient utilities are the servants of the housewife and the invisible partner of the business man. They light the lamps, cook the meals, provide the heat, call the doctor, the police or the fireman, make possible business and social intercourse, whether it be with next door or thousands of miles away, carry millions of workers to and from their employment, turn the wheels of great factories, making employment to millions possible, and at every turn, day and night, winter and summer, lighten the burdens, make for better health and bring happiness, convenience and prosperity to all of the people of the great busy city.

Today these genii smile at their far-reaching accomplishment. But the task is not done. It will never be done. With driving force, the work must go on. Not for an instant can the managers of the great utilities hesitate in their work of building, their constant planning, their untiring inventing and developing. For every baby that is born, for every new citizen who comes to the city and for every uplift in the standard of living, more pipes must be laid, more wires must

43

be strung, more tracks must be pushed out into sparsely settled parts of the city to be used in all manifestations of the social, business and industrial life of the great city.

As It Was and Now. How the Giant Grew

So tremendous a factor in the city's life has this great service become—so unfailing and intimate—that one might believe its bounties had always been available.

Yet it was only as late as May 25, 1882, that the Western Edison Light Company, the Commonwealth Edison Company's predecessor, was chartered. This little company, like the present gigantic electrical enterprise, was a distinctively home-owned Chicago institution.

But, with its eleven original stockholders it was a pigmy alongside of the great Edison family of today of more than 26,000 stockholders, more than 90 per cent of whom are residents of the city.

The company obtained a franchise authorizing it to distribute electricity throughout the then city of Chicago in 1887, this franchise being assigned to its successor, the Chicago Edison Company, in the same year. This latter company built its first generating station at 139 Adams Street (now 120 West Adams Street) from which the sale of electricity was begun in August, 1888. In 1898 the men in charge of the Chicago Edison Company secured control of the Commonwealth Electric Company, which, in 1907, was consolidated with the Chicago Edison Company to form the present Commonwealth Edison Company. With the parent Edison stem, many other electric central station companies have been united, including the Chicago Arc Light and Power Company and the Cosmopolitan Electric Company, the latter being absorbed in 1913. The scores of small and uneconomical plants in the 200 square miles of area of Chicago have thus, as the years passed, been succeeded by one city-wide organization for the production and distribution of electricity, to the great advantage of the people of the city, both in the character of the service and the low rates made possible by centralization of generation and distribution.

The tremendous growth in output of the Commonwealth Edison Company of 740 times since 1890 is largely accounted for by the great and manifold uses to which electricity is put in Chicago, both in the home and the factory. In 1890 the sales of electricity amounted to about two to three kilowatt-hours per inhabitant. In 1921 this had been increased to over 600 kilowatt-hours per capita. Electricity was something remote, strange and mysterious in 1890; now a child pushes a button and is its master.

As indicative of how electricity has been placed at the service of Chicago and the faith investors have had in the great city and its ultimate fairness to invested capital, some figures are illuminating.

In 1889 the output of the Chicago Edison Company was 874,000 kilowatt-hours.

In 1921, its successor, the Commonwealth Edison Company, reported an output of over 1,928,271,000 kilowatt-hours.

In 1888 the original rating of the Edison generating equipment was about 640 kilowatts.

At the end of 1921 the rating of the generating stations of the Commonwealth Edison Company, including storage batteries, was about 630,000 kilowatts, or 850,000 horsepower.

Half Million Homes and Factories Have Light and Power

In 1893 the number of customers was 4,452. Now more than 537,000 homes, factories, railways, stores and offices are being served.
to meet the demands for service. Always the utilities must keep ahead of the demand and stand ready to serve.

Utility Development a Wonder Tale

The bare historical facts of Chicago's public utilities, efficiently rendering service as they do at a cost second only in cheapness of all products to the two-cent postage stamp, is a wonder tale. Today the city's utility services of all kinds average probably higher than anywhere in the world.

A quarter of a million people—more than the total population of many important cities—derive their living today from the city's utilities, they being the great army of more than 51,000 employes and their families. Still hundreds ot thousands of others, constituting the men and women who have more than $600,000,000 invested in the stocks and bonds of these companies, and their families, rely for part of their family income from their thrifty investments. The vast sum they have invested so that every person, poor or rich, may equally benefit from these services, is equal to more than $229 for every man, woman and child in the city.

Utilities Exemplification of "I Will" Spirit

These great public utilities are not "accidents."

They have not, like Topsy, "just growed." They are the materialization of tremendous effort, an example of the great way in which the happiness and convenience of the giant Chicago's people are cared for, a striking commentary of the faith investors have in the city's fairness and their belief that savings invested in the public's benefit will be protected and a mute demonstration of the "I Will" spirit which moves the great city.

Succeeding pages offer a brief survey of the origin and development of the great utilities that serve the city.

ELECTRIC LIGHT AND POWER

Electrically, Chicago is the most interesting of all cities.

Its electric company—the Commonwealth Edison Company—has the largest individual electricity-supplying system in any city in the world.

The use of electricity, per capita, is probably greater than in any other large city.

Since 1890, the growth of Chicago's population has been two and one-half times. The output of the Commonwealth Edison Company has been expanded in the same period 740 times.

In 1921 the company reported the enormous station output of 1,928,271,940 kilowatt-hours. This figure is larger than the population of the world and one kilowatt-hour will keep twenty average sized incandescent lamps burning for an hour.

Into the maw of the great furnaces at the generating plants goes annually more than 2,150,000 tons of coal—practically all of it coming from the company's own mines—to be changed from latent energy into economic, indispensable electric power for factories, to make the electric transportation system operate, into light for homes, stores, factories, offices, hospitals, hotels—in fact,

JOHN M. ROACH

JOHN M. ROACH, former street railway president, was born in Lowell, O., Jan. 30, 1851; son of John M. and Sarah Ann (Mackey) Roach. He was educated in public schools of Beverly and Athens, O. Mr. Roach married Katie E. Lyon, Elmira, N. Y., July 4, 1872. Son, Frederick. Mr. Roach entered the employ of the North Chicago Street Railway Co. as conductor in 1872; assistant superintendent, 1887; superintendent, 1890; second vice president, and general manager, 1893; became vice president and manager, West Chicago Street Railway Co., 1897; was also president of Cicero and Proviso Street Railway Co., Suburban Railway Co., Chicago Union Traction Co.; president of Chicago Railways Co. from 1907 to 1913, when he resigned. He is now a director. Clubs: Union League, Chicago Golf, Exmoor Country, Press. Home: 436 Surf St.

MITCHELL DAVIS FOLLANSBEE

MITCHELL DAVIS FOLLANS-BEE, attorney, was born in Chicago, Jan. 23, 1870; son of Geo. Alanson and Susan Dana (Davis) Follansbee; ed., South Div. High School, Harvard School, Chicago; A. B., Harvard, 1892; LL. B., Northwestern Univ., 1894 (LL.D., 1915); married Julia Rogers McConnell, April 14, 1903. Children: Eleanor, Mitchell Davis, Jr., Rogers, Susan, Julie. Practiced in Chicago since 1894; mem. Adams, Follansbee, Hawley & Shorey; dir. Bucyrus Co., Met. Life Ins. Co., Erie R. R., North Avenue State Bank. Mem. Am. Bar Assn., Ill. State Bar Assn., Chicago Bar Assn. (pres., 1914-15). Law Club, Legal Club. Republican, Unitarian; Clubs: University, Chicago, Casino, City, Saddle and Cycle, Harvard (Chicago) University, Harvard (New York), Recess (New York), Harvard Union (Cambridge, Mass.), Associated Harvard Clubs (ex-pres.). Home: 65 Bellevue Pl. Office: 137 S. La Salle St.

The original capitalization of the Chicago Edison Company in 1887 was $500,000, and the first bond issue, authorized in 1888, was $130,000.

In the interim, thrifty investors have poured a golden stream of money into the city's great electrical enterprise, to provide service for rich and poor alike, until the capitalization in 1921 of the Commonwealth Edison Company was $113,184,750, of which $55,553,750 represented capital stock and $57,631,000 bonds and notes.

The largest electric generator in the system in 1888 was rated at about 80 kilowatts, a toy compared with the great generators of 35,000 kilowatt rating now in use.

In 1889, the income from sales of electricity of the Chicago Edison Company was $105,700. In 1920, the operating revenues of the Commonwealth Edison Company were $37,139,830.

In 1921, the company paid out in various forms of taxes and municipal compensation the sum of $3,816,259, it being the largest payer of personal property taxes in Cook County.

Chicago's Great Electrical Plants

Chicago's electricity is produced at several great generating plants—the most prominent being Fisk Street Station, West Twenty-second and Fisk Streets with a rating of 230,000 kilowatts; Northwest Station, Roscoe Street and North California Avenue, with a rating of 165,000 kilowatts, and Quarry Street Station, West Twenty-fifth and Quarry Streets, with a rating of 84,000 kilowatts. The Calumet Station, west bank of the Calumet River, near Commercial Avenue and East One Hundredth Street, a new plant designed to have an ultimate rating of 180,000 kilowatts, is under construction. The company has other generating stations and also fifty-eight sub-stations scattered throughout the city, which are the centers of distribution for their own neighborhoods.

When the new Calumet plant is fully completed the company will have a greater electrical horsepower than the developed capacity of Niagara Falls.

The Fisk Street Station is the largest electric generating station in the world under one roof. Its turbo-generator room is 635 feet long. This station is of historic interest, for it was the first in the United States, and probably the world, to be designed for exclusive operation by steam turbines.

All electric railways, surface and elevated, of Chicago are operated by electrical energy purchased from the Commonwealth Edison Company. The company supplies power for factories, for the operation of elevators, for newspaper establishments, for the familiar electric fan, the helpful electric washing machine and all of the varied industrial requirements of Chicago. Its electric heat is in demand for the popular electric flat iron, cooking apparatus, household heaters and for countless other operations. At least 90 per cent of all the ice used in Chicago is manufactured by the use of Edison power. The company is officered by men who have grown up in its own ranks. It is "owned in Chicago."

CHICAGO'S GAS SERVICE

Hardly a person lives a single day in Chicago without being served in some way by gas. A person eats or drinks something cooked with gas; he comes into contact with gas lighting or he uses something that was manufactured with the assistance of gas.

RUSH CLARK BUTLER

RUS: CLARK BUTLER, lawyer, was born in Northwood, Ia., Aug. 27, 1871; s. Lindley S. and Julia (Pickering) Butler; Ph.B., Iowa State Univ., 1893. Married Isabelle Crilly of Chicago, June. 6 1901. Children: Rush Clark, Jr., Crilly, Milburn. Admitted to bar in 1894. Member of Butler, Lamb, Foster & Pope (specializing in practice of interstate commerce, federal revenue and Sherman law cases). Mem. Am., Ill., and Chicago Bar Assns., Chicago Law Inst., life mem. Chicago Historical Society and Art Inst. of Chicago; charter mem. Committee of Fifteen. Congregationalist. Mason. Clubs: Chicago, Union League, University, Industrial Law, Indian Hill, of Chicago, and Metropolitan and Chevy Chase of Washington, D. C. Author (with Cornelius Lynde) of The Federal Trade Commission and the Regulation of Business Under the Federal Trade Commission and Clayton Laws, 1915. Home: Winnetka, Ill. Office: 1414 Monadnock Blk.

FREDERICK H. WICKETT

FREDERICK H. WICKETT, president of Sapulpa Refining Co., was born June 23, 1868, in Devonshire, England, and taken by parents to Canada in 1871. Graduated in law, Ontario, Can. Came to Chicago, May, 1893 as assistant attorney for Northern Pacific R. R. Married Alice Wiswell, Morgan Park, 1893. Children: Kenneth Llewellyn, Dorothea Huszagh, Marjorie. Engaged in practice of corporation law for a number of years, quitting practice in 1910 to head Sapulpa Co. and other oil companies. Director Drexel State Bank and other corporations. Independent in politics. Episcopalian. Clubs: Mid-Day, Chicago Golf, Old Elm Golf, Chicago club. Office: 134 S. La Salle St. Residence: 229 Lake Shore Drive.

Chicago's supply of manufactured gas comes from the largest gas company operated as a single unit in the world, The Peoples Gas Light & Coke Company.

So efficient has been its operation and so painstaking has been preparation for the future, that today Chicago citizens enjoy gas service that is unexcelled anywhere in the world. Every day upwards of 705,000 homes in Chicago—practically all—have only gas as fuel for cooking. Preparation of the evening meal begins in these homes at practically the same hour every day—all begin using gas at about the same moment—yet the supply never fails day or night.

During 1921 the company manufactured 22,005,445,000 cubic feet of gas and purchased 6,474,786,000 cubic feet from other producers, or a total of 28,480,-231,000 cubic feet. The average daily distribution of gas amounted to practically 86,000,000 cubic feet.

To manufacture this gas for Chicago households and industries in 1920, the following raw material was required:

Bituminous coal .... 222,612 tons
Anthracite coal .... 95,332 tons
Coke .... 400,207 tons
Fuel oil .... 3,121,348 gallons
Enriching oil ....74,759,918 gallons

Miles of Mains Transport Your Gas

To "transport" the gas from manufacturing stations throughout the city requires an immense network of street mains—3,122 miles of them. Connected to these big mains are thousands of miles of smaller pipes, known as "services," which bring the gas to the consumer's premises.

How Chicago's Gas Company Grew

The first gas company in Chicago, the Chicago Gas Light and Coke Company, was organized in 1849, twelve years before the Civil War. In the years which followed several other companies were organized that supplied different parts of the city and also entered into disastrous and expensive competition with each other. In 1897 all of these companies were, by special provision of the legislature, consolidated with The Peoples Gas Light and Coke Company (which came into existence in 1855) and since then one great and efficient company has been the city's unfailing source of gas supply.

The total capitalization of the gas company is $84,786,000, of which $38,500,000 is capital stock owned by more than 7,000 men and women investors and $46,286,-000 is bonds. The present value of the company's property (in July, 1921) is in the neighborhood of $140,000.000.

How the City Is Efficiently Served

Chicago is served with gas manufactured at seven big gas making plants scattered throughout the city, which are coupled up with a number of distributing stations and all linked by the great network of gas mains.

DR. HENRY EUGENE IRISH

DR. HENRY EUGENE IRISH, noted pediatrician, treating children only, was born in Jackson, Mich., March 31, 1877; son of Diana (Moe) and David Irish. He was educated in Jackson public schools and received M.D. degree from the University of Illinois. In May, 1916, he married Elizabeth Blume, of Chicago. Children: Nellith C., D. Vernon, Rosemary Jean, Shirley Elizabeth, Keith Randall. Dr. Irish is associate professor of pediatries at the University of Illinois, attending pediatrician to University and Cook County hospitals and consulting physician for the Municipal Contagious hospital. He has written a number of articles on pharmacology, retrapharyngeal abscess and lumbar puncture. During the war, Dr. Irish served with exemption board No. 30 and as a teacher at Military school of University of Illinois. Member of A. F. & A. M., Maccabees, K. P., and O. E. S. Clubs: Town and Country, Riverside Golf. Home: 5312 Washington blvd. Office: 30 N. Michigan blvd.

C. C. LE FORGEE

ONE of the most prominent figures associated with the bar of Illinois is C. C. Le Forgee, of Decatur. Since the day he gave his valedictory glance to college, Mr. Le Forgee has built up a large clientele that numbers men prominent in life in every part of the state. When Gov. Len Small was placed on trial on a charge of embezzling funds from the state treasurer's office during his tenure of office as treasurer, he selected Mr. Le Forgee as one of his chief counsel. The confidence the state's chief executive had in Mr. Le Forgee's ability has since been merited. It was Mr. Le Forgee who helped clear the governor in the Waukegan trial of 1922. Mr. Le Forgee has his offices in Decatur, Ill.

A gas manufacturing plant is a highly complicated establishment, each consisting of eight or more large and small buildings. In a medium sized plant there are usually a dozen gas "machines," each consisting of three parts (generator, carburetor and superheater) which are either in one steel shell or in three separate shells according to the type of machine. After the gas has been "scrubbed," "condensed" and "purified," the tar and other chemical elements being extracted, it is put into great gas holders which operate somewhat like a collapsible tin cup. Each manufacturing station has two to three gas holders. To make certain that Chicago's gas pressure will be even throughout the city, nine storage or distribution holders and pumping machinery, are in operation away from the manufacturing plants. These holders store gas and at the periods of the day—meal times—when gas is needed the most, send out a supply. One distribution holder, recently built at Crawford Avenue and Thirty-first Street, is the second largest in the United States and has a capacity of 10,000,000 cubic feet.

Tremendous Addition to Insure City's Supply

On the Drainage Canal a great water gas plant and a by-product coal gas plant has been built at a cost of $18,000,000, adding upwards of 40,000.000 cubic feet of gas a day to Chicago's supply and also providing coke for existing plants. This was the second largest building project in the Middle West during the years of 1920 and 1921.

The main building of The Peoples Gas Light and Coke Company is a 21-story skyscraper at Michigan Avenue and Adams Street, which is said to compare with any office building in the world in beauty and general utility.

Gas has come into wide industrial use in Chicago because of its superiority as a fuel from the standpoints of uniformity, concentration, ease of control, cleanliness, lack of storage space requirements, expense of handling and financing the supply, all of which combine to make it a most desirable factory fuel. It is largely used to melt metals such as aluminum, babbitt, lead, brass, tin, zinc and linotype. Gas fired core ovens, wherein casting molds are baked, have proved very economical. Forging work is also a large consumer of gas; and porcelain enameling, brazing and japanning are other processes wherein it is widely used. Gas fired steam boilers for plating and pressing, gas fired lumber kilns, china kilns, coffee roasters, smoke houses and candy furnaces are also in common use. There are industrial customers of the company who use as high as 15,000,-000 cubic feet of gas monthly.

Big and Continuous Fuel Supply Necessary to Protect Gas Users

A continuing supply of oil, coke and coal, as well as other raw materials necessary in the making of gas, is one of the gas company's major problems. Unlike other businesses, public utility companies can not "close down" because prices of products they use are too high or shortages exist. An interruption would be a public calamity. Such enormous quantities of raw materials are necessary in the production of gas for a great city like Chicago that the future supply must be protected always with contracts. This is a handicap to economical buying when the tendency of prices is downward, but must be accepted in the public's protection.

Gas being sold directly from the producer (the gas company) to the consumer—without any middleman as in most businesses—the housewife, herself,

DR. BENJAMIN HARRISON BREAKSTONE

DR. BENJAMIN H. BREAK-STONE, president of West End Hospital and Training School for Nurses and National College of Midwifery, was born in Lithuania, 1877; s. of Esther (Semiatisky) and Judah Reubin Breakstone; ed. in N. Y. and Scranton pub. schs.; B. S. degree, Carnegie Univ.; M. D. degree, Rush Medical Col., 1898. Married Rose Friedman, Chicago, 1905. Children: Judah R., Blanch D., Irving L., Annette. Surgeon, Mary Thompson Hosp. since 1903; chief surgeon, Maimonides Hosp., 1912-16; Cook County Hosp., 1906-08; Jefferson Pk. Hosp., 1906-21; Douglas Hosp., 1915-17; German Am. and Chgo. Gen. Hosp., 1915-19; Municipal T. B. Sanitarium since 1916. At West End Hospital since 1916. Mem. Am. Medical Assn.; Ill. and Chicago Med. Socs.; Physicians' Economical League; Ill. Med. Soc. Author of Medical Treatises. Clubs: Covenant, Sheridan Park, Press, Rogers Park Physicians, West Side Physicians. Home: 1309 Lunt av. Office: 35 S. Hoyne av.

DR. WESLEY MORLEY SHERIN

DR. WESLEY MORLEY SHER-IN, physician and surgeon, was born in Dubuque, Ia., Feb. 15, 1875; the son of Susan (Naylor) and Rev. Samuel Sherin. He attended grammar and high school in St. Paul and graduated from the medical department of the University of Minnesota in 1897 and from the University of Illinois in 1898. Dr. Sherin was married on Nov. 28, 1901, to Jeanne MacArthur of Chicago. Daughter, Betsy Jeanne. In 1898 he began the practice of medicine and surgery in Chicago and has since formed a large clientele. His work, which has been chiefly in surgery, has won the attention of medical leaders of Chicago. Dr. Sherin is a Methodist. He is also a member of the Masonic lodge. His home is at 7401 Crandon av. and his office at 31 N. State st.

regulates her own bills. When she wishes to "purchase" some gas for the cooking of a meal or other household duties, she turns a lever and strikes a match. When she wishes to stop "buying" she merely turns the lever again, the flow of gas stops and her "purchase" is ended. In this way she has complete supervision over her gas bill.

The first gas company in Chicago was authorized in its charter to charge $3 per thousand cubic feet for gas. In the charter of The Peoples Gas Light and Coke Company, under which the company operates today, the rate authorized was $2.50 per thousand. During the Civil War and after, the price of gas in Chicago, including war tax was as high as $4.50 per thousand. During the last 25 years the trend of prices of most fuels—coal, coke, wood, oil—has been steadily upwards, some grades of fuel being twice or three times the prices during the World's Fair year. On the other hand, the price of gas has tended steadily downward due to perfections in the art of making artificial gas and economies in operation and distribution.

HOW CHICAGO TALKS

Chicago has more than 610,000 telephones in use—one for each five persons —embracing a system furnishing universal local service and facilities for long distance communication to more than 13,000,000 telephones on the North American continent.

There are more telephones in Chicago than there are on the continents of Asia, Africa and South America taken together; more than there are in France, Italy, Spain, Greece, Portugal and Norway combined.

If the calls made in Chicago in one day were formed into one continuous call it would consume 6,250,000 minutes, or 12 years.

If the calls made in 1920 were formed into one continuous call it would take about 3,920 years to complete the conversation.

It is estimated that in Chicago the use of the telephone saves 28,750,000,000 minutes daily.

The telephone renders incalculable service to fire and police departments, these calls being handled free to any person making such use of the telephone.

Chicago Wires Would Wrap Earth 76 Times

The Illinois Bell Telephone Company, which owns and operates Chicago's wonderful system, has in use within the city limits 2,000,000 miles of wire, sufficient to encompass the earth at the equator 76 times.

Beyond the city's boundaries to the south, west and north, the Illinois Bell Telephone Company operates an additional 250,000 telephones, affording a rapid, convenient and inexpensive "express" service to industrial centers and suburban residential communities

The company is a state-wide one. It started 1922 with 857,875 telephones. It connects with nearly 600 other telephone companies in the state, making a total of 1,200,000 telephones in the state system.

The company operates 233 central offices. It has 2,306,000 miles of wire in its state system, mostly in underground cables, which guard against delays caused by storms and other unforeseen happenings.

GEORGE ANDREW BARR

GEORGE ANDREW BARR, state director of trade and commerce, was born in Will Co., Ill., May 25, 1873. He attended Joliet pub. schs., and prep. dept. of Univ. of Ill.; A. B. degree from Univ. of Ill. in 1897, and was admitted to the state bar in 1899. Married Mary W. Speer of Joliet, Oct. 16, 1902. Children: James W. and Joseph M. Mr. Barr was state's attorney of Will Co. from 1908 to 1912; pres. of Joliet Assn. of Commerce, 1917-19; chmn. for Joliet in 2d Liberty Loan Drive; chmn. of Will Co. in 5th Victory Loan Drive. He is a member of the firm of Barr & Barr, Joliet. His residence is Joliet.

RUSSELL JOHN POOLE

RUSSELL J. POOLE, Chicago food expert and wholesale grocer, was born in Tuscola, Ill., Aug. 26, 1878; s. of Mary Ann (Connor) and John Francis Poole. His great grandfather edited two bibles in 1800 for use of Queen of England. Mr. Poole received his education in Tuscola grammar school. Married Anna C. Beecher, Chicago, 1903. He started career as a laborer for the Illinois Central and left this to enter grocery business, gradually becoming head of wholesale firm at 6836-8 S. Chicago av. In 1919 he was appointed director of Bureau of Markets, Foods and Farm Products. A year later he was made secretary of the City Council Committee on High Cost and High Rents. His work is generally credited with having broken sugar gouging in 1920. Pres. of R. J. Poole Co. and dir. of 79th and Halsted State Savings bank. Mem. of Masonic Lodge, Aryan Grotto, Assn. of Comm., Thompson Rep. Club. Clubs: Hamilton, Kiwanis. Home: 7027 St. Lawrence av. Office: 6836 S. Chicago av. and 1003 City Hall.

In the territory served by this system there is a population of 6,506,000. This means a telephone for each 5.6 persons.

How the great communication company has worked with Chicago and aided in its wonderful growth is illustrated by figures showing the service given the city. The figures show the growth in telephones as follows:

Year	Population	Telephones in Service	Ratio of Telephones to Population
1878	537,600	400	1 to 1,344
1880	596,358	2,971	1 to 201
1890	1,250,000	7,766	1 to 161
1900	2,010,000	34,414	1 to 55
1910	2,329,000	239,083	1 to 9
1921	2,884,000	610,000	1 to 5

Investment for Chicago's Use Is Tremendous

The Illinois Bell Telephone Company has, according to its books, spent approximately $115,000,000 for land, buildings, equipment and apparatus, to give Chicago and Illinois this wonderful service. It would cost more than double this sum to replace this property.

In the last ten years, the growth has been three times that of the preceding thirty years and so tremendous is the giant Chicago's expansion that the present plant, engineers say, must be doubled in the next ten years if the company maintains its present service for the city.

How Chicago leads the great cities of the world in telephone service is illustrated by comparison with European cities, showing the ratio of telephones to population:

	Population	Telephones	Ratio of Telephones to Population
Chicago	2,884,000	610,000	1 to 5
London	6,726,000	293,000	1 to 23
Paris	2,888,000	120,000	1 to 24

Chicago has 33 telephone exchange buildings, averaging 24,000 square feet of floor space each, located, planned and built to meet the demands peculiar to telephone operation, in which 64 central office units, each designated by a name, are located. The capacity of each unit is 10,000 lines.

The company has about 16 000 employes in Chicago and suburban territory and about 5,000 downstate, and a payroll of approximately $24,000,000 per annum, most of which is spent over the counters of Chicago and Illinois business men.

Great Employe Army Constantly on Job

It requires 9,000 operators to handle the city and suburban calls, which vary from 1,000 per hour after midnight, to more than 260,000 per hour during the busy periods of the day. The total number of calls made in Chicago averages 2,750,000 daily.

In addition there are 7,668 subscribers' private branch exchange switchboards in use, through which telephone service of the large business concerns is handled, and these concerns employ more than 10,000 operators.

An army of experts is employed to police the lines and equipment and keep them in working condition. These experts are prepared to meet at a moment's notice, night or day, emergencies of every character.

To facilitate the use of the telephone in Chicago, 1,250,000 directories are distributed annually. If placed end to end they would reach from Chicago to Toledo, Ohio.

55

RICHARD S. FOLSOM

RICHARD S. FOLSOM, attorney, was born in Chicago in 1872; son of Sarah T. (Sweet) and Charles Antoine Folsom. Educated in Chicago public schools and Racine Coll., Racine, Wis.; Columbia Coll.; A.B., Williams, 1894; and at Northwestern Univ. Married Dorothy Moulton, Chicago, in 1905. Admitted to Illinois bar, 1896, and has since practiced law in Chicago; mem. of law firm of Lewis, Folsom, Asay and Streeter. Master in chancery, Cook County Circuit Court, 1911-15; corp. counsel, City of Chicago, 1915; gen. counsel, board of education, Chicago, 1912-15. Member of Chicago Bar Assn.; Law Club; American Bar Assn. Democrat. Episcopalian. Clubs: University, Mid-Day and South Shore Country. Home: 2917 S. Michigan av. Office: 105 W. Monroe street, Chicago.

MICHAEL L. IGOE

MICHAEL L. IGOE, attorney, was born in St. Paul, Minn., April 6, 1885; son of Katherine (Sherin) and James F. Igoe. Educated in St. James School and De La Salle Institute, Chicago, and Georgetown University, Washington, D. C.; came from Minneapolis to Chicago in 1894. Member of the firm of Freeman, Mason & Igoe. Member Illinois General Assembly, 1912-14-16-18 and Democratic leader, 1918. He was Assistant U. S. Attorney, 1913-17. Director West Thirty-First State Bank, Chicago. Clubs: Illinois Athletic, Olympia Fields Country, Iroquois, Elks. Residence address: 5434 Cornell avenue. Business address: 69 W. Washington street, Chicago.

Chicago has the largest plant in existence manufacturing telephone apparatus and equipment.

History of Chicago's Big Phone System

The first telephone was installed in Chicago in 1877—a year after Alexander Graham Bell exhibited his telephone at the Centennial Exposition (only three months after the first one was made). The Atlantic and Pacific Telegraph Co., with which B. E. Sunny, now president of the Illinois Bell, was connected, obtained four telephones (receiver type) and placed them upon a line connecting the telegraph office on Washington Street, opposite the present County Building, with the home of John N. Hills in Ravenswood.

On Dec. 21, 1878, the Bell Telephone Co. of Illinois was chartered upon petition of H. H. Eldred, G. E. Stockbridge, G. G. Eagle and C. S. Squires, the capital stock authorized being $80,000. Mr. Eldred was made general manager and Gardiner G. Hubbard, the father-in-law of Mr. Bell, president. Mr. Sunny became superintendent early in 1879. The general office of the company was in the basement of an old building now 11 South LaSalle Street and the principal exchange was on the top floor. The lines were located mostly upon the roofs of buildings.

In January, 1881, the Chicago Telephone Co. was incorporated with a capital of $500,000. Norman Williams, a prominent attorney, was its first president, being succeeded a few days after his election by Gen. Anson Stager. The property of the American District Telegraph Co. and the Bell Company was bought and the two systems unified by means of several aerial cables connecting the tower of the Bell exchange on LaSalle Street with the tower of the A. D. T. company opposite—where the Hotel LaSalle now stands.

At the end of 1882 the new company had 2,610 telephones in Chicago and 392 in suburban towns. The growth of the system was slow, capital being hard to obtain and inductive interference, cumbersome switching apparatus, impracticable underground cables and high maintenance costs being some of the problems. It was not until 1896 that the great period of expansion began and Chicago's wonderful telephone system of today began to take definite form.

ELECTRIC STREET CARS

The Chicago Surface Lines is the largest system in the world under a single management. It is a combined operation of the Chicago Railways Company—the west and north side line—and the Chicago City Railway Company, the Calumet and South Chicago and the Southern Street Railway companies—the south side lines—so that the people might ride over the tracks of all companies for a single fare.

There are over 1,000 miles of single track and 3,085 double truck cars.

The double right of way, approximately 530 miles in length, paved with Belgian block, would reach almost to Buffalo and is maintained, cleaned and cleared by the company.

The Surface Lines have the most liberal transfer system in the world, the use of transfers being unlimited so long as the passenger continues to travel in the same general direction.

For every 100 cash fares collected there are 70 transfers issued and used

57

FREDERICK A. BANGS

FREDERICK A. BANGS, lawyer, was born in Lacon, Ill., April 3, 1865; s. of Harriet Cornelia (Pomeroy) and Mark Bangs. He is a descendant of Edward Bangs who came from England in second ship after Mayflower. Mr. Bangs was ed. in pub. schs. of Lacon and Chicago; L. L. B. degree from N. W. Univ. Admitted to Ill. bar in 1886; mem. of law firm of Bangs, Wood & Bangs until dissolved in 1904; practiced alone until he formed partnership with Ald. E. I. Frankhauser in 1920, which is still in existence. Director and gen. counsel for D. A. Stuart & Co. Served as colonel on Gov. Yates' staff during latter's term of office; pres. of West Chicago Park Comm. from 1900 to 1905. Mem. Chicago, Ill., and Am. Bar Assns. Home: 5838 Washington Blvd. Office: 522 First National Bank Bldg.

LLOYD DAVID HETH

LLOYD D. HETH, lawyer and former assistant state's attorney of Cook county, was born in Lena, Ill., July 7, 1886; s. of Mary Bickel (Davy) and Nathan Byron Heth. Received A.B. degree from Beloit Coll., 1908; grad., Univ. of Chicago Law School, 1913. While at Beloit, Mr. Heth won oratorical championship of eleven states. Coached Rockford, Ill., high school champion football team three years. Admitted to Ill. bar in 1913 and in 1919 was appointed assistant to State's Attorney Hoyne. His most famous case under Hoyne was the W. Bross Lloyd case, in which 20 anarchists were convicted. Under Hoyne's successor, Robert E. Crowe, he prosecuted Carl Wanderer, Tommy O'Connor, Glorianna Gang and Hyde Park bandits. He resigned in 1921 to resume private practice, but has been retained as special state's attorney to handle the Lloyd case appeal in supreme court. Author: "Civil Government in Illinois." Club: Hamilton. Home: 830 Galt av. Office: 38 S. Dearborn st.

Approximately 2,000,000 passengers (nearly one-third the number of the people in all Illinois) pay cash fares daily, and there are 1,500,000 rides furnished on transfers, or a total of 3,500,000 riders carried each day to and from work or pleasure.

The Surface Lines property devoted to public service, if reproduced new today, would cost about $250,000,000.

Over 16,000 Employes; Wages Over $30,000,000

For the year ended January 31, 1922, the Surface Lines paid out as operating wages $30,967,701, this being more than 66.58 per cent of the total expenses.

The Company has over 16,000 employes, of whom more than 11,000 are conductors and motormen.

The power used by the company during the past year amounted to 496,-579,296 kilowatt hours.

In 1893 there began a general change from horse and cable to electric operation. This was the year of the Chicago World's Fair and the Intramural Railway on the fair grounds was one of the first experiments with electric cars on an elevated structure. The first electric cars were largely remodeled horse and cable cars. Four wheel motor trucks carrying the motors were substituted for the old trucks. The cars were lighted and later were heated by electricity. The length of cars was from 12 to 18 feet, which was soon increased to 22 and 24 feet.

The first motors in Chicago were 15-horse power capacity. The cars and equipment weighed about 12,000 pounds which was soon after increased to 18,000 pounds. Longitudinal seats were the standard. There were no enclosed vestibules. In 1893 the first overhead trolley system in Chicago was built, and by 1896 most of the horse cars had been abandoned. By the end of 1906 all of the cable lines had been electrified.

Chicago's Transportation Progress Rapid

Interesting historical dates in the development of the city's great surface transportation system have been:

1858—Nov. 1—Ground broken at State and Randolph streets for first horse car lines.

1859—Four cars running (population of city about 108,000).

1864—Steam dummy running on Evanston Avenue (now Broadway) from Diversey to Graceland Cemetery.

1871—Steam dummy running on Cottage Grove Avenue from Oakwood to Fifty-fifth Street, and on Fifty-fifth east to Lake Avenue.

1882—Jan. 28—First cable line began operation on State Street as far south as Twenty-Second Street.

1887—The north side lines extended as far as Irving Park Boulevard by way of Clark Street and Evanston Avenue (now Broadway). The South Side lines as far as Fortieth Street. The West Side lines as far as Garfield Park.

1888—March—First north Side Cable on Clark street to Diversey Boulevard.

1890—July—First West Side cable on Madison Street (Population 1,099,850).

1893—First overhead trolley line put in operation by South Side company (Chicago City Railway Company).

1894-95-96—Various other lines electrified and numerous extensions built.

1906—All cable lines changed to overhead trolley.

EVAN EVANS

EVAN EVANS, president of the Moffett Studio and a number of other commercial enterprises, is another product of Ohio. from whence come presidents and big business men. The son of Jane and Griffith E. Evans, he was educated in Missouri Normal School. Although handicapped by the lack of capital, he made up for this deficiency by hard work and it was not long before he was heading a commercial photographic enterprise. Photography had always interested him and in the development of it he poured a great deal of his energy. Following the organization of the Moffett Studio, he formed the Drake and Matzene Studios, of which he is still the head. Mr. Evans is also president of the Ohio Building Company and the Stout Manufacturing Company. Mr. Evans was married to Pauline Hart in Chicago. Mr. Evans' clubs are Union League, Chicago Athletic, Exmoor Country, Forty and Arts; Lambs (New York). He resides at Ambassador Hotel. Office: 509 South Wabash avenue

1907—Feb. 11—"Settlement Ordinances" passed affecting surface lines. Nov. 24—Pay-As-You-Enter cars introduced on Cottage Grove Avenue.

1914—Feb. 1—Unified operation of all surface lines in city effective.

In 1859 car tracks were laid upon 9 miles of city streets. Early growth was not rapid.

In 1866 there were but 29 miles of track and in 1876 but 54 miles. In successive years the mileage was as follows: 1886, 131 miles; 1896, 344 miles; 1907, 385 miles; 1916, 475 miles and in 1921 there are 530 miles. In general these figures may be multiplied by two to give the miles of single track.

In 1866 a single fare would buy a 2-mile ride.

In 1886 a single fare would buy a 4-mile ride.

In 1896 a single fare would buy a 12-mile ride.

Now a single fare will buy a 32-mile ride, this being possible because of the liberal transfer system.

Surface Lines Lead World In Development

The Chicago Surface Lines exceed any other city railway, surface, elevated or subway in the world in number of miles of track, number of cars, number of car hours and car miles operated and of passengers carried.

Comparing this system with all the electric railways (surface, subway and elevated) in the United States, it has about 2.3 per cent of the total miles of track; about 3.7 per cent of all passenger cars; it employs 5.2 per cent of all the employes and about 7.8 per cent of all the motormen and conductors; it operates about 5.3 per cent of the total number of car miles and carries about 6.5 per cent of all revenue passengers and about 18 per cent of all transfer passengers.

Surface transportation in Chicago presents enormous difficulties because of the traffic congestion on the streets and because of the simultaneous movements of hundreds of thousands of people during the rush hours. In the morning and in the evening, this "rush" comes as people go to and from work, the demand for transportation at these periods being 100 per cent greater than during the normal hours of the day. To meet this requires the maintenance of a very expensive reserve equipment above that necessary for ordinary transportation demands.

The speed with which Chicago is given transportation in the rush hours is illustrated by one busy intersection. At the point where North Halsted Street and West Grand and Milwaukee Avenues intersect, there are operated over this crossing during the "peak" of the morning and evening rush hour a car every 6 seconds—10 cars a minute—this not taking into account the miscellaneous traffic over the crossing. At this same intersection, approximately 30,000 people transfer from one line to another during the course of a day.

ELECTRIC ELEVATED RAILROADS

Without equal in the world is the service of the Chicago Elevated Railroads, this either considered from the viewpoint of safety of passengers, high speed or distance which may be traveled for a single fare without change of cars.

Radiating from the "loop," or business heart of the city, the elevated lines extend far beyond the city limits on the North and West sides of the city and for a distance of ten miles on the South side. From the main line in each

LUIGI CARNOVALE

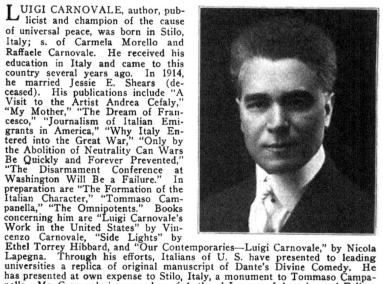

LUIGI CARNOVALE, author, publicist and champion of the cause of universal peace, was born in Stilo, Italy; s. of Carmela Morello and Raffaele Carnovale. He received his education in Italy and came to this country several years ago. In 1914, he married Jessie E. Shears (deceased). His publications include "A Visit to the Artist Andrea Cefaly," "My Mother," "The Dream of Francesco," "Journalism of Italian Emigrants in America," "Why Italy Entered into the Great War," "Only by the Abolition of Neutrality Can Wars Be Quickly and Forever Prevented," "The Disarmament Conference at Washington Will Be a Failure." In preparation are "The Formation of the Italian Character," "Tommaso Campanella," "The Omnipotents." Books concerning him are "Luigi Carnovale's Work in the United States" by Vincenzo Carnovale, "Side Lights" by Ethel Torrey Hibbard, and "Our Contemporaries—Luigi Carnovale," by Nicola Lapegna. Through his efforts, Italians of U. S. have presented to leading universities a replica of original manuscript of Dante's Divine Comedy. He has presented at own expense to Stilo, Italy, a monument to Tommaso Campanella. Mr. Carnovale is a member of Authors' League of America and Fellow of American Geographical Society. 30 N. Michigan Blvd., Chicago.

DR. MAX. THOREK

DR. MAX THOREK, surgeon, was born in Hungary, in 1880; s. of Sarah (Mahler) and Isaac Thorek. He removed with parents to America in 1900. He was educated in schools of Hungary and was graduated from Rush Medical College, University of Chicago, in 1904. He was married to Fannie Unger, in Chicago, April 16, 1905. Son, Phillip. Dr. Thorek was an organizer of the American Theatrical Hospital Association which takes care of numbers of theatrical people, free of charge, when they are in need of such services. He is now president of Board of Trustees of the Hospital. He has been invited to deliver a lecture before International Congress of Physicians, Rome, Italy, 1922. Member of Masons and Elks, Club: Press. Member Chicago Med. Society; Illinois Med. Society; Fellow American Medical Association; Teaches surgery to Post Graduates. Has been teaching surgery for many years. Late member of Consulting Staff, Cook County Hospital. Home: 646 Sheridan Road. Office: 30 N. Michigan Ave.

section of the city, one or more branches run off into business and residence neighborhoods, giving a fast and convenient service to practically every part of the city and adjoining suburbs.

The elevated railroads have 71.12 miles of roadway. There are 167.05 miles of single track on the main lines. The total mileage is 193.33 of single track.

Over these lines passengers can ride farther in one general direction for a single fare than in any other city in the country, one ride—from Linden Avenue, Wilmette, to Jackson Park—being 24 miles, this accomplished without changing cars and the running time being 77 minutes.

The average length of ride on the elevated is 6.48 miles compared with 4.16 miles on the New York Elevated and 5.57 miles on the New York subway. Express trains on the Chicago elevated make a little faster time than similar trains in the New York subway.

Over Half Million Ride "L" Daily

The average number of passengers carried daily on weekdays on the elevated railroads is 540,000. The record days have been: Nov. 11, 1918 (Armistice Day), 869,653 passengers; July 15, 1920 (strike on surface lines), 864,624 passengers.

The employes include 4,900 men and 600 women, a total of 5,500.

On April 29, 1920, a record was established when 953 elevated cars entered the "loop" in one hour.

The number of car miles run daily on the elevated lines averages 150,000, or equal to a distance of six times around the world at the equator.

Every 24 hours there are 5,232 trains of 16,812 cars run over the lines of the elevated railroads.

There are 206 stations on the lines, including 11 on the loop and 5 stub terminals.

There are 270 miles of copper cable in use and 23 miles of trolley wire, the copper required in power transmission alone weighing 5,201,000 pounds.

There are 35, 210 lights in elevated cars, which alone cost $10,998 a year to maintain and there are 16,225 lights in elevated stations, costing $16,352 a year. The cost of keeping passengers comfortable through heating of cars averages $166,800 a year, this being 10.65 per cent of the total power used.

The elevated lines have 1,664 cars in operation, it costing $1,202 per car for maintenance per year, as against $497 in 1914. The cost of a motor car is $23,500. They weigh 70,000 pounds and have 380 horse power motors. The elevated railroads pay taxes of approximately $900,000 a year.

Busiest Crossing In World on Elevated

The busiest railroad crossing in the world is at the elevated intersection of Lake and Wells Streets, where in the hour of maximum travel 218 trains of 1,100 cars pass this corner at the rate of 18 cars a minute. If these cars were coupled together they would make a continuous train of more than 10 miles in length.

The elevated railroads maintain 125 fully equipped first aid stations along their lines and a school for instructing first aid workers is conducted, which qualifies employes for this important work.

On regular routes the interval between trains in rush hours is two minutes and throughout the day six minutes, while after midnight trains operate 30 minutes apart. On the main lines where several branch lines use the same

GEORGE LANGER SCHEIN

GEORGE L. SCHEIN, lawyer, was born in Chicago, July 4, 1888; s. of Frances (Langer) and Louis Schein; ed. in Chicago pub. schs., Lake Forest Univ. for two years and Northwestern Univ. Law Dept. Married Louise Mayer, Chicago, Oct. 26, 1918. Children: George L., Jr., Louise. Mr. Schein was admitted to Ill. bar in 1910, becoming associated with late John E. W. Wayman. In 1914, he practiced alone, taking a leading part in the Chicago Tribune's anti-loan shark campaign. He then specialized in corporation law, being counsel for a number of big Chicago firms. In 1921, he became law partner of Ex-Judge Beckwith, former corp. counsel for City of Chicago. Dir. Oscar Mayer Packing Co., Victor May Co. Mem. Am., Ill., Chicago Bar Assns.; Assn. of Comm. Mem. of Masons, Elks. Clubs: Chicago Yacht, Lincoln, Press (Life), City. Home: 1310 Astor st. Office: Conway Bldg.

tracks for part of the distance, the interval between trains is one minute in rush hours.

For the safe conduct of passengers the elevated railroads have a record that stands unequalled on any transportation line. For more than 13 years there has not been a single fatal accident to a passenger on a train on the elevated. In that period the roads have carried more passengers than the entire population of the world.

How the "L" Grew From a "Dummy" Line

The first elevated railroad built in Chicago was the South Side Elevated Railroad. It began operation on June 6, 1892, with steam locomotives. The steam locomotives were abandoned and electric operation was substituted April 20, 1896.

The second line to begin operation was the Chicago and Oak Park, which first ran trains on a section of its line on Nov. 6, 1893. Steam locomotives were used until Sept. 20, 1896, when electric operation was instituted.

The Metropolitan West Side Elevated began operation May 6, 1895, on its main line, using electric power from the beginning.

The Northwestern Elevated began operation on its main line, May 31, 1900. On Sept. 3, 1901, the Northwestern purchased the Union Elevated Railroad Company (Union Loop), which had operated as a separate company from Oct. 1, 1897, and leased its lines to all the companies. The Loop is used jointly by the four companies.

Until Nov. 1913, the four elevated roads were operated separately, but on that date they were brought together under one management and through service operation was inaugurated between the Northwestern and South Side roads.

The elevated lines consist of several branches radiating, as do the surface lines, from the loop. On the South, the South Side Elevated line runs to Jackson Park and four separate branches extend to the stockyards, Kenwood, Englewood and Normal Park.

On the West, the Metropolitan West Side Elevated Railroad consists of a main line to Marshfield Junction and four branches from that point, these being the Logan Square, Humboldt Park, Douglas Park and Garfield Park lines, extending to the northwest side and far beyond the city limits to the west.

The Chicago and Oak Park Elevated runs west directly through Austin and Oak Park to River Forest.

On the North Side, the main line of the Northwestern Elevated parallels the Lake Michigan shore line from the heart of Chicago through Evanston, terminating at Wilmette. From the main line at Belmont Avenue, the Ravenswood branch runs northwest.

The Union Elevated Railroad (loop) forms a square in the business heart of Chicago and all lines use it.

The Chicago North Shore and Milwaukee Railroad, whose electric trains connect with points between the city and Milwaukee, enters the city over the Northwestern Elevated and runs around the loop. The cars of the Aurora, Elgin and Chicago Railroad enter the city over the Metropolitan Elevated, the terminal being at Quincy and Wells Streets. On the South and West Sides, the elevated and surface lines also connect with a number of other important interurban lines which serve wide sections of northern Illinois and Indiana.

65

DR. DEAN LEWIS

DR. DEAN LEWIS, Rush Medical College professor, was born in Kewanee, Ill., Aug. 11, 1874; s. of Winnie (Cully) and L. W. Lewis. He was educated in Kewanee schools; A.B., Rush Medical College, 1898; Sc. D., University of Cincinnati, 1920; LL. D., Lake Forest University, 1921. Married Pearl Miller, of St. Anthony, Idaho, Nov. 25, 1903. Dr. Lewis has engaged in practice of surgery since 1899 in Chicago. Asst. in anatomy, 1900-01, asso., 1901-03, instructor since 1903, Univ. of Chicago; prof. of surgery Rush Medical College. Mem. Am. Assn. of Anatomists, Am. Physiological Soc.; Eclat Club, Am. Surg. Assn., Am. Soc. Clin. Surg., Internat. Surg. Soc.; Western Surg. Assn.; Southern Surg. Soc.; Ill. State and Chicago Medical Socs. Clubs: University, City, Industrial, South Shore, Flossmoor. Frequent contributor to A. M. A. Journal. Home: 5757 Kenwood av. Office: 1454 Peoples Gas Bldg.

DR. WILL WALTER

DR. WILL WALTER, member of the senior staff of Evanston hospital and surgeon for Illinois Children's home, has gained eminence in specialized surgery, eye, ear and nose work through a keen curiosity to learn the advances of his science and years of research work following his graduation from University of Michigan in 1891. Dr. Walter's first hospital work was in St. Joseph's, Philadelphia. This he followed with study in Vienna and London for several summers since graduation. He is a fellow of American College of Surgeons, member of Oxford Ophthalmological congress, International Congress of Ophthalmologists at Lucerne and Illinois and Chicago Medical associations. Dr. Walter is an editor of the American Journal of Ophthalmology. He was born in Oakland County, Michigan, in 1866, married in Denver in 1893 to Frances George and has two sons, Will Hamilton and John Lorenzo. The doctor

is the organizer and president of the American Medical Golf Association. Clubs: Glen View Golf, University of Chicago and of Evanston, Evanston Country, North Shore Yacht. Home: Evanston.

WILLIAM J. HEALY

WILLIAM J. HEALY, realtor and trustee of the sanitary board of the District of Chicago, was born May 26, 1871, son of Margaret (Trant) and William Healy. He was educated in Chicago public schools, Worthington Business College and Kent College of Law. In 1900, he married Caroline Lynch, also of Chicago. Children: Rowena, George P. and Robert W. Following his graduation from law school, Mr. Healy entered the real estate business and his determination, energy and sound judgment soon placed him in the forefront of the business in Chicago. He has participated in and consummated many important transactions. He was a member of the City Council from 1910 to 1918, president of the sanitary board from 1920 to 1921, and is at present a trustee. Mr. Healy is the author of several important works treating with sewage construction both in the United States and in Europe. He is a member of the Elks and Chicago Lincoln Club. His clubs are the Illinois Athletic, Chicago Yacht, Westward Ho Golf. Home: 5562 Van Buren street. Office: Tower Building.

JAMES H. LAWLEY

JAMES H. LAWLEY, Member of the Board of Trustees of the Sanitary District of Chicago, was born in Chicago May 25, 1876, son of Sarah (Cameron) and James Lawley. He was educated in the public schools of Chicago, Bryant & Stratton Business College, and the Illinois College of Law. Member of the Chicago City Council for five terms, 1907-16. Member and chairman of the Board of Trustees of the Sanitary District of Chicago, 1916-22; member of Phi Alpha Delta; Hamilton Club. Politics, Republican. Home: 1925 W. Chicago Ave. Office address: 910 S. Michigan Ave., Chicago.

68

CHICAGO'S SANITARY DISTRICT

THE SYSTEM of sanitation in Chicago unquestionably is one of the most thorough, extensive and complete in the world. It covers a wider field, a greater expanse of territory, than that of any of the largest cities and in its entirety embraces an almost inconceivable diversity of ramifications and provides utilities for preserving public health unsurpassed in Europe or America. Chicago's health record has within recent years become a matter of world-wide comment, and the excellence of its sanitary conditions has stamped the Garden City as one of the healthiest on the Globe. All this, accomplished in the last twenty years under all but insurmountable difficulties, has excited the interest and wonderment of foreign municipalities whose officials have sent investigators to learn something of our great system and obtain a better knowledge of the difficult problem of preserving the health of their people.

Considering that Chicago is built upon ground that originally was a swamp, and now is largely artificial, the enormous amount of money and labor expended in perfecting its sanitary system can well be understood. Spots which within the memory of many of our older citizens bore signs displaying the warning, "NO BOTTOM," are today covered by fine pavements under which, are tunnels for freight from point to point to relieve the teeming street traffic.

Skyscrapers of twenty-two stories and over are reared upon foundations of steel and concrete which rest upon solid rock in some cases hundreds of feet below the surface. To construct tunnels and conduits through what formerly was marsh and quicksand called for the most scientific engineering and the indefatigable efforts of artisans of the highest skill. In many instances, work at the point of completion was destroyed by cave-ins or rendered insecure by softening of the earth, necessitating detours and reconstruction.

With the growth of the city arose imperative demands upon the resources of the sanitary department. The sewage facilities and the water supply had to be increased constantly to accommodate the phenomenal growth of the city's population. From year to year incessant increase of requirements taxed the resources of the department to the utmost and it was only by the exercise of the greatest ingenuity and financial wisdom that it was enabled to keep pace with the ever-increasing demands upon its resources. To divert the sewage of a city of a million from its water supply became a problem appalling in magnitude, not only because of the labor involved but also the great amount of capital required to carry it on. As the population grew from one to three millions the operatives and resources had to be increased in proportion.

The Sanitary District of Chicago was chartered in 1889 for the purpose of disposing of the sewage of the city by reversing the current of the Chicago river and causing it to flow from instead of into Lake Michigan with an outlet into the Illinois river, and further to provide for the disposal of sewage in any way practicable to prevent contamination of the water supply from the lake, and for the purification of the water by dilution. For many years, the river was a stream of filth which polluted the atmosphere of the entire city, spread diseases broadcast and discharging its deadly contents into the lake, befouled the water upon which the populace depended for its various hourly needs. Tunnels had been constructed miles out under the lake to obtain pure water, but the turgid tide of offal from the city became so voluminous that it forced its way to the cribs or intakes of the tunnels. The correction of this condition was the stupendous problem that confronted the Health Department of Chicago, and it was only through the establishing of the Sanitary District that the solution was achieved.

The area covered by the Sanitary District is 437.39 square miles, with a population, as given by the census of 1920, of 2,963,090, now over 3,000,000, and embracing forty-eight incorporated cities and towns. Within this area is an almost inconceivable network of tunnels and conduits, honeycombing the earth, which carry off the sewage and contain the wires of the great system. Through this area from the north flows the North Shore Channel which is flushed by pumping works with water from the lake. This channel carries the water down into the Main Channel through the great Sanitary Canal into the Des Plaines river. At Lawrence avenue, away north on the lake shore, are pumping works which add to the volume of water in the channel creating a current which draws the water through from the lake through the main channel of the Chicago river in to the South Branch, increasing the volume and accelerating the tide, and at the

MATTHIAS AUGUST MUELLER

MATTHIAS AUGUST MUELLER, vice-president and treasurer of the Gruene Mueller Coal Company, was born in Germany, 1864; s. of Sophie and Christian Mueller. When he was but a child, he removed with parents to Randolph Co., Ill. He received his education in county schools, and in 1883 came to Chicago. Married Minnie Warning, Chicago, Jan. 25, 1890. Children: Myrtle and Irene. By straightforward business methods he advanced in the coal business and became vice-president and treasurer of the Gruene Mueller Co. Mr. Mueller served as alderman for the 29th Ward under Mayor Busse, and as a member of the Sanitary District of Chicago for six years. Clubs: Hamilton, German. Home: 5017 S. Wood st. Office: 910 S. Michigan av.

70

southern end of the district is what is known as the Calumet Sag Channel which, drawing its water from the lake through the Calumet river, flows into the main channel, on into the canal and into the Illinois river.

The Chicago Drainage Canal is, in truth, one of the wonders of the world. It is thirty-one miles long, 160 feet wide and 26 feet deep. Work on it was begun in 1892 and the water was turned in eight years later, in 1900, and with its auxiliary channels, bridges, etc., cost more than $70,000,000. No public work in all the histories of the greatest cities of the world can compare with it, and beyond question it has preserved the health and saved the lives of countless thousands of people.

In addition to the preservation of health and life of Chicago's people, this great achievement of the Sanitary District has given them the benefits of bathing beaches, which before the sewage was diverted from the lake were unfit for use. These beaches during the summer are the daily resorts of thousands and add in great measure to the healthfulness and happiness of the people. Miles upon miles of concrete walks and driveways along the shore of a sweetscented lake, and a blue-green tide of odorless water in the Chicago river—marvelous! Which recalls the wonderment of a former citizen of Chicago, who had returned after a twenty-year residence in the East, as he stood upon the magnificent structure which replaces the old Rush Street Bridge, "Like a new world! You ought to see what used to float out of this river!" Ah yes, no longer is Chicago a withering stench in the nostrils of its people, and no longer can it justly be made a mark for the flippant shafts and wanton ridicule of the effete East. Our beautiful parks, our myriad miles of immaculate driveways, our architectural magnificence and, above all, our sweet waters. All, all attributable in largest measures to the efficacy of our great Sanitary System.

The Drainage Canal is the most important link in the long desired deep waterway between the Great Lakes and the Mississippi river. Along both sides of this channel and along its auxiliary, the Calumet Sag Channel are some of the best industrial sites in this section of the country. The Main Drainage Channel is paralleled by two railroads and the Calumet Sag is crossed by five, making these sites accessible by both rail and water. All told, there are approximately one hundred miles of water frontage. Some of the largest industries in the world have already taken advantage of long term leases on some of these sites and there is no doubt but that in the near future we will see along the banks of the Drainage Canal a vast industrial district. The growth of such a district will be hastened by the completion of the state waterway now under construction from the end of the Drainage Canal to the Illinois river.

To give in detail a description of the equipment, its extent and cost, would require the space of a sizable book in itself, which information is given in the literature issued by the Sanitary District at certain intervals. The great pumping stations, which draw many millions of gallons of water from the lake hourly for the dilution of the sewage that flows into the river, the bridges and dams of the Drainage Canal, the testing and treating stations, the miles upon miles of tunnels and conduits and all the adjuncts of the great system in their entirety attest the assertion that Chicago's Sanitary System is the greatest in the world.

The operation of this system has necessitated the selection of the most capable and experienced men in this country and many from foreign cities. From the ranks of scientists and skilled artisanry have been called adepts in all the various departments of operation, and the governing body is elected by the votes of the people. Politics have not been permitted to interfere with the efficiency of the system. The Board of Trustees consist of nine men of prominence and integrity, those now forming the present board being: Morris Eller, Matthias A. Mueller, James H. Lawley, Harry E. Littler, Lawrence F. King, Charles H. Sergel, William J. Healy, Willis O. Nance, Alexander N. Todd.

The officers are: Lawrence F King, president; Walter E. Schmidt, treasurer; William F. Mulvihill, attorney; Horace P. Ramey, acting chief engineer; William W. Smyth, clerk.

Horace P. Ramey is acting chief engineer; Edward F. Moore, assistant chief engineer; George M. Wisner, consulting engineer; Julius R. Hall, principal assistant engineer; Langdon Pearse, sanitary engineer; Samuel Moreell, chief structural engineer; H. I. Steffa, mechanical engineer; F. W. Mohlman, chemist; I. T. Roberts, electrical engineer.

The offices of the Sanitary District are located on the seventh floor at 910 S. Michigan avenue, Chicago.

71

W. H. FINLEY

W. H. FINLEY, president of the Chicago & North Western Railway Company, was born in New Castle County, Del., and was educated in the public schools at Wilmington. After private instruction in engineering, he entered the service of the Edge Moor Iron Company at Wilmington, in 1881, remaining with that company until 1887, when he accepted a position with the bridge and building department of the Chicago, Milwaukee & St. Paul, leaving the employ of that road in 1892 to go to the Chicago & North Western as engineer of bridges, from which position he was promoted successively to principal assistant engineer; assistant chief engineer and chief engineer. On June 11, 1918, he was elected President of the Chicago & North Western and on Sept. 19, 1922, was also elected president of the Chicago, St. Paul, Minneapolis & Omaha Railway, a subsidiary company. He is a member of the American Society of Civil Engineers; past president of the Western Society of Engineers and also the American Association of Engineers.

CHICAGO AS A RAILROAD CENTER

A TOTAL of 170,455 miles of freight cars are switched in Chicago railroads each year. That means a total of 15,000,000 freight cars, with mileage enough to belt the earth with a seven-standed necklace of the highly utilitarian vehicle that brings us everything we eat, wear and use.

These figures give a vague idea of the importance of the city recognized as the greatest railroad center in the world. They mean, for instance, that the total of more than 15,000,000 head of cows, sheep and hogs are hauled into the "yards" every year. They mean, again, that 400,000,000 bushels of grain—about two-thirds of the total consumed in the country—are brought here every year.

On the thirty-nine railroads entering the city, there are 1,500 trains a day and they carry into Chicago more than 190,000 persons. That is enough to make a good-sized city and the 1,500 trains a day mean more than a train a minute for the full twenty-four hours of the day. But most of the trains are run between daylight and dark, so as a matter of fact during the day there are two trains a minute entering Chicago carrying passengers and those trains, of course, have nothing to do with the thousands of miles of freight trains except to demonstrate the efficiency with which railroad departments of operation are able to systemize their work and keep the trains out of the way of each other.

Employes of Chicago railroads would make a city of more than 250,000.

One Chicago railroad yard is equipped to handle 10,000 cars daily and there are more than 100 yards here. That means possession of facilities for handling with system and dispatch the tremendous volume of business that flows toward Chicago every hour of the day and from every quarter of the world. Stop the railroads for a day and not only Chicago, but much of the rest of the country would feel the pinch of hunger.

The quarter of a million employes of the railroads draw down more than $1,000,000 a day in wages, which means more than $350,000,000 annually poured into Chicago channels of trade.

Every one of the thirty-nine railroads has its terminal in Chicago. One cannot cross the continent on any of the greatest trunk lines without stopping in Chicago, for the roads from the east end here, as do the roads from the west, and that means daily thousands of transient visitors who are here between trains and who leave some of their wealth on the way in and out.

With the possible exception of London, Chicago is the greatest distributing center in the world. The tonnage into and out of Chicago by rail is more than 600,000,000 annually. In connection with the 100 railroad yards, there are 177 freight distributing stations throughout the city, and more are being erected to facilitate the handling of the ever-increasing volume of business.

There are more than 1,400 miles of belt line trackage. Girding the city is the outer belt, which helps bring Chicago's daily supplies closer to the consumer.

These thirty-nine railroads have essential connections with more than half the entire railroad mileage of the country. Twenty-six of the roads are trunk lines, representing more than forty per cent of the mileage in the United States.

73

Within a night's ride of Chicago are 50,000,000 persons, a great percentage of whom get to the city with increasing frequency. Drawn by the facilities for shopping or buying in large quantities and for getting their purchases home, these people look upon Chicago as their "market town."

And to make their trip easy, the railroads have built, or are planning passenger terminal facilities that will be in keeping with the freight accommodations. There are seven main approaches by rail, of which four are east and south of the river and three are north and west.

There are six major railway passenger terminal stations—Northwestern, Union, LaSalle, Grand Central, Dearborn and Central. Of these, the Northwestern is comparatively new, and was erected at a cost of $25,000,000. Six main line elevated approach tracks and sixteen sub tracks enter it.

But the greatest railway terminal will be the Union station, the sub-structure work on which has been completed and the cost of which is to run high into the millions. It will serve the Pennsylvania, Burlington, Alton and St. Paul roads. Sixteen passenger tracks will enter the train sheds from the south and ten from the north. A subway will connect a large concourse on the east side of Canal street with the station.

One section of the new passenger terminal will extend almost from Carroll avenue on the north to Roosevelt road on the south. The Pennsylvania freight houses will cover space immediately north of Roosevelt road to Taylor street; The Burlington freight houses will be between Harrison and Taylor streets near Canal street.

The new Union station will be able to accommodate passenger traffic for years to come, as the original plans have been changed to permit the erection of a sixteen-story building over the station proper.

Included among the other railroad projects are the electrification of the Illinois Central and the straightening of the river from Van Buren street south, throwing into one piece of land much of the trackage that now is not wholly efficient because of existing conditions.

The lake front and electrification projects mean an expenditure of more than $80,000,000 by the city and the railroads.

The ordinances under which the railroads are granted rights in certain streets bind them to street improvements at an estimated total cost of $5,855,000. These will provide for thirteen viaducts, an elevated roadway at Canal and Kinzie streets, and the revamping of Canal street from Washington street to Roosevelt road. It was estimated that the last of these projects would alone cost $2,375,000.

In its turn, the city is pledged to erect the Monroe street bridge and a double-deck bridge at Kinzie street and to widen Canal street 100 feet, all at an estimated cost of $1,860,753.

The roads also agreed to pay $1,511,000 in cash. The total cost to the railroads, exclusive of money paid for land before the terminal ordinances were passed, was estimated at $65,000,000. All these estimates, however, were made several years ago. The actual costs will probably be appreciably greater.

74

BARTOW ADOLPHUS ULRICH

BARTOW ADOLPHUS ULRICH, lawyer, publicist and intimate of Abraham Lincoln, was born in Fishkill, N. Y., Feb. 12, 1840; son of Henrietta (Von Riesankompff) and Louis Augustus. In 1841, the family moved to Springfield, Ill., and the hospitality of their home attracted such men as Lincoln, Stephen A. Douglas, Lyman Trumbull, Browning, Shields and others. Mr. Ulrich was educated in private schools here and in Heidelberg and was graduated from the University of Michigan law department in 1864. He married Helen Amelia Russell, of Brighton, Mich., in 1864. Children: Victoria (Mrs. E. E. Noyes); Helen (Mrs. Achilles Alberti); Gertrude; Lela (Mrs. M. C. Grover); Russell, Perry and B. A., Jr. (deceased). Mr. Ulrich settled in Chicago in 1865, opening a law office and, as a diversion, engaging in real estate. He contributed to all Chicago papers on municipal and political questions. Mr. Ulrich is the author of the dramatic cantata "Victor" and seven essays on Christ Jesus; "Abraham Lincoln and Constitutional Governments" and "Abraham Lincoln and New Constitutional Governments." He is a member of Michigan Alumni, of Chicago, and life mem. of the Press club. Home: 1448 Bryn Mawr ave. Office: Press club.

75

(J. D'Esposito, chief engineer, Union Station Co.; Graham, Anderson, Probst & White, Architects)

CHICAGO'S NEW UNION STATION

THE accompanying illustration shows Chicago's great union passenger terminal as it will appear when completed. Work on this magnificent structure, which will surpass in beauty and grandeur any of the terminals of America, was started late in 1922.

The station is of twin or double-end design, with a transverse concourse between two sets of stub tracks for the railways entering from the north and south.

Surmounting the headhouse, which will occupy an entire city block, will be a twenty-story office building, thus utilizing the air rights for revenue purposes.

The new Union station will be occupied by the Pennsylvania system; the Chicago, Milwaukee & St. Paul Ry.; Chicago, Burlington & Quincy R. R., and the Chicago & Alton R. R.

76

THE PENNSYLVANIA RAILROAD COMPANY

THE Pennsylvania Railroad System, as it is constituted today, embraces what were originally about 600 constituent corporations. This number, by merger and otherwise, has been reduced to 142 corporations, whose separate identity, for various legal reasons, must still be preserved.

The parent company of the System is the Pennsylvania Railroad Company. It consolidates the System in a compact group of lines, under united management, through ownership of the majority of the stock of the subsidiary corporations, long term leases of their physical properties, or both. In most cases the ownership of the stock of the subsidiaries is substantially complete and long term leases have been made of all lines of importance, with one or two exceptions.

The Company also directly owns the principal lines of the System located in the State of Pennsylvania, and under its corporate organization directly operates the major portion of the entire System.

The Pennsylvania Railroad Company was chartered in 1846. It arose out of a movement to secure for the city of Philadelphia its proper proportion of the traffic of the new West, which was then opening up to development, through the Pittsburgh gateway at the head of the navigation of the Ohio River, and the natural inland waterway comprised in the Great Lakes.

Although it was thus a local enterprise in its inception, the Pennsylvania System has been extended until it is now a national, and in some respects an international, institution.

The Pennsylvania Railroad System

The Pennsylvania Railroad System traverses practically the entire middle belt of the United States of America, lying between the Atlantic Ocean on the east and the Mississippi River on the west, and stretching from the Great Lakes into the Southern States. This region is the most densely populated in the United States, contains the country's most important industries, as well as large areas of its most fertile agricultural lands, and embraces the largest cities in North America.

In consequence, the Pennsylvania System has an extremely dense traffic, both passenger and freight, and is very highly developed as to double and multiple trackage, large yards, terminals, etc.

The States actually served are thirteen in number, in addition to the District of Columbia, namely, New York, New Jersey, Pennsylvania, Delaware, Maryland, Virginia, West Virginia, Ohio, Indiana, Kentucky, Missouri, Illinois, and Michigan. The actual population of this territory, in the census of 1920, was 52,808,528, or 49.9 per cent of the population of the entire United States.

The Pennsylvania System directly serves eight out of the ten largest cities of the United States, namely, New York, N. Y.; Chicago, Ill.; Philadelphia, Pa.; Detroit, Mich.; Cleveland, Ohio; St. Louis, Mo.; Baltimore, Md., and Pittsburgh, Pa. The total population of these cities, in 1920, was 16,049,473.

Character of Traffic

The iron and steel industries and coal mining provide the backbone of the traffic of the Pennsylvania System. This is due, in part, to the position of the System as the dominant carrier in the Pittsburgh District, which produces about 40 per cent of all the iron and steel of the United States; and in part to the fact that the lines of the System traverse the great anthracite and bituminous regions of Pennsylvania and adjoining States.

In addition, the Pennsylvania System is also a very important carrier of

77

JOHN GILMOUR RODGERS

JOHN GILMOUR RODGERS, vice-president of the Pennsylvania System, was born in Philadelphia, Nov. 14, 1865, son of Isabel (Gilmour) and Samuel Morris Rodgers. He was educated in Lewistown Academy and under private tutors. On Feb. 4, 1901, he married Agnes P. Barney, of Dayton, O. Children: Louise Perrine, John Barney, Agnes Mac Aulay and Sidney Maurice. Entered service of Pennsylvania Railroad as rodman in 1882. In 1889, he became assistant supervisor; in 1893, supervisor; in 1900, superintendent; in 1909, assistant to general manager; in 1911, general superintendent; in 1917, assistant to the president; and since 1920 vice-president, in charge of the northwestern region. Served as Lieutenant-Colonel, Engineers, U. S. A., in 1918. Member of Archaeological Society of Chicago, Historical Society of Pennsylvania. Republican. Presbyterian. Clubs: Mid-Day, Onwentsia (Chicago); Rittenhouse (Philadelphia); Engineers (New York). Home: 40 Bellevue place, Chicago. Office: 841 Insurance Exchange Building, Chicago.

lumber from both the West and South, of fruits and vegetables from the Southern States to northern and eastern markets, and of grain, packing house products, etc., from the West, Northwest and Southwest to the consuming centers of the East and seaboard.

It has also an immense tonnage of miscellaneous manufactured articles, and from the fact that it reaches four leading eastern seaports—New York, Philadelphia, Baltimore and Norfolk—it handles a very large proportion of the country's import and export trade.

Volume of Public Service Rendered

In 1921 the Pennsylvania Railroad System performed public service equivalent to carrying one ton of freight 34,589,953,448 miles, and one passenger 6,323,-414,240 miles. These, however, were not the highest recorded figures owing to the general business depression in the United States last year. The peak for freight traffic was reached in 1917 with 48,594,643,624 ton miles and for passenger traffic in 1920 with 7,325,202,158 passenger miles.

The average revenue for hauling a ton of freight one mile in 1921 was 1.208 cents; per passenger mile, 2.875 cents.

Mileage and Trackage

The Pennsylvania System as of December 31, 1921, embraced 11,643 miles of line and 27,341 miles of track. On the entire System 4,175 miles are double-tracked, 919 miles have three tracks, and 694 miles have four tracks.

Between New York and Philadelphia, a distance of 91 miles, the Pennsylvania System has a six-track line of railroad. Between Philadelphia and Pittsburgh, a distance of 348 miles, it has a four-track railroad. Between Philadelphia and Washington, a distance of 137 miles, it also has a four-track railroad. Between Pittsburgh and Chicago, a distance of 468 miles, it has a two-track railroad; while large portions of the line between Pittsburgh and St. Louis, a total distance of 612 miles, are also double tracked.

There are many other multiple track lines of lesser extent, but the foregoing cover the main arteries of the System. The extent of multiple trackage and the high development of yards and terminals, sidings, etc., account for the fact that the track mileage of the Pennsylvania System is practically two and one-half times its line mileage.

Capitalization and Investment

The Pennsylvania Railroad System represents an investment in road and equipment of $2,102,421,811, as shown upon its books. Against this sum there are outstanding in the hands of the public securities, both stocks and bonds, amounting to $1,420,775,280.

Equipment

The rolling stock of the Pennsylvania System consists of 7,781 locomotives, 8,225 passenger equipment cars, 271,066 freight equipment cars, and 5,409 work equipment cars. The locomotives have a total tractive power of 315,981,785 pounds.

The seating capacity of the passenger cars is 335,607 persons. The carrying capacity of the freight cars is 14,035,593 tons. In addition to the cars and locomotives, there are in use 436 vessels of various kinds.

The total valuation of all equipment is $596,241,643.

Earnings

The total operating revenues of the Pennsylvania System in 1921 were

79

$662,756,803, or approximately one-ninth of the operating revenues of all railroads in the United States.

Employes and Wages

The number of employes on the System as of December 31, 1921, was 218,859. The total payroll in 1921 was $362,135,423.

Employe Representation

Following the close of the World War and the return of the railroads to their owners, after their utilization for war purposes, numerous problems of a most serious character arose with reference to relations between employes and management. In an endeavor to solve this problem, the Pennsylvania System management, in co-operation with the working forces, has instituted a plan of employe representation. Under this plan, differences between the employes affected and the management are referred to Joint Reviewing Committees. Each Committee consists of an equal number of representatives of the management and of the employes. Each side has equal voting power.

The plan was first put into effect with the Engine and Train Service employes on January 1, 1921. Later the same year it was extended to the Shop Crafts, the Telegraph and Signal Department, the Maintenance of Way Department, the Clerical Employes, and the Miscellaneous forces.

During the first year of its operations, over 6,000 grievances and controversial questions with employes were satisfactorily adjusted by the several committees. Recently wage agreements affecting more than 140,000 employes have been negotiated in a series of conferences under this plan, and the results obtained show conclusively that the employe representation plan, carried out in the proper spirit on both sides, provides a means for the amicable settlement of all differences and will wholly prevent strikes.

Stockholders

The Pennsylvania Railroad Company has outstanding $499,265,700 of capital stock, divided into shares of $50 each. These shares, owing to the position of the Company as a holding corporation, represent substantially the ownership equity in the entire Pennsylvania System. It is, therefore, an interesting fact that they are more widely distributed among the public than the shares of any other railroad company.

At the close of 1921 there were 141,699 stockholders whose average holdings were approximately seventy shares each. About 47 per cent of the stockholders are women. Formerly about 15 per cent of the stock of the Pennsylvania Railroad was held abroad, but owing to events in connection with the war this is at the present time less than 4 per cent.

Pensions

Every employe, of whatever grade, is pensioned at the age of seventy years. Between the ages of sixty-five and seventy he may be pensioned upon disability. The method of computing pensions is uniform. The average earnings of the last ten years of service are ascertained and 1 per cent of this sum, multiplied by the total number of years of service, gives the amount of the annual pension, which, like wages and salaries, is paid in monthly installments.

The pension system was established January 1, 1900. Since then 14,513 employes have been retired under its terms. Of these, 7,828 had died up to March 1,

1922, leaving the total number receiving pensions on that date 6,685.

Pension payments of the Pennsylvania System now amount to approximately $2,900,000 a year.

Plan of System Organization

The executive offices of the Pennsylvania Railroad System are located in Philadelphia, Pa. The System administrative organization consists of: Samuel Rea, President; Lewis Neilson, Secretary; W. W. Atterbury, Vice-President in Charge of Operation; G. D. Dixon, Vice-President in Charge of Traffic; Henry Tatnall, Vice-President in Charge of Finance; A. J. County, Vice-President in Charge of Accounting; M. C. Kennedy, Vice-President in Charge of Real Estate, Purchases, and Insurance; F. I. Gowen, Vice-President and General Counsel (Legal Department).

In addition, there is also a Vice-President in Pittsburgh (J. J. Turner), who is in charge of the corporate affairs of that portion of the System lying west of Pittsburgh; a Vice-President in Charge of Personnel (G. L. Peck), who is a staff officer of the System Vice-President in Charge of Operation; and four Regional Vice-Presidents.

The Treasury is under the jurisdiction of the Vice-President in Charge of Finance.

Regional System of Operation

In order to secure a greater unification of the System lines for operating purposes, the Board of Directors, on March 1, 1920, established a regional system of organization affecting all departments. From that date, so far as its service to the public is concerned, the Pennsylvania Railroad System has been a single unit.

The Pennsylvania Railroad System was divided into four regions, each in charge of a Vice-President. These regions are designated "Eastern," "Central," "Northwestern," and "Southwestern." The headquarters of the respective regions are in Philadelphia, Pa.; Pittsburgh, Pa.; Chicago, Ill., and St. Louis, Mo.

The main track mileage is: Eastern Region, 4,250 miles, Elisha Lee, Vice-President in charge; Central Region, 3,650 miles, James A. McCrea, Vice-President in charge; Northwestern Region, 1,750 miles, J. G. Rodgers, Vice-President in charge; Southwestern Region, 1,750 miles, Benj. McKeen, Vice-President in charge.

Each Regional Vice-President has a complete staff of officers, including a General Manager in charge of operation, a Traffic Manager in charge of all matters pertaining to traffic and rates, and of other officers representing the Financial, Accounting, Engineering, Legal, Real Estate, and Purchasing Departments.

The Regional Vice-Presidents report to the System Vice-President in Charge of Operation, and each is directly responsible for the efficient operation of his Region and for maintaining better and closer relations between the Railroad and its employes and the public.

While the reconstructed organization is based on the theory that the Pennsylvania Railroad is practically a united System, yet the various constituent companies not fully owned or operated by the Pennsylvania Railroad Company retain their corporate identities.

GEORGE ANDERSON COOKE

GEORGE ANDERSON COOKE, attorney and former judge of Illinois Supreme Court, was born in New Athens, O., July 3, 1869; son of Vanceline (Downing) and Thomas Cooke. Ed. in Aledo, Ill., Schs. Received A. B. degree from Knox Coll., 1892; LL. D. degree Knox Coll., 1922. Read law in office of Pepper & Scott at Aledo and admitted to Ill. bar 1895. Began practice in Galesburg, where he remained until Aug. 1, 1896. Married Sarah Blee, Oct. 20, 1896, at Aledo. Children: Mrs. Marjorie McBride, Martha, George Blee, Thomas Blee. In 1896, Mr. Cooke formed law partnership with Guy C. Scott at Aledo. This partnership continued until 1899, when he formed partnership with John F. Main, later judge of Supreme Court of State of Washington. In 1900, Mr. Cooke took as his partner Alexander McArthur. In 1905 he became associated with John M. Wilson. Elected judge Ill. Supreme Court, to succeed Guy C. Scott, deceased, in 1909, and re-elected in 1912 for 9-year term. Resigned December, 1918, and has since practiced law in Chicago as head of firm of Cooke, Sullivan & Ricks. Was secy., State Dem. Central Comm., 1908-1909; mem. Ill. House of Rep., 1902-1906. Mem. Beta Theta Pi. Clubs: Univ., Ill. Athletic, Yacht, Mid-Day, Sangamo (Springfield). Office: 38 S. Dearborn St. Home: 3030 Sheridan Rd.

CHICAGO & NORTHWESTERN RAILWAY CO.

HUMAN progress is fundamentally linked with the development of transportation. Rome was made the world's capital because of her unexcelled system of roads, and Venice once ruled the earth through her control of the world's highways of maritime commerce. In this modern age of progress, Chicago, the wonder metropolis on the shores of Lake Michigan, is the greatest commercial and industrial center because it has the best transportation facilities of any city in the world.

Chicago began her first period of active growth simultaneously with the beginning of service over its first railroad, the Galena and Chicago Union. Every mile of railway that has been added to the mighty systems that center in this city has added new progress and prosperity to Chicago by adding to her trade territory and by increasing the productive efficiency and purchasing power of the inhabitants of the Mississippi Valley.

The outstanding factor in Chicago's marvelous development from the very outset, however, is the railroad which has constantly kept a step ahead of this city's progress. That railroad is the Chicago and North Western Railway, now one of the greatest railway systems in the world. Like the Galena and Chicago Union, the first railroad to afford the city transportation, the Chicago and North Western, of which the Galena and Chicago Union became a part, maintained the position of being the premier railroad in meeting Chicago's transportation needs during the period of her unprecedented growth. It links her with the rich country to the west and north and has at all times extended to her the fullest co-operation.

Actual work on the Galena and Chicago Union, the pioneer road of the Northwest, was started in September, 1847, and the first shipment of freight into the city, which consisted of hides and hogs, was made the following year. It was a very insignificant system, compared with its present greatness. Instead of 110-pound rails, rock-ballasted roadbed, monster locomotives, all-steel electric lighted equipment and palatial terminals, it consisted of forty-odd miles of strap rails, over which was operated one locomotive and thirteen light, wooden cars.

This lone locomotive, called the Pioneer, was as crude as the strap rails which supported it. The Pioneer had cylinders ten inches in diameter, an eighteen-inch stroke, and weighed ten tons. The superstructure of the road was composed of cross-ties, nine feet long and six inches thick, which were laid thirty inches from center to center. On these were placed longitudinal rails of Norway or yellow pine, a portion six inches square and a portion seven inches square, fastened in place by triangular blocks or knees of scantling, firmly spiked to the ties on each side. Upon the longitudinal rails was an oak ribbon one and one-quarter by three inches square, and on this ribbon was an iron plate rail, two and a half by three-fourths or seven-eighths inches, weighing about thirty tons to the mile.

Gradually this strap rail road reached out its lines, tapping the fertile valleys of the Great Northwest, keeping a step ahead of the progress of Chicago—

A. C. JOHNSON

A. C. JOHNSON, vice president of the Chicago & North Western Railway, with direct charge over traffic, was born in Crawford county, Pa., May 20, 1861, and was educated at Meadville College. He began service with the Chicago & North Western Railway in 1894 as special agent, which position he held until 1899, when he became general agent for South Dakota and Minnesota. In May, 1910, he was appointed general traffic manager, serving in this capacity until the government assumed control in 1917. During the period of war-time control by the government, Mr. Johnson served as chairman of the Western Freight Traffic Committee, which had jurisdiction over all freight matters in western territory. When the Chicago & North Western personnel was reorganized, following the return of the road to private control, Mr. Johnson again assumed the position as traffic manager. In 1920, he was elected vice president. Mr. Johnson is a Thirty-second degree Mason, Knight Templar, Shriner, Elk, Woodman and a member of Phi Delta Phi. His clubs are the Union League, Hamilton, Traffic, Mid-Day and Highland Park.

84

and today that system—the Chicago and North Western—operates over 10,000 miles of modern railway, with thousands of locomotives and tens of thousands of cars, any one of which will carry more than the entire rolling stock of the first road.

The great states of Illinois, Wisconsin, Minnesota, the Dakotas, Iowa, Nebraska, Michigan and Wyoming, have virtually been brought to Chicago's doors in its marvelous development. These commonwealths have been definitely and permanently added to the trade territory of Chicago by the Northwestern line's connections that make this city their logical market center.

. Always mindful of the fact that Chicago would look to it to meet the demands of the city in the development of its commerce and industry, the Chicago and North Western has at all times displayed unusual foresight in providing facilities to take care of the city's needs in transportation to and from the Northwest. In 1880 the Chicago and North Western erected the Wells Street passenger station, which at that time was the largest and finest structure of its kind in the city. But this was merely a stepping stone in its progress, because the North Western system grew so rapidly that the Wells Street station became inadequate to accommodate the road's patrons. In consequence, the North Western took another characteristic step to show its interest in the city by building its present superb passenger terminal at Madison and Canal Streets in 1911. This terminal is one of the greatest and most mod-

Chicago Passenger Terminal—Chicago & North Western Ry.

ern passenger stations in the world. With its construction the North Western also kept a step ahead of the city's progress by elevating its tracks and enlarging its huge freight yards.

From the beginning the Chicago and North Western Railway has observed its present policy of affording its patrons the highest standard of service. Its phenomenal growth is indicative of its success in transportation by always furnishing the "BEST OF EVERYTHING."

CHARLES H. MARKHAM

C HARLES H. MARKHAM, president of Illinois Central railroad, was born on May 22, 1861, at Clarksville, Tenn., and received his education in public schools of Addison, N. Y. In 1881 he joined the Atchison, Topeka & Santa Fe railroad, and worked for them for several months. He then became connected with the Southern Pacific and rose rapidly, being assistant freight traffic manager, which he quit in 1901 to become vice-president of the Houston & Texas Central Ry. and executive head of the Harriman lines in Texas. In 1904 he was made general manager and vice-president of the Southern Pacific. The latter part of that year he became general manager of the Guffey Petroleum Co. and retained that position until 1910, when the Mellon interests made him head of their oil companies in the southwest. In Dec., 1910, Mr. Markham was elected president of Illinois Central and the following year president of Central of Georgia Ry. and Ocean Steamship Co. Mr. Markham, in 1918, was appointed railroad director in the southern region by Director General McAdoo, of the U. S. Railroad Administration. Later he severed all railroad connections and was appointed regional director of the Allegheny district. He remained in this position until 1919, when he was re-elected president of Illinois Central and chairman of board of Central of Georgia and Ocean Steamship. Clubs: Chicago, South Shore, Old Elm, Chicago Golf. Home: Chicago Beach. Office: 135 E. 11th place, Chicago.

ILLINOIS CENTRAL RAILROAD COMPANY

THE Illinois Central System, with 8,157 miles of lines serving fifteen states, had its beginning in a railroad 705 miles long, which was built in Illinois between 1851 and 1856. The building of the parent road was made possible through a grant of lands from the Government. The project of connecting the Great Lakes and the Gulf of Mexico with a railway line paralleling the Mississippi River was a question of national importance, and the proponents of the plan succeeded in inducing Congress to cede federal lands to the states of Illinois, Alabama and Mississippi, to be used in encouraging the proposed railroad. In granting a charter to the Illinois Central Railroad Company, in February, 1851, the legislature of Illinois ceded its granted lands to the road, in payment wherefor the company is required to pay into the state treasury, in lieu of other taxes, seven per cent of the gross revenue from its charter lines. The Government retained alternate sections and disposed of these at $2.50 an acre, instead of $1.25, the price asked prior to the grant. The land received by the Illinois Central was sold for $23,218,611, and payments to the state under the charter tax have aggregated, to date, more than $50,000,000.

In 1851 the longest railroad in the United States had only 300 miles of line. There had been practically no railway construction at a distance from the Atlantic seaboard, and, as much of the material had to be brought from England, the engineering difficulties encountered were considerable. At that time, the interior of Illinois was largely untouched by industrial development. much of the land traversed was wholly unexplored, and very little of it had been settled.

Surmounting the many difficulties, the builders of the charter lines completed their work September 27, 1856. The main line of the railroad was between Cairo and Galena, with a branch extending off the main line into the small town of Chicago. The railroad thus built formed the nucleus of the present Illinois Central System. In 1867, western lines were leased, eventually connecting the Illinois road with Omaha, Sioux City and Sioux Falls. Extensions south of the Ohio River date from 1882, with the lease of the Chicago, St. Louis and New Orleans Railroad, furnishing a line south from Cairo through Jackson, Tenn., Canton, Miss., and Jackson, Miss., to New Orleans. In 1897, the lease of the Chesapeake, Ohio & Southwestern connected Louisville with the system and gave it a northern entrance into Memphis. Five years prior to that, the Illinois Central had purchased the capital stock of the Yazoo and Mississippi Valley Railroad, extending through the Mississippi Delta country from Memphis, south to New Orleans, through Greenville, Greenwood, Vicksburg and Natchez. In 1909, the Illinois Central purchased the capital stock of the Central of Georgia Railway, a road whose birth antedates that of the parent road of the system. The Central of Georgia has developed from a road of 191 miles built in 1843. The Central of Georgia, in turn, controls the Ocean Steamship Company of Savannah, which operates a coastwise trading service between Savannah, Ga., and northern Atlantic ports. The Central of Georgia itself extends from Birmingham, Ala., where it connects with the Illinois Central, to Savannah, Ga., and also serves the cities of Atlanta, Ga., Montgomery, Ala., and Chattanooga, Tenn.

87

A number of men who figured prominently in the Civil War had been connected with the Illinois Central, notably, Abraham Lincoln, who had been an attorney of the road, General George B. McClellan, General P. G. T. Beauregard and General A. E. Burnside.

As the railroad always exercises its influence in the development of the territory it serves, the Illinois Central System has played a prominent part in building up the Mississippi Valley. Industries followed the railroad, and the settlement of farming communities has been encouraged. The road has done much to bring the South to the forefront in agriculture.

Although Chicago was originally the terminus of a branch from the main line of the Illinois Central, its development has made it the principal northern terminal point of the system.

The Illinois Central built into Chicago in 1852. Trackage rights were obtained along the lake front south of the mouth of the Chicago River upon condition that the railroad should take over the burden of protecting the lake shore from the ravages of storms, which prior to that time had wrought much damage, even threatening to wash out Michigan Avenue in places. It became necessary for the railroad to spend $2,500,000 in protecting the lake shore, but the obligation was carried out in its entirety.

A suburban service was inaugurated in 1856 between South Water Street and Hyde Park (Fifty-third Street), and later extended to Matteson, South Chicago and Blue Island. During the Columbian Exposition, between May 1 and October 31, the suburban service carried 8,780,000 passengers to and from the exposition grounds, in addition to its regular passengers. It now handles nearly 30,000,000 passengers a year on 342 suburban trains each twenty-four hours.

The project of electrifying the operation of the Chicago terminals is already under way. As a part of this project, the Illinois Central will rebuild its passenger and freight terminals in Chicago, and the South Park Commissioners will construct a lake front park connecting Grant and Jackson parks with land reclaimed from the lake. South of the present Field Museum of Natural History, which was completed last year on ground provided by the Illinois Central, to the east of the proposed Central Station, there will be built an immense stadium and two bathing beaches.

The passenger terminal which will replace the present Central Station will be the largest in the world. Subways will be provided for Roosevelt Road surface line cars, and a connection will be available for the proposed subway lines.

The present Illinois Central System employs more than 72,000 individuals, and in 1920 it performed a service equivalent to carrying 17 billion tons of freight one mile and 1½ billion passengers one mile. It stands sixth among the railroads of the country in originating coal traffic. In its passenger service, the Illinois Central System is especially noted for the on-time operation of trains.

The present officers are: Charles H. Markham, president; Charles M. Kittle, senior vice-president; J. L. Beven, assistant to senior vice-president; L. W. Baldwin, vice-president, operation; F. B. Bowes, vice-president, traffic; M. P. Blauvelt, vice-president, finance and accounting, and A. C. Mann, vice-president, purchases.

88

CHICAGO, MILWAUKEE AND ST. PAUL RY.

EVER since its inception, the Chicago, Milwaukee and St. Paul Railway has been distinguished by its enterprise in penetrating new countries and seeking out new resources to develop. The opening scenes of its operations were in southeastern Wisconsin at a time when the first settlers were beginning to straggle in and the rich and fertile prairies were virgin soil. Extending gradually north and westward year by year, it played a vital part in the development of the northern Mississippi Valley; and then reaching out farther to where the Missouri River country was practically unknown, it did notable pioneer work for the plains and prairies, helping to transform them into the richest grain-bearing country in the world.

The Chicago, Milwaukee and St. Paul Railway is a Wisconsin corporation. It received its charter at Madison, in 1863, under the title of the Milwaukee and St. Paul Railway Company.

The next succeeding decades with the Chicago, Milwaukee and St. Paul Railway form a record of constant advancement into new territory and a continual development of the territory contiguous to its new lines.

As the settlement of the country progressed, the volume of business increasingly demanded a Chicago outlet, and accordingly, in 1878, work began on an extension to Chicago. In 1874, the corporate name was changed to the Chicago, Milwaukee and St. Paul Railway Company.

At the close of the century, its mileage had expanded to over 8,000 miles, its rails gridironed the states of Wisconsin, Minnesota, South Dakota and Iowa and reached out into rich sections of North Dakota, Missouri, and penetrated the upper peninsula of Michigan. It had bridged the Mississippi River at five different places and touched the Missouri. Under its developing influences, vast areas teemed with busy life, magnificent fields of grain, great industries and big cities had become the speaking evidence of its fostering policies—for always this railroad had blazed the trail for the people whose product and labors are the support of its traffic.

Following the Spanish-American, the trade possibilities of the Pacific Coast and the desirability of an expanded commerce with the countries of the Orient began to dawn on business men. All the railroads of the Middle West felt the necessity of closer affiliations with the Pacific Coast lines, but the Milwaukee line was the only one to strike out for and push ahead to the Coast on its own rails.

Probably the most progressive step taken by any railroad was the electrification by the Chicago, Milwaukee and St. Paul Railway of approximately 700 of its main lines through the mountain districts. It now operates 660 of its main coast line.

The Milwaukee has always been a leader in introducing modern improvements into its service. It owns and operates its sleeping and dining-cars. It was the first railroad to install electric lighting of trains, and it introduced the electric reading-lamp into sleeping-car berths. It was the first Western railroad to operate solid steel trains in transcontinental service. The excellence of its passenger service has given the road a world-wide reputation, travelers from almost every country of the world having had, at one time or another, personal acquaintance with the luxuries of the Pioneer Limited between Chicago and the Twin Cities; or the two fine trains, The Olympian and Columbian, in coast-line service between Chicago and Seattle and Tacoma, the Milwaukee being the only line into that territory to operate through trains over its own rails between those cities.

EDWARD JACKSON BRUNDAGE

EDWARD J. BRUNDAGE, attorney general of Illinois, was born in Campbell, N. Y., May 13, 1869; s., Victor and Maria L. (Armstrong); removed with parents to Detroit, Mich., 1880; ed. pub. schs. of Campbell and Detroit until 1883; employed in railroad office in Detroit and Chicago and studied law at leisure; admitted to Ill. bar 1892; LL. B. Chicago Coll. of Law 1893; m. Germaine Vernier, of Caen, France, Dec. 17, 1913. Children: Edward J., Jr., Robert, Margaret. Practiced law in Chicago since 1893; mem. Ill. legislature, 41st and 43rd gen. assemblies, from 6th senatorial district.; pres. Bd. of Cook County Commrs., 1904 and re-elected 1906; resigned 1907 to become Corp. Counsel of City of. Chicago; appt. judge of Court of Claims 1915; resigned to become atty. gen. of Ill. for term 1917-21; re-elected in 1921. Was vice-pres. for Ill. of Pan-Am. Expn., Buffalo, N. Y. Mem. Am. Bar, Chicago Bar, State Bar Assn., Chicago Lawyers Assn., Mason (32d deg., K. T.); mem. K. P. Clubs: Chicago Athletic, University, Industrial, Hamilton, Sangamo Illini Country and Evanston Golf Club. Home: 617 Arlington Pl., Chicago. Office: 734 Otis Bldg., Chicago, and Supreme Court Bldg., Springfield.

THOMAS D. HUFF

THOMAS D. HUFF, lawyer, was born in Eldora, Iowa, January, 1872; son of Hon. Henry Lewis and Elizabeth D. (Diven) Huff; educated in the public grammar and high schools of Eldora and Grinnell, (Ia.) Academy and Grinnell College. LL. B. Northwestern University Law School, 1895. Married Evelyn K. Allen of Helena, Montana, 1903. Children: Emorie Cannon and Curtis Allen. Has practiced law in Chicago since 1895; makes a specialty of corporation law in all its branches. Member of the firm of Huff and Cook; formerly assist. corp. of Evanston; Western counsel of U. S. Corp. Editor of (Ill.) Corporation Manual. Member American, Illinois State and Chicago Bar Associations, Chicago Law Institute. Republican. Episcopalian. Club: Hamilton. Home: 624 Noyes street, Evanston. Office: 29 S. La Salle street, Chicago.

CHICAGO, BURLINGTON AND QUINCY RAILROAD COMPANY

ON SEPTEMBER 2, 1850, the Burlington Railroad began to serve the public. It was 12 miles long and had one "iron horse," one coach, and two baggage-and-freight cars. Built to meet a requirement of a purely local nature, it was beyond the imagination of the owners that the road ever would be extended beyond the boundaries of the sovereign state of Illinois.

Expanded to fulfill a vision of economic development and present-day requirements, this little 12-mile railroad has become the West's most dependable transportation machine—an unusual example of what a railroad should be, providing service (both passenger and freight) about as you would have it if it had been your own railroad; with 9,389 miles of splendidly equipped and carefully manned road and through traffic agreements with connecting lines so comprehensive that it embraces practically every point of real scenic or commercial importance in our entire West.

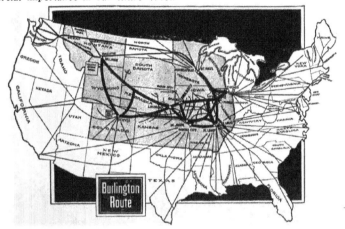

The territory served now includes eleven great states, Illinois, Iowa, Wisconsin, Minnesota, Missouri, Nebraska, Kansas, South Dakota, Colorado, Wyoming, and Montana. Here is produced about 50 per cent of the wheat, 52 per cent of the corn, 60 per cent of the oats, 50 per cent of the alfalfa, and 42 per cent of the sugar beets, and about 41 per cent of the cattle, 45 per cent of the hogs, and 31 per cent of the sheep in this nation. These eleven great states comprise an area almost equal to that of England, Wales, Scotland, Ireland, France, Spain, Italy, Portugal, Switzerland, Belgium, Holland, Denmark and Germany combined. Ponder, for a moment, the significance of that and the myriad opportunities wrapped up in such a tremendous empire.

Before you travel or ship, take the nearest Burlington representative into your confidence. Burlington service is "At Your Service." Try it next time and judge for yourself.

Officers of the Chicago, Burlington and Quincy are: Hale Holden, president; O. M. Spencer, general counsel; L. B. Allen, general manager, Chicago; W. F. Thielhoff, general manager, Omaha; II. II. Holcomb, freight traffic manager; P. S. Eustis, passenger traffic manager; C. I. Sturgis, vice president, secretary and treasurer. The directorate is composed of the following: William W. Baldwin, Chicago; Ralph Budd, St. Paul; Charles Donnelly, St. Paul; Claude G. Burnham, Chicago; Robert J. Dunham, Chicago; Howard Elliott, New York; Louis W. Hill, St. Paul; Hale Holden, Chicago; Charles I. Sturgis, Chicago; Arthur Curtiss James, New York; Charles E. Perkins, Burlington, Ia.; Frederick H. Rawson, Chicago, and Oliver M. Spencer, Chicago.

LOUIS L. EMMERSON

LOUIS L. EMMERSON, secretary of state of Ill., was born at Albion, Edwards Co., Illinois, Dec. 27, 1863. Ed. in Public Schs. of Albion and moved to Mt. Vernon in 1887. There he engaged in mercantile business until 1901, when he organized Third National Bank of Mt. Vernon of which he is president. He entered politics 20 years ago becoming chairman of Rep. Co. Central Comm. of Jefferson Co., in which capacity he served for 12 years. Served as chairman of Cong. Comm. of 23rd Dist. and as mem. of Rep. State Central Comm. Also served as mem. of State Bd. of Equalization and on Bd. of Comm. of S. Ill. Penitentiary. Candidate for Rep. Nomination for State Treas. in 1912. Elected Secy. of State in 1916 and re-elected in 1920. He is a Mason, mem. of K. of P., I. O. O. F., Red Man, Woodman, Elks, Moose. He is married and has two daughters.

CHICAGO, ROCK ISLAND AND PACIFIC RAILWAY COMPANY

THE Rock Island Railway, which represents 70 years of service, not only was the pioneer railroad in the fourteen states through which it now oper ates, but its early history was probably more closely associated with the Indian period of the Middle West than any other road now in operation.

This fact has been brought out in connection with investigation conducted by the Rock Island in the formulation of an historical sketch of that line, incident to the observance on October 10, 1922, of the Seventieth Anniversary of the Rock Island Lines.

It was discovered that, in general, the main lines of the Rock Island follow the trails originally made by the Indians in the days before the coming of the immigrant wagons into the Great West. This is particularly true of the main line out of Chicago to Rock Island, Ill., and Davenport, Iowa. This was the original line opened to traffic in 1852-1854.

In general, the right of way is along an old Indian trail, made by the Red Men in their hunting pilgrimages across the prairies. Later, this trail was followed by the immigrant covered wagons, and finally by the railroad. The Rock Island has now in its possession, an old map showing these ancient Indian trails.

It has been determined that the Indians were wont to cross the Mississippi river at the point where the Rock Island in 1856 built the first bridge, the pier of which still stands on the present grounds of the Rock Island Arsenal and is plainly seen from the trains as they pass over the present steel bridge which was built between Rock Island and Davenport 50 years ago.

The same general following of the ancient Indian trails occurred in the construction of the first railroad into Iowa, formerly known as the "Mississippi & Missouri," and now a part of the Rock Island main line from Davenport to Omaha, Nebraska. This "first railroad in Iowa" was opened to traffic in 1855 and the arrival of the "first trains" in the various towns in Iowa was the occasion for celebrations that are still the talk today of the older generation of that state.

The Oklahoma lines, likewise, follow the trail originally made by an Indian scout in 1860 when he led the federal troops out of the old Indian Territory to Fort Leavenworth, Kas., at the outbreak of the Civil War. The trail thus established later was followed by the immigrants, and afterwards, the railroad. Accordingly, the Rock Island is looked upon as the "Pioneer Road of the West." In fact, the first locomotive to pull a train out of Chicago seventy years ago was called "The Pioneer."

Much of this early history of the Rock Island already has been collected and by the Seventieth Anniversary the Rock Island hopes to preserve this early record by erecting permanent markers at the various historic spots along its lines, giving the important events of the development of the Middle West.

The Rock Island started 70 years ago with but 40 miles of railroad in operation. In the "span of life" since 1852, this railway has increased its mileage to over 8,000 miles or 200 times its original trackage. This has been at the average rate of 115 miles a year. The road began operation at a time when there were no telegraph lines and when a day's journey by rail was often not more than eighty miles.

Today, the "Rocky Mountain Limited" makes the run from Chicago to the Colorado Rockies in a day and a night and the "Golden State Limited" takes its passengers from Chicago to California in less than three days, with utmost comfort and convenience. These two famous trains played an important part in the Seventieth Anniversary celebration.

One of the reasons for the Rock Island's growth is the fact that courtesy and comfort are one's fellow travelers on this line.

The company's officers are: J. E. Gorman, president; M. L. Bell, vice president and general counsel; L. C. Fritch, vice president, in charge of construction, maintenance and capital expenditures; T. H. Beacom, vice president and general manager; S. H. Johnson, vice president and freight traffic manager; L. M. Allen, vice president and passenger traffic manager; Carl Nyquist, vice president, secretary and treasurer; W. H. Burns, vice president and general auditor, and F. D. Reed, vice president and general purchasing agent.

ANDREW RUSSEL

ANDREW RUSSEL, Auditor of Public Accounts for State of Ill., was born in Jacksonville, Ill., June 17, 1856; s. of Wm. and Emily Gallaher Russel. Ed. in Pub. Schs. and at Ill. Coll., Jacksonville. Married Clara Robbins. Vice-Pres. of Ayers National Bank, Jacksonville. Treas. of City of Jacksonville 5 terms; Chmn. of State Bd. of Pardons from 1901 to 1906; also for number of years Pres. of Jacksonville Pub. Lib. Bd. Now Chmn. of Bd. of Trustees of Ill. Coll. Pres. Ill. Bankers Assn., 1902 and 1903; now mem. of Executive Council. Was State Treas. from 1909 to 1911 and from 1915 to 1917; elected to office of Auditor of Public Accts. in 1916 and re-elected in 1920. Mem. Masons, Odd Fellows, K. of P., Woodman, B. P. O. E., Moose. Clubs: Union League, Hamilton, and Mid-Day of Chicago and Sangamo of Springfield. Home: Jacksonville. Office address: Springfield.

ILLINOIS TRACTION SYSTEM

ONE of the most highly developed systems of interurban railways and public utility properties in the central west is that of the Illinois Traction System. The pres.dent of this organization is William B. McKinley, of Champaign, Ill., and at present one of the two U. S. Senators from Illinois. The operating head of the company is H. E. Chubbuck, vice president executive, with headquarters in Peoria.

The application of electricity to the transportation problems of Illinois with subsequent construction of the most highly developed electric carrier in the mid-dle west has made the name of McKinley synonymous with energy, progressive-ness and stability.

McKINLEY BRIDGE, ST. LOUIS, MO.

The Illinois Traction System is now operating through electric trains over greater distances than any other electric railway and is an important factor in transportation in central Illinois. The northern terminus of the main division is at Peoria, with southern terminal at St. Louis, Mo. The McKinley bridge at St. Louis is the largest electric railway bridge in the world.

These electric lines connect Springfield on the east with Decatur, Champaign and Danville; and also Peoria with Decatur. There is a northern division, known as the Chicago, Ottawa & Peoria Railway, which operates between Joliet, Ottawa, Bureau and Princeton, and in affiliation with other electric lines, affords electric service from Chicago to these points through what is known as the historic Illinois river valley.

The Illinois Traction System offers such refinements of service as parlor and sleeping cars, automatic block signals, belt lines around cities for handling of freight, direct connection with mines, elevators and large industries, physical connection and traffic relations with all steam roads and handling of standard railway equipment, both freight and passenger.

While developing this vast interurban system the company has acquired and modernized a group of public utilities which now extends into five mid-western states. The company furnishes electric light and power to eighty-four cities and villages, operates street railway service in twenty-four cities, provides gas service in 14 cities, heating service in 9 cities, as well as several miscellaneous water and ice plants.

JAMES A. PATTEN

JAMES A. PATTEN, capitalist, was born in Freeland Corners, Ill., May 2, 1852; s. of Agnes (Beverage) and Alexander R. Patten. Ed. in country schools. Married Louise Buchanan, of Chicago, April 9, 1885. Children: Agnes, Thomas Beverage (deceased), John, Lowrie. Clerk in country store, 1869-71; on grandfather's farm, 1871-4; employee of state grain insp. dept., Chicago, 1874-8; with G. P. Comstock & Co., 1887-80, and with brother, George W., in grain comm. business as Patten Bros., 1880-1903; mem. of firm of Bartlett, Frazier & Carrington, 1903-10; retired. Dir. Continental and Commercial Nat. Bank, City Nat. Bank of Evanston, Chgo. Title & Trust Co., People's Gas Co., Diamond Match Co., Advance Rumely Co., Commonwealth Edison Co., C., R. I. & P. R. R. Dir. of Presbyterian Hosp., Evanston Hosp., Old People's Home of Chicago. Presbyterian. Mayor of Evanston, 1901-5. Clubs; Union League, Chicago, Glen View, Westmoreland, and Evanston Country. Home: Evanston. Office: Western Union Bldg., Chicago.

CHICAGO—THE BANKING CITY

NEW wealth from the soil, the forest and the mine is the wellspring of Chicago's happy condition. Although Chicago may never hope to displace New York City as the country's money center, the day is dawning when it may, at least, share honors more evenly than now.

The right of the older city to retain all of the advantages and give none may well be challenged. Chicago's power to distribute investments and to parallel every power now held by New York may seem remote, but the steady increase in the wealth of the Central West, it is believed, will soon usher in the time when Chicago will demand equal rights with respect to all forms of financial operation.

As the financial center of the West, with banking resources high and expanding, Chicago is meeting realized requirements and lending proportionate aid to the country's development.

Discussing the strength of the Chicago money system, a famous Chicago banker had this to say: "The thing we are most proud of in our local banking situation is our system of clearing house examination, organized immediately after the Walsh failure in 1905. This system of clearing house supervision has grown into the most complete and effective supervision enjoyed by any city in the world, and there has not been a single failure of any bank under this supervision in fifteen years. Of course, there is no pretense of guaranteeing deposits or doing anything more than giving intelligent and careful supervision, but the results are very impressive. Speaking of our promotion of foreign trade, the banks of Chicago have been very slow to encourage trade in South America, and the experience of the seaboard banks has fully demonstrated the wisdom of the Chicago banks."

On June 1 of 1921, the twenty-four national and nearly 120 state banks of Chicago reported aggregate banking facilities as follows: Capital employed, $265,446,592; deposits, $1,741,444,311; loans and discounts, $1,493,178,193; cash resources, $481,885,562. Corresponding items accounted for June, 1920, were as follows: Capital employed, $1,805,228,994; loans and discounts, $1,548,299,008; cash resources, $474,529,476. One of the important changes has been the growth and distribution of savings deposits throughout the city, the total in 1921 reaching $497,315,100, of which more than fifty per cent was in the banks of the central business district. The increase in savings deposits has been greatest in the outlying banks.

Chicago is purchasing and distributing more and more the securities of this richly productive central region, although the resources of the eastern money center will for an indefinite time be employed in national development, Chicago is gradually becoming able to meet financial needs of the great commercial and manufacturing area, the Mississippi Valley. It is now said that always can be formed a group of financial men to swing any deal that is too large for a single institution and always producers' representatives work well with bond houses or other financial agencies. One famous producer goes so far as to say that every sign points to Chicago's ultimate supremacy as a financial center.

Today Chicago can handle its own great projects—a $60,000,000 flotation has been accomplished here—and offer financial facilities throughout the country. In the last four or five years, Chicago has enjoyed a significant growth in respect to the sale of investments and it is felt that the city is doing a reason-

JOHN CORNELIUS CANNON

JOHN CORNELIUS CANNON, Collector of Internal Revenue for the Northern District of Illinois, embracing thirty counties, was born in Chicago, Sept. 11, 1863; son of Ellen (Dooner) and Cornelius Cannon. His education was received in public schools of Chicago. In 1890 he was married to Anna Redell in Chicago. Children: Irene and Clara (Mrs. John V. Walsh). Mr. Cannon is a member of the firm of Cannon, Carolan & Ringer, Inc., 111 W. Washington St., dealing in surety bonds. He was Superintendent and Secretary of the Lincoln Park Commission for ten years and a member of the City Council, 1897-8. Mr. Cannon was also Chairman of the Board of Election Commissioners. In 1921 he was appointed Internal Revenue Collector. Home: 4521 N. Paulina Ave. Office: Federal Bldg.

able percentage of the volume of business which Chicago could expect to do in this class of banking.

As to Chicago bank stocks, these have won an established place among investors, and as for Chicago as a banking training school not alone are the distinction and authority of its banking veterans striking evidence, but other evidence exists in the contributions which this city has made to the banking personnel of New York.

Up to 1920, the United States had issued five Liberty loans with subscriptions which greatly exceeded allotments and aggregated $24,016,141,750. Of this amount, Chicago contributed $3,293,183,450.

The resources of Chicago banks have kept pace with the general growth of the city. In 1861, when the Chicago Clearing House Association was first organized, the deposits of members totalled $17,000,000. These had risen to $31,-000,000 in 1871 and by 1896 to $138,000,000, while now they exceed $1,600,000,000. In the meantime, the capital and surplus of all the Chicago banks has increased from $14,500,000 in 1871 to more than $234,000,000.

Foreign trade has not played as important a part in Chicago as it has in some of the cities on the seaboard whose entire business prosperity depends on the export and import trade of the country. Nevertheless, although an interior city, Chicago has not neglected trade with countries outside of America. Especially in the handling of bills of exchange based upon exports of raw materials, Chicago banks have been of primary importance. And in this connection they have not failed to make use in an ever-increasing degree of acceptances, an instrument of credit relatively new to this country. The acceptance market, which plays such an important part in the financing of the foreign trade of European countries, is steadily growing in favor, and Chicago banks have been doing their best to develop a broad acceptance market in this region.

Another institution for which Chicago is noted is the Chicago Stock Exchange, which is second only in importance in the United States to the New York Stock Exchange.

MARQUETTE NATIONAL FIRE INSURANCE CO.

THE Marquette National Fire Insurance Company, with assets of $2,000,978, is the largest company of its kind in Illinois. Its officers have brought the company to the front by strict adherence to honorable business methods.

In 1919, the Marquette company founded the Great Western Fire Insurance Co. in order to take care of the growing volume of business. In 1921, the two companies formed the Great Western Underwriters, which has a combined capital of $875,000 and assets of approximately $3,000,000. The company further added to its holdings in 1922 by the purchase of the Pittsburgh Fire Insurance Co., of Pittsburgh, Pa., and the Firemen's and Mechanics' Fire Insurance Co., of Indianapolis.

Marquette company officers are Anthony Matre, president; Dr. Henry Reis, Joseph Berning and F. J. Matre, vice presidents; Napoleon Picard, secretary and treasurer. Directors are Anthony Matre, Napoleon Picard, Dr. F. Gaudin, Joseph Berning, James F. Houlehan, Dr. Henry Reis, Francis J. Matre, Hugh O'Neill and Archibald A. McKinley. Main offices are at Insurance Exchange building, Chicago. It has branches and agencies in twenty-one States.

HAROLD FOWLER McCORMICK

HAROLD FOWLER M'CORMICK, Capitalist, was born in Chicago, May 2, 1872; son Cyrus Hall (inventor of reaping machine) and Nettie (Fowler) McCormick; A. B., Princeton, 1895; married Edith, daughter of John D. Rockefeller, Nov. 26, 1895; children: John Rockefeller (died 1901), Harold Fowler, Jr., Editha (died 1904), Muriel, Mathilde. Gen. Agt. McCormick Harvesting Machine Company, Council Bluffs, Iowa, 1896-97; Vice-President International Harvester Co., 1902-18, Treasurer, 1906-16, President since Dec. 16, 1918; Trustee Chicago Exchange Bldg. Co.; Trustee University of Chicago, McCormick Theological Seminary. Clubs: Chicago, Commercial, University, Chicago Athletic, Onwentsia (Chicago); University, Princeton, Racquet and Tennis (New York). Office: 606 S. Michigan Ave.

THE CONTINENTAL AND COMMERCIAL BANKS

THE group known as the Continental and Commercial Banks is an individual banking unit, composed of four corporations, the Continental and Commercial National Bank, The Continental and Commercial Trust and Savings Bank, the Continental and Commercial Securities Company and the Continental and Commercial Safe Deposit Company. They are housed in their own building at 208 South LaSalle Street, occupying the larger part of the first floor, all of the banking floor, the entire third and fourth floors and parts of the fifth, sixth and seventh. The main banking room is undoubtedly the largest in the country. It is 362 feet long with a skylight over the central part 62 feet above the floor. The ceiling in this room is supported by 48 taverndelle marble columns.

The invested capital, which includes capital, surplus and undivided profits, exceeds 55 million dollars. On March 10th, 1922 the total deposits were over 444 million dollars. Of this amount 50 million was in the savings bank and the commercial accounts of both the banking units were 394 million dollars of which 367 million dollars was in the National bank.

The entire institution has approximately 150,000 customers. Of these, about 122,000 are savings depositors. The National Bank has over 17,000 commercial accounts, while 5,200 banks carry deposits with it. Aside from the Safe Deposit Company and the Securities Company, the departments of the bank consist of commercial, foreign, savings, trust and bond and investment. Within these departments, there are many other departments and divisions. The National bank alone has 52 departments, including one which is run by and for women. The Foreign Department has over 6,000 correspondents located in various parts of the world.

The purpose of the directors and the management of this banking institution is to provide banking facilities to meet every possible financial demand under a single roof. It takes a staff of 2,100 employes to perform the needed banking service.

Of the internal ramifications of a large banking institution, little is known to the general public which is familiar only with the floors where actual contact is had with the employes. In the Transit, or out-of-town check collecting department of this bank, there are 300 employes whose entire time and attention is devoted to that work. The mail room, in which both outgoing and incoming

JOHN F. SMULSKI

JOHN FRANKLIN SMULSKI, banker and lawyer; was born in Posen, Poland, Feb. 4, 1867; s. William and Euphemia (Balcer) Smulski; ed. Govt. Mil. High Sch., Germany, 5 yrs.; St. Jerome's Coll., Berlin, Can., 2 years; law dept., Northwestern Univ., Chicago; m. Harriet Mikitynski, of Chicago, June 7, 1899. Was 5 yrs. in the newspaper and publishing business with his father, who established, in 1869, the first Polish newspaper in the U. S.; admitted to bar, 1890; mem. law firm of David, Smulski & McGaffey to 1905; organizer, 1906, and president North Western Trust & Savings Bank; alderman, Chicago, 1898-1903; city atty., 1903-5; state treas. of Ill., 1905-7; mem. Bd. of West Park Commrs., Chicago, 1907-13 (ex-pres.). Treas. Chicago Assn. of Commerce, 1911 (chmn. Conv. Bur., 1914). Decorated by French Government Chevalier Legion d' Honneur, Dec. 1921. Clubs: Press, Chicago Athletic, Union League. Home: 2138 Pierce Av. Office: 1201 Milwaukee Avenue.

mail is handled, has 275 employes and the banks postage bill exceeds $125,000 a year. For the employes, there is a rest room for women, a club room for men, a fully equipped gymnasium and a lunch room where 1,500 persons eat every day. The bank has its own print shop in which, however, only its own forms are printed, and in the supply room there is rather more stationary than would equip an ordinary retail store.

The Continental and Commercial group is the product of a number of combinations and mergers of banking institutions. These combinations centered around the Continental National Bank and the Commercial National Bank. The latter two were brought together in 1910 since which time there has been only one addition. The Fort Dearborn National Bank and the Fort Dearborn Trust and Savings Bank were taken over by this institution in January, 1922. The National Bank, whose stockholders own all the stock of the other three corporations, has 42 directors and about 2,000 stockholders.

FOREMAN BROTHERS BANKING CO.

FOUNDED in 1862, Foreman Brothers' Banking company has survived the strains of three wars, the great fire and the crises and panics that have beset banks during the long period.

The company's steady growth has been won by its own efforts and not through consolidations with other banks.

Since 1897, when the bank became a state institution, deposits have increased from $977,914.95 to over $35,000,000. The bank's capital and surplus is $4,000 000. It is a member of the Federal Reserve System and the Chicago Clearing House Association.

Oscar G. Foreman is chairman of the board of directors. Other officers are Harold E. Foreman, president; George N. Neise, Alfred K. Foreman, Gerhard Foreman, William J. Fickinger, Charles A. Burns and John Terbough, vice-presidents; Andrew F. Moeller, cashier; Edwin G. Foreman, Jr., Max J. Thies, Frank B. Woltz, J. E. Sullivan and James S. Rodie, assistant cashiers; James A. Hemingway, secretary; Edwin G. Neise, assistant secretary; and John H. Bartelme, auditor. Neil J. Shannon is trust officer, and John W. Bissell is assistant trust officer.

The bank's quarters are located at La Salle and Washington streets, Chicago.

STANDARD TRUST & SAVINGS BANK

THE STANDARD TRUST & SAVINGS BANK, one of the growing Loop institutions, was founded by Charles S. Castle and a number of his friends and business associates in September, 1910. The Bank was formerly located at 29 South LaSalle street, now occupying the banking floor of the Standard Trust & Savings Bank Building, and part of the ground floor where its Savings, Trust, and Bond Departments are operating.

The paid in capital and surplus of the Bank was $1,250,000. Its present capital, surplus, and undivided profits are over $1,800,000, having been increased to that amount from earnings. Deposits are now in excess of $11,000,000.

The officers of the Bank are Charles S. Castle, President; Ward C. Castle, Vice-President; Robert M. Campbell, Vice-President; Walter J. Kuhn, Cashier; Martin A. Olson, Assistant Cashier; Leo J. Talleur, Assistant Cashier; Frank R. Curda, Assistant Secretary.

The directors are W. J. Carney, Robert F. Carr, A. R. Marriott, Charles S. Cutting, George A. Eddy, Charles R. Street, Oliver M. Burton, F. J. Lewis, P. D. Castle, Jacob Mortenson, Fred F. Bullen, Frederick A. Hill, James D. Murphy, William P. Worth, Walter H. Jacobs, Eugene N. Strom, James B. Beckett, Ward C. Castle, and Charles S. Castle.

ROBERT P. LAMONT

ROBERT PATTERSON LAMONT, president of the American Steel Foundries, was born in Detroit, Dec. 1, 1867; s. of Robert and Isabella (Patterson) Lamont; B.S., C.E., Univ. of Mich., 1891. Married Helen Gertrude Trotter, of Chicago, Oct. 24, 1894. Children: Robert P., Jr., Dorothy and Gertrude. Engineer at World's Columbian Exposition, 1891-2; secretary and engineer of Shailer & Schinglau, contractors, 1892-7; vice pres. Simplex Railway Appliance Company, 1897-1905; vice pres. American Steel Foundries, 1905-12, and pres. since 1912; dir., First National Bank and Morris Plan Bank. Clubs: Chicago, Union League, University, Mid-Day, Shore Acres, Old Elm. Home: Lake Forest, Ill. Office: 332 S. Michigan Av., Chicago.

THE FIRST NATIONAL BANK OF CHICAGO

T HE FIRST NATIONAL BANK of Chicago was organized immediately after the passage of the National Bank Act and opened its doors for business July 1, 1863, having received charter number eight from the Comptroller of the Currency. The initial capital of the bank was fixed at $250,000, and its first statement published September 30 of the year of its organization showed deposits of $273,089.49.

The bank was originally located at Clark and Lake Streets, but the rapid growth which attended its early history necessitated larger quarters; and in 1868, it occupied a new building at State and Washington Streets. This building was erected as fire-proof, but could not withstand the great fire of 1871, though the vaults and their contents were unharmed. The building was restored after the fire.

Despite the fire and the depression of 1873, the bank continued to grow, its balance sheet on November 1 of that year showing loans in excess of $3,000,-000, capital of $1,000,000 and deposits of nearly $3,500,000.

In 1882, the bank occupied its then new building at Dearborn and Monroe streets, which has been its location continuously for the past forty years; its present building, erected in two sections, being finally completed in 1905.

The capital of the bank in 1882 was increased to $3,000,000 and again in 1900 to $5,000,000, two years later being made $8,000,000 and in 1910 increased to $10,000,000. The present capital is $12,500,000 with a surplus fund of the same amount and undivided profits of $4,486,403.

During its existence there have been merged with the First National two other banks: The Union National in 1900 and the Metropolitan National in 1902. In 1903 the First Trust and Savings Bank was organized under direction of First National interests. The stock of both banks is owned by the same stockholders and both banks are governed by the same board of directors. The growth of the First National Bank has been reflected in the First Trust and Savings Bank, the latter's capital having been increased from $1,000,000 at the time of organization to $6,250,000 with a surplus fund of the same amount and undivided profits of $1,983,350. The deposits of the First National Bank at the close of business March 10, 1922, were $189,810,438, and those of the savings bank $91,534,069.

The National Safe Deposit Company, having a capital of $3,500,000, is also affiliated with the two banks and operates safe deposit vaults on the ground floor of the building.

There are six official divisions in the First National bank and one major department, the Foreign Exchange. The First Trust and Savings Bank has four principal departments: the Banking, which includes savings, the Bond, the Trust and the Real Estate Loan. The affiliated institutions are thus enabled to render a complete and highly specialized service to customers.

During its entire history the First National Bank has had but five presidents. The first, Edmund Aiken, who had been a private banker prior to the National Bank Act, served the institution until his death in 1867. He was succeeded by Samuel M. Nickerson, who was chief executive from 1867 to 1891 and again from 1897 to 1900. The period intervening marked the administration of Lyman J. Gage, who resigned to become secretary of the Treasury. James B. Forgan was elected president in 1900 and served until 1916, assuming the position of chairman of the board upon the election of Frank O. Wetmore, the present incumbent.

By reason of the excellent management which it has enjoyed, the high financial policy which it has strenuously advocated, and the respect and esteem of the community which it has never sacrificed, this institution has attained a reputation well merited by its record.

WARREN WRIGHT

WARREN WRIGHT, president of the Calumet Baking Powder Company, was born in Springfield, O., in 1875; son of Clara and W. M. Wright. He was educated in the public schools of Springfield and Chicago. He was married to Lucille Parker in Chicago. The Calumet Baking Powder Company was founded by W. M. Wright in 1889. Today the company has three plants, each of them the last word in mechanical triumph, and the management has passed from W. M. Wright to his son, Warren Wright. Under the latter's direction, the sales of Calumet Baking Powder have increased each year until it is by far the largest selling brand in the world. Mr. Wright is also an official of the Calumet Chemical Company and the Calumet Can Company. His clubs are the Chicago Athletic, Chicago Yacht, Bob O' Link Golf, Exmoor Golf, and South Shore Country. Home: 230 E. Walton place. Office: 4100 Fillmore street, Chicago.

CENTRAL TRUST COMPANY OF ILLINOIS

WHEN the Central Trust Company of Illinois opened for business on July 8, 1902, on the main floor of the old Howland Building, on the present site of the Westminster Building—Dearborn and Monroe Streets —its staff numbered seven officers and eighteen employees. The President, Charles G. Dawes, had previously made an enviable record as Comptroller of the Currency during President McKinley's administration and was ably qualified not only by experience, but by an unusually keen mind, sound business judgment and a wide acquaintance to assume the leadership and responsibility of the new institution, which engaged to do a general commercial banking business, although including other branches of banking in its services.

That the new bank was destined to prosper and had the confidence of the community was evidenced by the steady increase in its deposits. These on the opening day stood at $4,984,055. More ample quarters were deemed advisable in the course of several years, and the bank accordingly purchased the building it now occupies at 125 W. Monroe St.—just east of LaSalle—taking possession of the greater portion of the main floor in 1906 and leasing the remainder of the space to various tenants. After five years of business, its deposits reached $11,778,890. Keeping step with this increase, the bank gradually broadened its facilities in order to better its service. Separate departments specializing in the distinct branches of its business were formed, necessitating the occupancy of further space. As a result, by 1912, the entire building was given over to the uses of the bank, the Commercial, Savings and Bond Departments being located on the main banking floor; the Trust Department on the second and the Real Estate Loan Department on the third.

By July of 1912—ten years after its organization—the bank's deposits stood at $43,009,654, an increase for the period of over $38,000,000.

So pressed had the bank become for working space by 1915 that upon the completion of the Borland Building, adjoining to the west, a part of the ground floor was leased for the accommodation of the Savings Department, with an entrance directly on La Salle St.; and, more subsequently, additional space was taken for the foreign and other departments. As evidence of continued growth, deposits of $55,912,165 were on the bank's books July 8, 1917. Approaching its twentieth anniversary, the figures shown in its latest published statement best reflect its position at this time—the item of deposits standing at $67,141,075. With employees now totaling close to the 500 mark, the bank is serving—in its Commercial and Savings Departments—more than 80,000 customers.

With the news of the entry of the United States into the Great War, in 1917, the stand of the Central Trust Company was immediately felt. The President himself secured a leave of absence to enter the service of his country, placing the affairs of the bank in charge of Mr. Joseph E. Otis, then Senior Vice-President. Mr. Dawes' first commission was that of Lieutenant-Colonel of the 17th Railway Engineers, which after a brief period of training arrived safely in France. It did not take long for those in command to recognize in Lt.-Col. Dawes the unusual qualities of a leader, combined with keen business judgment, and he was soon appointed General Purchasing Agent for the U. S. Army, greatly facilitating the movement of supplies to all the allied forces, his services in this connection earning for him the rank of Brigadier-General. Fifty-one stars in the service flag of the bank testify to the fact that that number of its employees likewise did honor to their country, no direct fatalities occurring and most of them returning to the places that had been held open to them.

Shortly after Gen. Dawes' return to his banking business, he was elected chairman of the Board of Directors, being succeeded to the Presidency by Mr. Otis. The need of his presence in public affairs, however, was still felt and, subsequent to the election of Mr. Harding to the presidency of the U. S., Gen. Dawes was appointed director of the budget of the United States, in which position he is succeeding in materially paring down the country's expenses.

It is under leadership such as this that the Central Trust Company of Illinois has gained a strong foothold in the banking world and is able to offer to a growing number of depositors a banking service meeting all of their business needs.

R. E. WILSEY & COMPANY

ROBERT E. WILSEY is president of R. E. Wilsey & Company, organized as a partnership in 1914 to engage in the purchase and sale of investment securities. The other members of the firm are W. B. Egan, B. J. Clarke and Wilbur Helm. Offices are in the Harris Trust and Savings Building.

All of the members of the organization have had several years of experience with financial institutions, principally along the line of originating and selling securities of well known and established utility companies.

The soundness of their judgment has been fully verified by the excellent record which public utility issues have established as to prompt payment of their obligations and the further fact that there is a continuing and increasing demand from the large and small investors for securities of this character.

108

THE MERCHANTS' LOAN AND TRUST COMPANY

PERHAPS no more unpropitious period for the founding of a financial institution ever existed in the history of Chicago than in the year 1857 when The Merchants' Loan and Trust Company was established. Business was at a' low ebb; finance was in a chaotic state and banks which could build and uplift the financial and business conditions of Chicago did not exist But the forward-looking merchants and business men of Chicago recognized the need for such a banking institution and they founded it well; they built on firm foundations and established a bank which has now been identified with Chicago's commercial growth and progress for sixty-five years.

Those years have covered many trying times,—first the Civil War, then the era of reconstruction, the many periods of financial and business depression and the great Chicago fire, which laid waste almost the entire city; but Chicago came through all those trying experiences, constantly advancing in commercial importance, and The Merchants' Loan and Trust Company has continued to be an important factor in the business development of the city and surrounding territory. The experience gained during those times has had much to do with the present stability of the bank. The character which was thus built into its structure is responsible in large measure for its present-day strength and influence.

During its corporate existence, The Merchants' Loan and Trust Company has witnessed practically the entire business development of Chicago and the Middle West. In 1856, the year prior to the establishment of the bank, the city's population was 84,113. Today Chicago numbers more than 2,700,000 inhabitants. In 1857 the total capital and surplus of all the banks in Illinois was less than four million dollars, only one-fourth of the present capital, surplus and undivided profits of The Merchants' Loan and Trust Company. The deposits of all the banks in Illinois in 1857 were barely a million and a half dollars as against one billion, eight hundred sixty-four million dollars for the city of Chicago alone in 1922. The value of real and personal property in Chicago in 1856 was about thirty-one million dollars. Today these two items are estimated to exceed three and one-half billion dollars.

As the founders of The Merchants' Loan and Trust Company were the business leaders of their day, men whose names stand high in Chicago's history, so are the men who direct its affairs and guide its policies today. On its board of directors may be found the present leaders in Chicago's commerce and industry. We find manufacturing business represented by such men as Cyrus H. McCormick, Chairman of the International Harvester Company, and Edward L. Ryerson, Chairman of Joseph T. Ryerson & Son. Mercantile business we find represented by John G. Shedd, President of Marshall Field and Company; Albert A. Sprague, Chairman of Sprague, Warner and Company and James P. Soper, President of the Soper Lumber Company. Representing transportation we find Marvin Hughitt, Chairman of the Chicago and North Western Railway Company; Hale Holden, President of the Chicago, Burlington and Quincy Railroad Company and John S. Runnells, Chairman of the Pullman Company. The law we find represented by Clarence A. Burley and by Robert W. Campbell, while finance and investment is represented by John J. Mitchell, Chairman of The Merchants' Loan and Trust Company and the Illinois Trust and Savings Bank; Ernest A. Hamill, Chairman of The Corn Exchange National Bank; Edmund D. Hulbert, President of The Merchants' Loan and Trust Company, the Illinois Trust and Savings Bank and The Corn Exchange National Bank; Orson Smith, Chairman of the advisory committee of The Merchants' Loan and Trust Company and the Illinois Trust and Savings Bank; Marshall Field of Marshall Field, Glore Ward and Company and Chauncey Keep, Trustee of the Marshall Field Estate.

The personnel of the official family of The Merchants' Loan and Trust Company is as follows:

Chairman of the board, John J. Mitchell; president, Edmund D. Hulbert; vice presidents, Frank G. Nelson, John E. Blunt, Jr., C. E. Estes, F. W. Thompson, and H. G. P. Deans; cashier, John J. Geddes; assistant cashiers, F. E. Loomis, A. F. Pither and W. A. Hutchison; secretary and trust officer, Leon L. Loehr; assistant secretary, A. Leonard Johnson; manager bond department, G. F. Hardie; assistant manager bond department, Cuthbert C. Adams; assistant manager foreign department, H. J. Sampson.

JAMES B. McDOUGAL

JAMES B. McDOUGAL, governor of the Federal Reserve Bank of Chicago, was born in Peoria, Ill., 1866; s. of Mary (Gray) and John Mc-Dougal. Educated in public schools of Peoria. Married Laura Gray of Painesville, Ohio, in 1896. Entered Central National Bank at Peoria and remained there until 1901, when he was appointed national bank examiner for five years. In 1906 he became official examiner of associated banks of Chicago and organized and operated department of examination of Chicago Clearing House. In 1914 he was elected governor of Federal Reserve Bank of Chicago. Clubs: Bankers, Industrial, Mid-Day. Home: Riverside, Ill. Office: Federal Reserve Bank of Chicago.

FOSTER C. SCOTT

FOSTER C. SCOTT, president of the Stony Island Trust and Savings Bank, 68th st. and Stony Island av., was born in Ohio, Ill., Oct. 24, 1889; son of Nellie R. and John L. Scott. He was educated in public and private schools of Washington, D. C., and graduated from the law department of George Washington University in 1913. Mr. Scott married Irene S. Bohnenkamp, of Chicago, April 7, 1920. Mr. Scott, with several associates, purchased the Stony Island bank from the Armour interests in 1921 and since then the bank's deposits have increased $600,000. The rise in business has made larger quarters imperative and the bank has started construction of a $350,000 home. Mr. Scott is a member of the South Shore Country, Olympia Fields Country and the Hamilton clubs. He resides at 2234 E. 70th place.

CORN EXCHANGE NATIONAL BANK OF CHICAGO

THE strength of four big financial institutions has been infused into the Corn Exchange National Bank of Chicago, Monroe and La Salle streets, and today it stands as one of the most formidable banking houses in the entire Chicago district.

The Illinois Merchant and Trust Company building on the block bounded by Clark, La Salle, Jackson and Quincy, is now in process of construction and will house the combined institutions. In the new edifice will be embodied every facility for meeting any demand in the banking business. The pressing need for space, which was accentuated by the rapid rise in business, has made the new building imperative.

In September of 1870, the Corn Exchange National Bank of Chicago came into being, with but a small capital. It passed, unscarred, through the trying financial times of the Spanish war and subsequent depressions and in 1900 it was amalgamated with the Northwestern National Bank. Two years later came the merger with the Merchants' National Bank. An affiliation was consummated with the Merchants' Loan and Trust Company and the Illinois Trust and Savings Bank on September 30, 1919.

Figures best tell the story of the rise of the Corn Exchange Bank. On December 31, 1901, the capital stood at $2,000,000; on December 31, 1921, it was $5,000,000. The surplus on December 31, 1921, which was $10,000,000, represented an increase of 1,000 per cent over the 1901 figure. The report of the bank's condition on June 30, 1922, showed that it had resources of $113,078,534.85 and liabilities of the same amount.

A management—whose members are not only made up of banking experts but also of leaders in other fields of endeavor—is one of the chief assets of the bank. The institution has earned high esteem, which is merited by its record, because of the policy of fair dealing, strenuously advocated by the management, and because it has never violated a trust placed with it by a customer.

Another of the assets is the staff of employes. They work with a unit spirit and discharge their work quickly, accurately and always with a view to rendering the best service.

The officers of the Corn Exchange Bank are Ernest A. Hamill, chairman of the board; Edmund D. Hulbert, president; Charles L. Hutchinson, vice-president; Owen T. Reeves, Jr., vice-president; J. Edward Maass, vice-president; Norman J. Ford, vice-president; James G. Wakefield, vice-president; Edward F. Schoenbeck, cashier; and Lewis E. Gary, James A. Walker, Charles Novak and Hugh J. Sinclair, assistant cashiers.

The directors are Watson F. Blair; Chauncey B. Borland, manager, Borland Properties; Edward B. Butler, chairman, board of directors of Butler Brothers; Benjamin Carpenter, president, George B. Carpenter & Company; Clyde M. Carr, president, Joseph T. Ryerson & Son; Henry P. Crowell, president, Quaker Oats Company; Ernest A. Hamill, chairman of the board; Edmund D. Hulbert, president; Charles H. Hulburd, president, Elgin National Watch Company; Charles L. Hutchinson, vice-president; John J. Mitchell, chairman of board, Illinois Trust & Savings Bank; Martin A. Ryerson; J. Harry Selz, president, Selz, Schwab & Company; Robert J. Thorne, and Charles H. Wacker, president, Chicago Heights Land Association.

JACOB KULP

JACOB KULP, financier and president of Jacob Kulp & Co., dealing in investment bonds, was born in Verbollen, Poland, Aug. 28, 1878; s. of Flora (Gedansky) and Lee Kulp. Educated in pub. schs. of Clinton, Ia., and Chicago. Married Hattie Harris, Chicago, Sept. 19, 1905. Son; Lee. In employ of Sears, Roebuck Co. 11 years, Gen. merchand. mgr. Harris Brothers 11 years; vice-pres. and mgr. invest. dept. Madison and Kedzie State Bank six years, organized Jacob Kulp & Co. in 1921. Dir. of U. S. Building Corp. and 22nd Street Station Building Corp. Club: Idlewild Country. Home: 1146 Hyde Park blvd. Office: 105 W. Monroe st.

RAY & COMPANY

RAY & COMPANY, dealing in bonds and investment securities, was founded in 1921. It was formerly the Cammack Ray Company. Its officers today are: H. T. Ray, president; H. D. Draper, vice-president; P. K. Sims, vice-president; L. M. Bonheim, treasurer. These officers are directors, together with the following: C. F. Packer, secretary; G. J. Bader, president of the Indiana Harbor National Bank; A. J. Morse, president of A. G. Morse & Company; E. D. Norton, member of the Chicago Board of Trade; E. W. Pratt, consulting engineer; and C. W. Robertson. Ray & Company has branches and correspondents in all the principal cities of the country. Its Chicago offices are located at 108 S. La Salle St.

LEE M. BONHEIM

112

TAYLOR, EWART & CO.

TAYLOR, Ewart & Company, through many years of reliable service, has attained a high position in the brokerage business of this section of the country. It prides itself on the fact that it has never violated a trust.

The company had its inception in 1911, under the name of Yard, Otis and Taylor. It became Taylor, Ewart & Company in 1917, following the withdrawal of F. A. Yard and the entrance into the firm of C. B. Ewart.

The firm specializes in government, municipal, corporation, railroad and public utility bonds. It selected this type of securities because of the protection offered to the purchaser and ample evidence of the wisdom of this choice is to be found in the fact that the company is daily adding to its clientele.

Business increases brought the establishment of branch offices at New York City and Kansas City. Originally started with the purpose of covering the Chicago district, the company's activities have extended into Indiana, Wisconsin, Missouri, Michigan, Minnesota, Iowa, Nebraska and Kansas.

Officers are B. F. Taylor, president; C. B. Ewart, vice-president and treasurer; L. A. Munger, vice-president; Thomas K. Carpenter, secretary; I. L. Billett, assistant secretary. B. F. Taylor, C. B. Ewart, Thomas K. Carpenter are the directors. Main offices are at 105 S. La Salle st.

THE HANCHETT BOND COMPANY

THE HANCHETT BOND COMPANY, in twelve years, has built up an investment business which has for its patrons many of the largest banks and insurance companies in America, as well as many fraternal orders, hundreds of trust companies and estates, as well as a host of individual investors.

A highly-developed executive force, plus a system of careful investigation, forms one of the reasons for the Company's success. The business is confined exclusively to Municipal Bonds, all of which are purchased outright by the Company for its own account after careful investigation and after the legality has been established by eminent bond attorneys..

The Hanchett Company has branches in several of the principal cities of the country, with the largest located at Detroit, New York, St. Louis and Philadelphia. Its Chicago correspondents are the First National Bank and the Central Trust Company of Illinois. Its New York correspondent is the Chase National Bank.

The firm was incorporated in 1910. The officers are: L. A. Trowbridge, president, William F. Hanchett, vice-president and treasurer, and Harold G. Hanchett, secretary.

THE JOHN McGILLEN & CO.

ORGANIZED in 1910, is the general agent for the Fidelity & Deposit Co. of Maryland. John McGillen, president of the company, served with the Chicago Title & Trust Company, Agnew & Company and Berudes Paving Company before entering the insurance business. He was a delegate to four Democratic national conventions. Offices of the McGillen Company are at 105 S. La Salle st.

FRANK C. RATHJE

FRANK C. RATHJE, lawyer and banker, was born in Bloomingdale Township, Illinois, Aug. 20, 1882; son of Louisa (Ehlers) and William Rathje. Educated in St. John's Military Academy, Delafield, Wis.; Armour Institute and Northwestern University Law School, graduating in 1907. On Oct. 16, 1915, he married Josephine Logan, Chicago. Children: Theron L., and Josephine. Mr. Rathje's first work was as a clerk for the Live Stock Exchange National Bank. From this bank, he transferred to the Chicago Title and Trust Company, being abstract counter clerk for three years. In 1908, he began practice of law, opening office in the Roanoke building. His rise was steady and today he is president of the Mutual National Bank of Chicago; chairman of the board of directors of the Alliance National Bank; and general counsel for the Chicago City Bank and Trust Company, and Kimbell Trust and Savings Bank. He is a member of the Medina Temple Commandery of the Shriners. Home: 6522 Harvard av. Office: 29 S. LaSalle street.

FRANK ALBERT ALDEN

FRANK ALBERT ALDEN, president of Garfield Pk. State Savings Bank, was born in Janesville, Wis., Aug. 21, 1870; s. of Albert Warner and Caroline (Case) Alden; descendant of John and Priscilla Alden of Mayflower. Ed. in pub. schs. of Chicago. Married Caroline S. Larsen, June 16, 1891, Chicago. Children: Charles Frank, Earl Russel, Mildred Gladys. Mr. Alden began with Commercial National Bank in 1888, continuing 12 years; in coal business 1900-07; entered employ of Prairie State Bank 1907 and continued with its successor, Central Trust Co., 1912-13; dir. and cashier, Liberty Trust & Savings Bank, 1913-19; pres, Garfield Pk. State Savings Bank since 1919. Mem. Pilgrim Congregational Church, Oak Park. Pres. Alden Kindred of Am. Republican. Clubs: West Town Bankers (pres.), Pilgrim Boosters, Garfield Park, Active Club, Butterfield Country. Pres. of Garfield Park Historical Soc.

and treas. of West Side Boy Scouts. Office: 4004 W. Madison St. Home: 621 S. Euclid Av.

MADISON & KEDZIE STATE BANK

ALTHOUGH it is one of Chicago's outlying banks and is comparatively an infant in years, the Madison & Kedzie State Bank has developed a nation-wide investment business.

The story of the Madison & Kedzie State Bank needs no embellishment to make it interesting. Organized in 1913, its primary aim was to better the community in which it was located by merchandising and making thrift more profitable.

Although the original staff was, perforce, small, it was made up of specialists, men who had long and intensive training in their particular branches of banking. They were as thoroughly aware of conditions in New Zealand as in Chicago. Their introduction of the human element into banking, taking each patron into their confidence, and stripping the business of its austerity, soon brought a steady flow of money into the bank, which to this day has not abated.

The bank's banner year was 1920, when the deposits increased $1,379,900. This was followed by still another increase of $1,008,476 in 1921. The same year, the bank moved into its new building at Madison St. and Kedzie Ave., which is seven times the size of its first building at 3131 W. Madison St. The thirteen large display windows of the new building are utilized in bringing before the public more poignantly the advantages of thrift.

H. H. Baum is the bank's president; A. H. Smith, vice-president; E. R. Mullen, assistant vice-president; J. T. Mammoser, cashier; P. A. Schroeder, W. F. Gleason, Henry Finholt, J. C. Meyer, Howard Huff, assistant cashiers; R. W. Hutchinson, auditor. Directors are J. A. Barkey, H. H. Baum, H. N. Bruns, David W. Clark, John P. Collins, Benjamin Kulp, F. B. Malcolm, H. V. McGurren, Otto Rice, H. L. Schroeder, A. H. Smith, G. D. Wilkinson, R. B. Wilson; J. T. Mammoser, secretary of the board.

STONY ISLAND TRUST & SAVINGS BANK

SINCE the purchase of the Stony Island Trust and Savings bank by Foster C. Scott and associates from Armour and Co. in 1921, the bank has increased its deposits more than $600,000.

The rise in business has been so great as to make larger quarters imperative and the company has started construction of a $350,000 home, which is expected to be completed in 1923. Proper facilities for a trust department will be embodied in the new edifice.

Located at 68th street and Stony Island avenue, in the center of the South Shore district, the bank draws its trade from one of the wealthiest residential districts in Chicago. Building department figures show this district enjoyed the greatest building activity in 1922.

The Stony Island Trust & Savings bank was founded in 1917 and was one of the first to join the Chicago Clearing House Association.

The present officers are Foster C. Scott, president; A. W. Broecker, vice president; Harry H. Cavin, vice president; Edward F. J. Lindberg, cashier; Oliver B. Cottle, assistant cashier; Carl Newgreen, assistant cashier. Board of directors: Foster C. Scott, chairman; Hon. Charles S. Deneen, Charles G. Blake, J. T. Russel, J. M. Delaney, A. W. Broecker, Edward I. Bloom, P. J. McShane, Ben Hunding, Frank Burke, David Wiedemann, Jr., George J. Bohnen and Henry P. Reger.

KASPAR STATE BANK

THE things that go into the making of a successful financier are ofttimes overlooked in the heat of business. Not only must he be a man fitted by nature and training for the handling of money other than his own, but he must have a long and varied experience, and be able to pass decidedly and firmly upon matters of moment. By his decisions, many large enterprises and the general well-being of the community are affected.

WILLIAM KASPAR

It is not often that men are trusted in so important an office as the presidency of a banking institution unless they have earned the right to such an honor, and there is no exception to the rule in the case of William Kaspar, president of the Kaspar State Bank.

Under the administration of Mr. Kaspar, the bank has developed into the

116

largest Bohemian financial institution in the United States, with resources of $12,929,306.

Mr. Kaspar was born in Hollitz, Bohemia, September 1, 1835; son of Anna (Michaleck) Kaspar. He reached the United States, November 2, 1852. Nine years later, he enlisted in the Northern Army in defense of the liberties of his new country. He was assigned to Company I, Fourth Massachusetts Volunteer Infantry and was drilled for service at Camp Joe Hooker at Middleboro, Mass. He left camp in December of that year for New Orleans. On June 14, 1863, his military career was abruptly halted by a severe wound in the leg during the attack on Fort Hudson and he was honorably discharged as sergeant, August 23, 1863.

It was at this time that Horace Greeley uttered his famous pronunciamento, "Go west, young man." Mr. Kaspar was impressed and the year 1864 saw him in Chicago.

After engaging in various enterprises, he entered the banking business, organizing a private bank in partnership with a Mr. Karel in 1888. Following Mr. Karel's withdrawal, Mr. Kaspar, in 1905, incorporated the bank as the Kaspar State Bank with a capital and surplus of $225,000 and which now has been increased to $1,250,000.00.

A steady growth marked the bank's course. To handle overflow business, Mr. Kaspar organized the First National Bank of Cicero, of which he is now president.

During the many years he has been connected with Chicago banking, he has never failed to serve the interests of his patrons, no matter how small. Mr. Kaspar has attained the distinction of a successful banker through merit, guarded by conservatism, which is the essential rule of banking, and has consequently gained the utmost confidence of the public.

His two sons, who have inherited much of their father's financial ability, have taken their places in the banking business. Mr. Otto Kaspar is at present chairman of the board of directors and vice-president of the Kaspar State Bank and the First National Bank of

OTTO KASPAR

Cicero. Mr. Eugene W. Kaspar is vice-president and cashier of the First National Bank of Cicero and vice-president of the Kaspar State Bank.

The officers of the Kaspar State Bank are William Kaspar, president; Otto Kaspar, vice-president; Charles Krupka, vice-president; Eugene W. Kaspar, vice-president; Emil F. Smrz, cashier; August Filek, Stanley L. Chleboun, Anton Jecmen, and Alvin O. Wiese, assistant cashiers.

The directorate is comprised of Otto Kaspar, William Kaspar, Eugene W. Kaspar, Adolph Karpen, Charles Krupka, William Oetting, H. E. Otte, Joseph Peschel, William C. Schreiber, Walenty Szymanski and George C. Wilce.

The bank's offices are at 1900 Blue Island Avenue, Chicago, Illinois.

117

CLARENCE BENNETT CHADWICK

PRESIDENT of The Bankers Supply Company since 1907, offices in Chicago, Denver, Atlanta, New York, Des Moines and San Francisco, the largest manufacturers of bank checks in the world.

Mr. Chadwick was born and educated in Green Bay, Wisconsin, and in the University of Wisconsin. His clubs are the Hamilton and Flossmoor Country. He is a member of Oriental Consistory (Shrine) and Sigma Chi.

Mr. Chadwick knows every phase of the bank supply business from the ground up, having started in as a salesman, selling checks in practically every section of the country.

This broad experience and intimate contact with bankers' needs throughout the United States enabled him to invent, develop and perfect the Super-Safety Insured Bank Check now widely advertised in the leading magazines and adopted in thousands of banks throughout the country. Before the development of these positively safe checks, Mr. Chadwick says, "In spite of all the ingenious methods used for protection, there has been a $30,000,000.00 annual loss through fraudulent checks." Seeing the futility of ingenuity as protection against such losses, he conceived the idea of forever eliminating this fear in the minds of bank depositors by positively protecting them with insurance. An arrangement with the Hartford Accident & Indemnity Company made it possible for him to protect the bank and each of its depositors on all Super-Safety Insured Checks with an individual bond without charge to them.

118

CALUMET NATIONAL BANK

A SOUND banking business, built upon a policy that is consistent with the times and a service which is noted for its dispatch and unerring accuracy—that is the Calumet National Bank, with headquarters at 9117 Commercial avenue.

An excellent management which it has the good fortune to possess; a high fnancial policy which it has ever advocated, and the respect and the esteem of the community, which it never has sacrificed, have made the Calumet National Bank one of the largest neighborhood banks in Chicago. Organized with a capital of $300,000, it has been the company's purpose, through all the periods of its development and changes, to house under one roof sufficient facilities to meet any demand in the banking business.

Serving mainly workers in the steel mills of the South Chicago district, it has started many on the road to independence by pointing out to them the benefits that accrue from thrift and by providing them timely loans. The Calumet National Bank has been an important factor in the building boom which is transforming the Chicago district into a bustling spick-and-span community and which is providing better living facilities.

The bank has never held itself aloof and its attaches are taught that courtesy is the key to higher dividends.

To the perspicacity of Emil G. Seip, its president, does the bank owe much of its success. It was he who brought it unscarred through slack times and depressions. Although occupied with a number of important offices in other commercial institutions, Mr. Seip has given a great deal of his time to the development of the Calumet institution. To act in his absence, he has provided an organization of capable clerks and officials, each of whom has had previous experience in banking.

Mr. Seip was born in Chicago, Oct. 8, 1876, the son of Fredrika (Maier) and Charles Seip. He was educated in Chicago public schools and Bowen high school and in 1897 received the degree of bachelor of law at Valparaiso University. On June 26, 1900, he was wed to Minnie Schottler, of Milwaukee Children: Willamine Estelle and Antoinette.

He practiced law from 1897 to 1904, when his services attracted the Illinois Improvement and Ballast Company, which made him secretary and treasurer. Today he holds the post of president. Later came the organization of the Calumet National Bank and to him was assigned the office of president. Mr. Seip is affiliated with three other banking institutions. He is chairman of the board of directors of the Interstate National Bank; director of the Roseland State Bank and director of the First National Bank of Gary, Ind. Mr. Seip is a member of the South Shore Country club.

Besides Mr. Seip, the officers of the Calumet National Bank are Marcus Aurelius, vice president, and F. A. Tinkham, cashier. The board of directors is composed of E. G. Seip, W. E. Schmidt, William Seip, Charles Seip, Charles Reuger, George E. Rose, Louis Kahn, T. J. Peden, Martin Hausler, Martin Furwan, F. X. Rydzewski, M. R. Driscoll, P. H. Moynihan, R. E. L. Brooks, W. E. Colburn and Marcus Aurelius.

119

JAMES F. STEPINA

JAMES F. STEPINA, banker, was born in Kuttenberg, Bohemia, Sept. 21, 1863; s. of August and Anna (Drtina) Stepina; came to U. S. with parents in 1864. Educated pub. schs., Chicago; Athenaeum Bus. Coll.; Union Coll. of Law; LL. B., Ill. Coll. of Law. Widower. Children: Mabel (widow of W. J. Shannon), Ida (Mrs. Fred W. Niemann). Engaged in mortgage loan and real estate business, 1883-1911; organized in 1911 the Am. State Bank of Chicago of which he is president. Co. commr. of Cook County, 1891-92; West Town Collector, 1897; West Chicago Park commr., 1904-7; pres. Bohemian Press Assn. of U. S. Mason (Chicago) Command. No. 19 K. T., Oriental Consistory 32, S. P. R. S., Medinah Temple Mystic Shrine. Life mem., Chicago Art Inst. Clubs: Bohemia, Bohemian Masonic, Press, Ill. Athletic, Adventurers. Office: 1825 Blue Island Av. Home: 616 Waveland Av.

OSCAR ARMIN KROPF

OSCAR ARMIN KROPF, lawyer, was born in Vienna, March 10, bank, was born in Vienna, March 10, 1872; son of Ferdinand Michael and Eleanor Johanna (Wehrhofske) Kropf; came to U. S. with parents, 1877; grad. Washburn Acad., Topeka, 1891; B. A. Washburn Coll., 1895 (Valedictorian); M. A., 1897; LL.B., Northwestern Univ. Law Sch., 1901. Married Edith Alfred Anderson, Chicago, Oct. 21, 1908; two children, Richard Thomas, Eleanor Arletta. Supt. pub. schools, Hays City, Kan., 1897-98; admitted to bar, 1901; mem. firm Paden & Kropf since 1904; dir. Prudential State Savings bank; mem. Am., Ill. State, Chicago Bar Assn. Republican; Lutheran. Mem. Phi Alpha Delta, Mason, Lincoln Park Lodge (Worshipful Master, 1909), Lawn Chapter, Lincoln Park Commandery; Red Cross of Constantine (Sovereign, 1921), Medinah Temple, A. A. O. N. M. S. (Potentate 1913-14); mem. ex. comm. bd., Chicago Masonic Relief Bd.; Grand Orator, Masonic Grand Lodge, 1916-17. Clubs: Union League, Ridgmoor Country, Law, German Club of Chicago (pres., 1914-15) Home: 1404 Sherwin Av. Office: 1752 Jackson Blvd.

MARSHALL FIELD, GLORE, WARD & CO.

MARSHALL Field, Glore, Ward & Company, transacting a general invest-ment banking business, was established in Chicago on March 1, 1920, as a partnership, under the name of Glore, Ward & Company. The partners then consisted of C. F. Glore, Peirce C. Ward, Allen L. Withers, and Earle H. Reynolds, president of the Peoples Trust and Savings Bank.

Toward the close of the company's first year, Marshall Field became a member and the name was changed to Marshall Field, Glore, Ward & Company. No changes in personnel were made at that time, with the exception of the addition of Mr. Field.

To accommodate its constantly growing eastern clientele, the company established a New York office at 14 Wall st. in 1921. Edward P. Currier and J. Taylor Foster, of New York, were added to the organization and placed in direct charge of the New York office.

Mr. Field recently purchased the building at 38 Wall st. as a permanent home for the company's New York office.

Through the company's many changes, the founders have remained with it and are bending every effort to place it in the lead in the banking business. The company's Chicago offices are 137 S. La Salle st.

JOHN NUVEEN & CO.

JOHN Nuveen started in the bond business for himself in 1898. His primary move was to adopt the policy of dealing only in the bonds issued by political subdivisions of the United States and payable from direct taxes.

The name technically given to such securities is "direct-obligation municipal bonds" and while they are of the highest grade and safest investments, many persons predicted Nuveen would not make a success of dealing exclusively in them because of the small margin of profit they offer.

He has remained true, however, to his original policy and in the past twenty years has built up one of the largest bond businesses in the country, dealing almost exclusively in municipal bonds. Nuveen & Co. has handled bond issues of municipalities in forty states.

Within recent years, when the nation's international position deemed it advisable to do foreign financing, the company broadened its policy to include bonds of Canadian municipalities and South American governments. Not one of the issues, supervised by Nuveen & Co., has failed to fulfill its promises.

Mr. Nuveen came to Chicago in 1886 and has resided here ever since. In addition to being sole proprietor of the bond business, he is vice president and director of the Columbian Bank Note Co. He is a member of the Union League, Mid-Day, Hamilton, Quadrangle and Olympic Fields Golf Clubs. Mr. Nuveen is also a trustee of the Y. M. C. A. college and a director of the Sunday Evening club.

John Nuveen & Co. offices are at 1000, First National Bank building.

HYNEY, EMERSON & COMPANY, INC.

R. S. HYNEY

THE investment banking firm of Hyney, Emerson & Company, Inc., began as a co-partnership March 1, 1918. The partners were Ralph S. Hyney and Guy L. V. Emerson, and the firm succeeded to the business which Mr. Hyney had previously established with a former partner in 1916.

The activities of the firm are confined solely to the purchase and sale of entire original issues of municipal and corporation bonds. Its particular specialty has been the financing of established Chicago and Middle Western industries and numbered among the enterprises which the firm has financed are such well-known concerns as The Cooper Underwear Company, Kenosha, Wis.; The Kilbourne & Jacobs Mfg. Company, Columbus, O.; The Clark Equipment Company, Buchanan and Battle Creek, Mich.; The Filer Fibre Company, Manistee, Mich.; W. Mc-Millan & Son, Chicago, and Bedford, Ind.; and the LaSalle Steel Company, Chicago, and Hammond, Ind. The firm has also kept pace with the growing demand for Chicago first mortgage real estate bonds and has recently underwritten bond issues for the Lexington Hotel and the Union Fuel Building, the latter a well-known loop office building.

The growth of the firm's business during the past few years has resulted in many additions to the personnel of the organization, and in order to facilitate transactions with its rapidly growing out-of-town clientele, branch offices are maintained in Kalamazoo, Mich., and Milwaukee. A department for women investors is also maintained at the Chicago office under the management of Mrs. Elizabeth H. Cobb.

COOPER-STITT & CO.

EARL K. STITT

THE Cooper-Stitt & Co., dealing in investment bonds, was founded in 1919 by Foster C. Scott and Earl K. Stitt. Since its organization, the volume of business has more than doubled. The Scott-Stitt Co. are large stockholders of the Stony Island Trust & Savings Bank, having acquired the Armour interests in that bank. The officers of the company are Foster C. Scott, president; Earl K. Stitt, vice-president; Herbert W. Cooper, vice-president; John H. Bierma, vice-president; C. J. Morgan, secretary and treasurer. Chicago offices are located at 111 W. Monroe st.,

HILL, JOINER & CO.

HILL, JOINER & CO., dealing in Investment Bonds, grew out of a business started under the name of McDonald, McCoy & Company in 1901. Later the name of the corporation of McDonald, McCoy & Company was changed to McCoy & Company, and in 1921, to Hill, Joiner & Co.

The corporation has a capitalization of $1,000,000.

W. W. Hill, President of the Company, was formerly with the Continental National Bank of Chicago. After several years with that bank, he joined the New York bond house of Messrs. Redmond, Kerr & Company, in charge of their western business.. Upon the dissolution of that firm, he went with one of their successors, Messr. Plympton, Gardiner & Co., first as Manager of their Chicago office, then as partner in their New York office. In 1914, he became affiliated with Messrs. McCoy & Company, and when the name of that corporation was changed to Hill, Joiner & Co., he became President.

Theodore E. Joiner, Vice-president, has spent practically all of his business life in the bond business in Chicago. Prior to joining Hill, Joiner & Co., he was with the firm of Messrs. Farson, Son & Company, and later, with the Continental & Commercial Trust and Savings Bank.

Henry H. Pahlman, Secretary and Treasurer, has been affiliated with the house for a number of years.

The directors are: Samuel Insull, Bernard E. Sunny, L. E. Myers, Theodore E. Joiner and W. W. Hill.

The general offices are at 105 South La Salle Street, Chicago, Ill.

STEVENSON BROS. & PERRY, INC.

ONE of the reasons for the success of the Stevenson Bros. & Perry, Inc., is the fact that its affairs are directed by men who have had thorough training in the rudiments of the brokerage business.

Robert Stevenson, Jr., its president, spent more than twelve years learning the fundamentals of the business before he branched out for himself. From 1906 to 1912, he was office manager for Lee Higginson Co. and for the next six years western manager for Kissel, Kinnicutt & Co. When war broke out, he was made deputy federal food administrator for Illinois, in recognition of his administrative ability. At this post he remained two years.

John A. Stevenson, vice president, was a member of the staff of White, Weld & Co. from 1908 to 1914 and associate western manager for Kissel, Kinnicutt & Co., 1914-18. He threw aside his business interests when war was declared, serving as captain in the American Expeditionary Forces for two years.

Before becoming vice president of the Stevenson Bros. & Perry, Inc., I. Newton Perry was affiliated with Lee Higginson & Co. and McCoy & Co. He served with the Red Cross in France.

Robert B. Whiting, secretary and treasurer, has also had years of brokerage training.

The company was incorporated in 1920, with a capitalization of $500,000. It confines its trade to railroad, municipal and corporation bonds. It has a direct private wire to Brown Brothers & Co. of New York, Boston and Philadelphia.

The directors are A. Watson Armour, W. V. Kelley, Robert P. Lamont, C. M. Leonard, John A. Spoor, Albert A. Sprague, Robert W. Stewart, George A. Ranney, Robert Stevenson, Jr., John A. Stevenson and J. Newton Perry. General offices are at 105 S. La Salle street.

123

WALTER E. SCHMIDT

WITH the administrative and banking ability of Walter E. Schmidt as one of its assets, the Illinois Improvement and Ballast Company has built up a million-dollar business and today it serves municipalities, real estate owners and builders throughout the middle west. It has plants in Chicago and Joliet. Since the company's incorporation in 1889, Mr. Schmidt has given lavishly of his time and energy to it, and the wisdom of his judgments is reflected in the rapid rise of the firm. Others who make up the governing body of the concern are E. G. Seip, president; L. E. McDermit, treasurer, and E. H. Kuttner, secretary. Mr. Schmidt, in addition to his post with the Illinois Improvement company, is president of the Roseland State Bank. He resides at 7315 South Shore Drive and his office is at 208 S. La Salle st.

R. LeRoy Huszagh   Rudolph D. Huszagh   J. H. Musson

HUSZAGH-MUSSON & CO.

THE firm of Huszagh-Musson & Co., bonds and mortgages, 69 W. Washington st., Chicago, has transacted a conservative business in first mortgage real estate securities for 37 years. It is composed of the following partners: Rudolph D. Huszagh, R. LeRoy Huszagh, and J. H. Musson.

The business was established in 1884 by Mr. Rudolph D. Huszagh, then an attorney specializing in real estate transactions. Later the real estate bond and mortgage business was developed. In addition to the active part taken by him in the bond and mortgage business of the firm, Mr. Huszagh gained a high reputation as an attorney, representing some of the largest corporations and individuals in Chicago. His knowledge of law and real estate, and his conscientious and conservative methods in doing business, give the firm the advantage of the best legal talent obtainable which is one of the most important factors in the operation of a conservative bond and mortgage business.

Mr. R. LeRoy Huszagh, son of Mr. Rudolph D. Huszagh, who has had fifteen years' experience in real estate, renting, building construction and the real estate loan business, is known as one of the best posted men in Chicago on ground values, renting·values and type of construction suited to location, especially in the Lake Shore District of the North Side, in which territory this firm specializes.

Mr. J. H. Musson, who joined the firm in 1921, was formerly an official of the Central Trust Company of Illinois, with which he had been associated for twenty years. Mr. Musson, who has had a wide experience as an investment banker, is well known in Chicago as a conservative man of high business principles.

The firm transacts its banking business with Foreman Brothers Banking Company, Central Trust Company of Illinois, Sheridan Trust and Savings Bank, and Mechanics and Traders State Bank, Chicago. The two banks first mentioned represent an association of thirty years and twenty years respectively.

The personnel of Huszagh, Musson & Co., and their long record of conservatism, have established them as one of the highest-grade bond and mortgage houses in Chicago.

WILLIAM L. ROHRER

WILLIAM L. ROHRER was for many years actively engaged in investment banking and is now largely interested in western banks, railroads, copper mines, and lumber interests. He was born in Illinois and is a descendant of Sir John Rogers, of Mayflower fame. He received his education in the schools of Illinois. He is a staunch Republican and has been for many years active in national politics. He was formerly secretary of the National Republican League. Mr. Rohrer has resided in Chicago for about twenty-five years. He has traveled extensively, visiting nearly all parts of the world. In December of 1921, he was married to Mrs. Josephine Hamon in Chicago. National recognition has been given to Mr. Rohrer's valuable work in securing more cordial relations between Spanish-American countries and the United States.

H. D. FELLOWS COMPANY

H. D. FELLOWS Company, by committing itself to a policy of distributing only bonds of a thoroughly conservative type, has forged its way to the top of the municipal bond business in the middle west and daily is adding to its clientele.

Issues sponsored by the Fellows Company are carefully guarded and safety of principal and interest is its first consideration. The company takes pride in maintaining its trusts inviolate. Its motto is "The Bonds We Sell Are the Ones We Ourselves Have Bought."

Fellows Company customers get the benefit of a service of specialists. Officers of this company have had ten or more years of specialized training in the departments for which they are responsible.

The company is capitalized at $100,000. Officers are H. D. Fellows, president; T. M. Kerkhoff, vice president, and F. A. Grosser, secretary and treasurer, L. J. Montgomery, L. E. Hicks, H. D. Fellows, T. M. Kerkhoff and F. A. Grosser comprise the directorate.

General offices are located at 29 South La Salle street.

STACY AND BRAUN

THE firm of Stacy and Braun, dealing in investment bonds, was founded on March 1, 1910, the original partners being Charles L. Stacy and Walter M. Braun.

The first two years of the firm's history was attended by a rapid growth in business and they began looking about with a view to widening their territory and opening new offices. In 1912, the Cincinnati office was opened. This was followed by the establishment of a New York office in 1915. Chicago and Detroit offices were opened in 1921 and in the early part of 1922 steps were taken for the establishment of offices in Boston and St. Louis.

As business grew, the partnership was extended. Robert Hixon was admitted as partner May 1, 1915; Warren J. Hoysradt, January 1, 1920; Erwin P. Bosworth, January 1, 1922. Mr. Braun and Mr. Hixon are located in Toledo, Mr. Hoysradt in New York, Mr. Bosworth in Cincinnati, and Mr. Stacy in Chicago.

The firm confines its dealings almost exclusively to municipal bonds. The Chicago offices are located at 108 S. La Salle st.

UNION SECURITY CO.

THE Union Security Company, organized in 1900, has had a part in the financing of many of the leading industrial firms of the middle west.

One of its most successful enterprises was consummated in 1922 in the financing of J. L. Kraft & Brothers Co., manufacturers of Elkhorn cheese in tins. From an humble start, this concern has grown to be the largest food manufacturing company of its kind in the world.

Underwriting and selling on a commission basis issues of preferred and common stock of industrial companies is the specialty of the Union Security Company. It also finances going concerns that require additional capital for expansion.

The Union Security Company was incorporated with a capital of $100,000. Its affairs today are in the hands of the same men who organized it. They are F. A. Meidinger, president; O. A. Benson, vice president; J. D. Meidinger, secretary. General offices are at 29 S. La Salle st.

CHARLES SINCERE

CHARLES SINCERE, broker in grain, stocks and bonds, was born in Chicago, July 3, 1874; s. of Rose (Friedman) and Henry Sincere. His education was received in public schools of Chicago. He married Mayme Wershinski, in Mendota, Ill., Oct. 11, 1900. Children: Charles, Jr., Roslyn Rae. Mr. Sincere started work at the age of 14. He spent five years in employ of Corn Exchange National Bank. In 1906, he launched the Charles Sincere and Company, Brokers, which has grown into one of the largest and most reliable brokerage firms in the country. Mr. Sincere served 7 years in the 1st Regt., Ill. National Guard, and is still a member of Vol. Co., 1st Regt. Mem. of B'Nai B'rith; Mason; Elks. Clubs: Ill. Athletic, Northmoor Golf. Home: Glencoe, Ill. Office: 141 W. Jackson blvd.

L. L. WINKELMAN & CO.

THE L. L. Winkelman & Co., by years of conscientious trading, has attained an enviable position among American brokerage firms. Founded in New York a number of years ago, its organization has rapidly expanded and today it has branches in many cities. It does a general business in stocks and bonds, specializing in Standard Oil securities and also those of independent companies. L. L. Winkelman and A. K. Nicholson are the heads of the company. The main offices are at 62 Broad street, New York City. Harold F. Ruster is manager of the Chicago offices, 309 S. La Salle street. The company's branches are located in Philadelphia, Cleveland, Pittsburgh, Baltimore, Akron, Zanesville, Findlay, Marietta, Parkersburg, W. Va., and Uniontown, Pa.

MANUFACTURERS & DEALERS' FINANCE CORP.

THE organization of the Manufacturers' & Dealers' Finance Corporation in 1921 marks the third period in the evolution of American financing. The first brought the national and state banks; the second, trust companies and the third, the so-called "discount" and commercial and finance companies. To meet the demand for the new form of financing, large corporations are being organized throughout the country.

The interests behind the Manufacturers' & Dealers' Finance Corporation are steadily establishing affiliations with other commercial finance houses in various parts of the country. It is their aim to establish a chain of similar companies for financing manufacturers and merchants on a national scale.

The company deals principally in notes given in payment for business and household necessities sold on the time-payment plan. The notes usually extend over a period of a year, with monthly payments, so that the average maturity is about six months. Back of the notes usually are a chattel mortgage on the property, the dealer's endorsement and a repurchase agreement with the manufacturer, in case of default of payment of any of the notes.

Chauncey B. Blair, son of the late Chauncey J. Blair, vice president of the Corn Exchange National Bank, was one of the leading factors in the organization of the corporation. He is now its president. Associated with him are George B. Caldwell, Charles H. Burras, Charles R. Vincent, James C. Johnson, Sidney W. Worthy, William Mitchell Blair and Leonard L. Marshall.

The capital of the company is $1,000,000 8% cumulative preferred stock and 20,000 shares of common stock having no par value. General offices are 716 Wrigley building.

GEORGE H. TAYLOR, JR. & CO.

GEORGE H. TAYLOR, JR., & CO. has been engaged in the bond business since 1918. Each year has seen its clientele grow and today its business activities extend throughout the middle west.

The company was organized by Mr. Taylor, September 1, 1918. To this organization he brought the fruits of twenty years' training in leading investment bond houses of the country and, under his administration, the company has firmly established itself in the business sphere of Chicago.

Officers are George H. Taylor, Jr., president, and O. Le Neve Foster, secretary and treasurer. George H. Taylor, Jr., O. Le Neve Foster and Frank A. Ford are the directors.

The general offices are located at 111 W. Monroe street, Chicago.

G. F. REDMOND & CO. INC.

EVERYTHING which tends to place service on a more efficient plane and which provides a staff or guide for the investor in the maze of finances has been provided by the brokerage firm of G. F. Redmond & Co, Inc, for its clientele. One of the conveniences is the maintenance of a private wire service. Another is "Redmond's Financial Weekly." This is not merely a house organ. Its primary aim is to give the investor or trader a clearer perspective of the financial world and to acquaint him with the latest shiftings of the market. The paper reports the movement of all stock and bonds and not only those handled by the Redmond company. The Chicago office of the Redmond firm is located at 166 W. Jackson boulevard. Other offices are maintained at New York, Boston, Cleveland, Detroit and Baltimore.

129

LINGARD TINDALE ROUNTREE

LINGARD TINDALE ROUN-TREE, president and general manager of the Randolph Box and Label Company, was born in Las Vegas, N. M., May 15, 1882; son of Anna (Tindale) and Greenville Rountree. At an early age, he removed to Nashville, Ill., where he received a public school and high school education. In 1900, he came to Chicago and from 1903 to 1914 he served as treasurer and superintendent of the H. S. McCracken Box and Label Co. In 1914, he reorganized the Randolph Box and Label Co. Mr. Rountree was married to Margaret Florence Harrison, June 26, 1907, in Chicago. Daughter, Constance. He is a member of the A. F. & A. M., Kenwood Lodge. Clubs: Illinois Athletic, Old Town, South Side Tennis. Home: 6842 Chappell av. Offices: 843 W. Van Buren st.

ARCHIE ROY WEBB

ARCHIE ROY WEBB has been engaged in the Security Business in Chicago for more than fifteen years. Mr. Webb was born in Whitehall, Wis., May 2, 1881; the son of Ella (Lake) and William John Webb. He was educated in the public schools of Whitehall and in Brown University, where he received the degree of Bachelor of Science. Mr. Webb was married to Nina Spencer Brown Aug. 16, 1919, in Chicago. Son, William John. Offices are at 76 W. Monroe st. Mr. Webb resides in Evanston.

130

BAKER, FENTRESS & COMPANY

BAKER, FENTRESS & COMPANY, successors to Lyon, Gary & Company, organized in 1891 to finance going concerns in the timber and lumber industries, have gained an unchallenged position among Chicago financial institutions. Their successful operations in the north, south and west have attained a total of over $35,000,000 loaned without the loss of a cent of interest or principal. The principle on which the business of this house rests is that lumbermen who own their timber resources ought to finance their operations by long-time amortizable funded loans, rather than by hand-to-mouth borrowing on general credit. The application of this principle enables lumbermen to cover their capital requirements for the entire period required to realize the commercial value of forest areas.

Lucius K. Baker, president; Calvin Fentress, treasurer; Frederic T. Boles, vice-president; and Fred E. Gary, director, are men of large experience as lumbermen. The other officers, W. W. Gurley, Clark M. Cavenee and Walter A. Graff, vice-presidents; and A. Merrill Coit, secretary, are highly rated in "the Street" as legal and financial consultants of the first order. The personnel of the company thus comprises talents and experience ample to reach the correct solution of any problem of forest financing.

TOBEY & KIRK

THE brokerage house of Tobey & Kirk was founded by Salathiel H. Tobey and Edward C. Kirk in 1873. The business has been conducted during all this time, under the same name.

The firm has memberships in the New York Stock Exchange, the Chicago Stock Exchange, and the Chicago Board of Trade. Its main offices are 25 Broad st., New York City, and it has branch offices at 208 S. La Salle st., Chicago, and Liberty Bldg., New Haven, Conn. It has direct private wires from its New York office to its branches and also to correspondents in various cities, including Cleveland, Detroit, Grand Rapids, and Pittsburgh.

The firm originally specialized in unlisted stocks and bonds, but in the last seven or eight years the business has been enlarged. It now comprises general brokerage activities in stocks, bonds, grain, provisions, and the handling of old underlying railroad and industrial bonds. Also, at times the firm participates in some of the leading bond underwritings. The firm today is composed of Harold Tobey, Allen Tobey, Clarence J. Blaker, John J. Moylen, and W. Kempton Johnson.

W. G. SOUDERS & CO.

W. G. SOUDERS & COMPANY, dealing in investment securities, public utilities, industrials, municipal and corporation bonds, are located at 208 S. La Salle street, Chicago. The company has branches in New York, Detroit, Milwaukee and Grand Rapids.

Its officers are W. G. Souders, president; John J. Murphy, treasurer, and Charles O. Reynolds, secretary. Directors are W. G. Souders, Charles O. Reynolds, John J. Murphy, all of Chicago; and John I. Beggs, of Milwaukee, Wis.

DR. LEWIS WINE BREMERMAN

LEWIS W. BREMERMAN, surgeon, was born in Washington, D. C., Aug. 12, 1877; s. Laban Trout and Helen Kate (Rhinehart) Bremerman; ed. in pub. schs., Washington; A.B., Central High Sch., Phila. 1897, A.M., 1905; M.D., Jefferson Med. Coll., Phila., 1900. Married Helen Tope of Oak Park, Ill., Sept. 26, 1905 (died Sept. 13, 1906), married 2d 1912, Mrs. Margaret E. Alexander, nee Thomas. Interne Pa. Hosp. For Injured Persons, Fountain Springs, Pa., 1900; W. W. Backus Hosp. Norwich, Conn., 1901; practiced surgery in New York, 1902-7, in Chicago, since 1907; specialist in diseases of the kidney and bladder. Asso. prof. Urology, 1904-5; prof. 1905-7, New York Sch. of Clin. Medicine; prof. Urology, Bennett and Practitioners' Med. Colls., Chicago, 1910; prof. Genito-Urinary Surgery, Univ. of Iowa, 1914-15; late surgeon to Oak Park Hosp.; late consulting Urologist, I. C. R. R.; Director of Bremerman Urological Hosp.; late Lieut- Col., U. S. A. for two years. Mem. Chicago Med. Soc., Mississippi Valley Med. Assn., pres. Ohio Valley Med. Assn., Chicago Urological Soc., Am. Urological Assn. Clubs: Illinois Athletic, Olympia Fields Country. Written over 150 articles for medical journals and have a text book on surgical subjects in preparation. Office: 1919 Prairie av. Home: Metropole Hotel, Chicago.

FRANKLIN LIFE INSURANCE COMPANY

THE FRANKLIN LIFE INSURANCE COMPANY, with home offices in Springfield, Ill., has established a record for the achievement of insurance ideals. Its aim of rendering life insurance safe in order that the protection of the beneficiary might be absolute has attracted to the Franklin company the best of executive insurance talent. As a result, the company has experienced the steadiest and most substantial growth known to the insurance world.

Aggressiveness each year has brought to the company an increase in its assets, its legal reserve and outstanding business. Insurance in force up to Jan. 1, 1922 totalled $130,000,000; legal reserve, $11,689,468; and assets, $13,263,-529.36. Conservatism in its management has reserved for this company the boast that it has never lost a dollar of investment funds or interest or closed a year with a dollar of either in default.

George B. Stadden is president. Other officers are: Henry Abels, vice president; H. M. Merriam, vice president; Will Taylor, secretary; Herman Abels, assistant secretary; Edgar S. Barnes, treasurer; I. L. McKinnie, assistant treasurer; James Abels, assistant treasurer; F. R. Jordan, actuary; J. A. Budinger, assistant actuary; Dr. O. F. Maxon, medical director; Joseph W. Jones, agency director; and C. B. McCreary, conservation director.

H. W. JOHNSON

ONE of the reasons why the Central Life Insurance Company of Illinois has grown into a corporation with $40,000,000 business in force in a little over a decade is H. W. Johnson. He has been its president since its organization. Its investment records for ten years show no losses and it has paid a liberal dividend each year since its formation. How this was accomplished is told on the next page.

134

CENTRAL LIFE INSURANCE COMPANY OF ILLINOIS

THERE is the romance of business in the figures of the Central Life Insurance Company of Illinois, Ottawa, Ill. Organized but fifteen years ago, its business totals $40,000,000 and the company holds assets of between four and five million dollars. Its operations reach into nine states.

Unbroken continuity of management, supported by efficiency and energy, has contributed much to the success, which, in many ways, is unparalleled in business annals. The organization of the Central Life Insurance Company of Illinois was effected by the same officers who now control its destinies.

The company was organized in 1907. Its first $100,000 of capital stock was sold at par and not one cent of the cost of organizing was levied against the stockholders. Twenty-two months were consumed in organization, during which period it sold twenty-year term insurance at old-line rates under an assessment charter. This business was rewritten to standard forms on the old-line basis and profits of $14,500 were turned over to the new organization, thus obviating the necessity of organization expense.

The consulting actuary at the time of the organization was Major Brinkerhoff, for many years connected with the Illinois Insurance Department. He was succeeded by George Graham, president of the American Institute of Actuaries. The policy of the company has not been to show a large volume of business in force, at the risk of future stability and permanency of the organization.

For this reason, the company made no headlong rush for business, but confined its earlier efforts to carefully covering the rural districts. Today, it is entering by a careful way some of the larger centers of population, where it is prepared to meet all competition on the strength of its record.

The management is composed of H. W. Johnson, president; W. F. Weese, vice president and agency director; Charles Nadler, vice president; S. B. Bradford, secretary and treasurer; W. H. Hinebaugh, general counsel and T. W. Burrows, medical director. They have brought to the company a wide business experience, although they were not men trained especially along technical insurance lines, but possessed of the qualities which enabled them to grasp high ethical standards of business.

It has been their plan to invest the company's reserves in states and communities where the business has been originated. At present, 75 per cent of the firm's assets are invested in first farm mortgages and its investment record for a decade shows not a dollar of loss of principal or interest.

The company has paid a liberal stock dividend each year since organization and has maintained a very satisfactory dividend scale to policy-holders. Since 1917, it has paid a first-year dividend, contingent on the payment of the succeeding premium. It also writes non-participating insurance at a low rate.

The company is now admitted and is operating in Illinois, Michigan, Minnesota, South Dakota, Iowa, Nebraska, Missouri, Kansas and Texas. It is expected that the headquarters of this company will be removed to Chicago within the next year.

135

ALFRED CLOVER

A LFRED CLOVER, founder, chairman of the board of directors and general manager of the Public Life Insurance Company of Illinois. General offices 1400 Washington Boulevard, Chicago.

FRED. S. JAMES & CO.

FIFTY-EIGHT years ago, seven years prior to the Chicago fire, Fred S. James, a youth of fifteen, began as an office boy in the insurance agency of his brother. A half century ago and immediately following the great fire Fred S. James opened a-below-the-sidewalk office at 152 La Salle St. Thus was created the firm, Fred S. James & Co., which has continuously for fifty years, borne that name.

In 1874, because of the rapid growth of business, new offices became a necessity, and new quarters were secured in the Old Bryan Block. Later the second and third floors of the New York Life Bldg. were taken over. In 1912 the offices were moved to the new Insurance Exchange Building, where now the entire twelfth floor is occupied.

Because of the expansion of business and to improve service to clients in the east, a New York City office was opened in 1904 at 23 Liberty St. At present, the New York office occupies over 22,000 square feet at 123 William st. A Pacific Coast office was established in 1918 at 362 Pine st., San Francisco.

When the agency was started and up to 1902 only fire insurance was written. In 1902, the first step was made toward the handling of other lines of insurance, and today all lines except life are written.

From the beginning, the various departments have been created and maintained, so as to give maximum service to clients. The underwriting department protects the interests of the assured and safeguards the companies. The loss department aids greatly in the establishing better understandings between the assured and the insurance companies.

So with the Marine, Lloyds, Automobile, Casualty, Bonding and other departments.

Always a pioneer and readily recognizing progressive ideas, Fred S. James & Co. established in 1900, one of the first engineering and inspection departments in the insurance field. Through this department, the underwriting department and the companies are furnished with complete and accurate knowledge of the risks involved, and at the same time clients are given information pertaining to rate reductions and to fire protection and fire prevention devices.

From the time of the founding of the Fred S. James & Co. agency, its members have been recognized as capable and efficient company managers. As early as 1873, Fred S. James was appointed general agent of the Boston Underwriters. He later became Western General Agent of the Washington Fire and Marine Insurance Company and George W. Blossom was appointed assistant general agent.

When the General Fire Assurance Co. of Paris commenced writing insurance in the United States in 1909, Fred. S. James & Co. was appointed their U. S. managers. In 1912, the firm became U. S. manager for the Urbaine Fire Insurance Co. of Paris. Again in 1916, Fred. S. James & Co., was appointed U. S. manager of the Eagle Star and British Dominions of London.

These three companies show an excellent growth and financial condition while under the management of Fred S. James & Co., which substantiates the confidence of the home offices when the appointments were made.

A healthy and rapid growth has been enjoyed by the firm, and its members have created and developed a national institution with an international reputation.

OLD COLONY LIFE INSURANCE COMPANY

JACKSON BLVD. QUINCY AND WELLS STS.

THE skyscraper home of the Old Colony Life Insurance Company, covering the block at Jackson boulevard, Quincy and Wells streets, will always
stand as a monument to the ability of the company's officers. These
officers, B. R. Nueske, president; Joseph McGauley, vice president and treasurer,
and R. C. Van Dyke, vice president and secretary, have built up in the Old
Colony company one of the largest insurance firms centering in Chicago. This
they accomplished by gathering for their associates leading insurance men of the
middle west and by giving the pubilc a line of insurance fitted to its needs and at a
low price. The company today has $25,000,000 of life insurance in force and is
insuring also children from the age of two up under annual premium policies, so
that it is in a position to insure "the entire family" on the non-industrial plan.
The company commenced business in 1907.

PEORIA LIFE INSURANCE COMPANY

THE Peoria Life Insurance Company is recognized as one of the leading institutions of its kind in the country. Organized in 1908, its growth has been so rapid that it has far outdistanced many similar organizations of much longer standing. It has recently completed the fourteenth year of its existence with the remarkable total of $70,000,000 of business in force.

The company was organized as an old line legal reserve company and has always pursued the policy of conducting its business along well-established and conservative lines. It has never attempted any of the fancy or startling features of life insurance. On the other hand, it has constantly kept abreast of the most up-to-date and approved methods known to the insurance world.

Its business has been built on the watchword of Service. It is known in

MR. EMMET MAY
President Peoria Life Insurance Company

insurance circles as "the Company with a Big Happy Family of Satisfied Policyholders." It enjoys the reputation of offering the most liberal policies and policy features, consistent with sound substantial insurance practice.

The motto of service is illustrated in the fact that every death claim is allowed and a check is on its way to the beneficiary within 30 minutes after proofs are received at the home office. This feature is also shown in the fact that it paid its war claims in full and refunded to its policyholders all extra premiums paid on account of military service. It is well known by its slogan, "Policies as Strong as Farm Mortgages Can Make Them," because its funds are invested in first mortgages on carefully selected farm property, in no case for more than 50 per cent of its value, thus furnishing its policy-

holders with the safest and most profitable security obtainable.

The sole exception to this rule is the Company's Home Office building. This magnificent 17-story structure, one of the most complete and elegantly appointed office buildings in the country, is the sole property of the Company. It was erected entirely out of current receipts, without lien or encumbrance of any kind, and without disturbing the company's farm loan investments. It represents a very profitable and satisfactory investment of the Company's funds.

The record of success of the Peoria Life must be attributed in a large degree to the wise and careful management of its officers, and the conscientious and active character of its agents in the field. Emmet C. May, president, has been connected with the company since its beginning and has served as president since 1913. He is a well known and popular figure in life insurance circles. Henry Loucks, vice-president and superintendent of agents, George B. Pattison, secretary and actuary, and George Parker, medical director, have likewise been associated with the company since it was first organized. All are prominent in the various leading insurance organizations.

The excellent policies, far-sighted methods, and dependable management of the company guarantee a continuance of its remarkable progress as one of the rising and popular insurance companies of the Middle West.

HOME OFFICES IN PEORIA

ILLINOIS FIRE INSURANCE CO.

IN 1876 the Illinois Fire Insurance Company of Peoria was founded by a number of prominent citizens under the leadership of the late Bernard Cremer and received its charter from the State under the name and title "German Fire Insurance Company of Peoria."

In 1918 its charter was amended and the company's name was changed to the "Illinois Fire Insurance Company of Peoria."

After the great Chicago fire in 1871, there was a scarcity of fire insurance companies all over the United States. Business men were looking around for more protection against loss by fire.

In the spring of 1876 a number of Peoria business men, after several preliminary meetings, decided to start a Peoria fire insurance company and adopted the name "German Fire Insurance Company of Peoria". The first officers were: president, Louis Green, vice president, Bernard Cremer, secretary, Fred H. Wagner, treasurer, Michael Pfeifer. The directors were Louis Green, Samuel Woolner, Gustav Harsch, William Oberhauser, Erhard Kramm, Bernard Cremer, Michael Pfeifer, Valentine Ulrich and M. F. Meints.

The first secretary, F. H. Wagner, was an experienced insurance man, having served as assistant secretary of the old German Fire Insurance Company of Freeport, Ill., for a number of years. In 1886 Mr. Wagner resigned and moved to Minneapolis, where he had bought an interest in one of the largest agencies of that city.

The first president of the company, Louis Green, who was one of the leading wholesale grocers of the city, died in 1882 and was succeeded in office by Bernard Cremer, who also was the largest stockholder at that time. Cremer served the company until his death Sept. 9, 1918.

The immediate successor to Mr. Wagner in the secretaryship was F. D. Weienett, who served only a very short time. He was killed in a wreck near Chatsworth, Ill., Aug. 10, 1887. The then assistant secretary, Theodore J. Muller, was chosen secretary and remained in office until 1893, when he ventured into local agency business. The late Charles Cremer, brother of the president of the company, was elected secretary of the company to succeed Mr. Muller.

Under the management of Secretary Cremer, the company expanded its business into new territory until it was represented from the Atlantic to the Pacific. The expansion of business also brought an increase in losses, which were promptly met.

The company has paid nearly $7,000,000 for fire losses. Of this amount $102,000 was sustained in the great Baltimore fire in 1904 and $470,000 represented the company's loss at San Francisco in 1906. The company's office was destroyed by fire in 1915, which burned the records of the company. This proved a great handicap to the business and was one of the main reasons for the company curtailing the business by leaving a number of States where they were doing business up to the time of the fire and confining their territory to the middle Western States. The company's funds are largely invested in gilt-edge bank securities of Peoria, Chicago and New York City.

The present business territory comprises Illinois, Wisconsin, Indiana and Pennsylvania and care is exercised to so place policies as to reduce to a minimum possibility of serious losses recurring in instances of large, general conflagrations.

The president of the company, Mathias S. Cremer, has been a member of the company for twenty-three years. He became president following the death of his brother, Bernard Cremer, who was the company's head for over thirty years.

The secretary, Henry F. Tuerk, has "grown up" in the fire insurance business. The vice president of the company, Robert Zimmermann, is a prominent local merchant, who has been a stockholder and director of the company for a number of years. The treasurer, Adolph Cremer, is a brother of the president.

The company has had an honorable career, never failing to do its duty and fulfilling its obligations toward its patrons. Although it does not claim to be one of the largest companies, it does claim to be one of the best and safest fire insurance companies in the middle West.

T. F. BARRY

BACKED by a rich fund of experiences both here and abroad and invested with many original and practical ideas, T. F. Barry has maintained a high record of achievements as secretary and manager of the Globe Mutual Life Insurance Company of Chicago. The record, translated in practical terms, is a 270 per cent gain in income in the last five years; a 350 per cent gain in assets and a 240 per cent ga.n in insurance in force. Mr. Barry was the organizer and has directed its operations from its organization in 1895. Its business has been built almost without capital and with intense competition. The policies are made attractive and a liberal interpretation is given the total and permanent disability clause. Mr. Barry was born in Ireland and his schooling took him through all the higher courses. Since becoming an American citizen, he has received a degree of L. L. B. and has been untiring in improving his education. His first insurance was with the Prudential, of London. In 1882, he was engaged by Metropolitan Life of New York and served with them for a number of years, at the end of which time he began organizing his own company. Mr. Barry's office is at 431 S. Dearborn street.

ILLINOIS MUTUAL CASUALTY COMPANY

THE Illinois Mutual Casualty Company was organized by O. L. McCord in Danville, Ill., in 1912. Before its organization, Mr. McCord was county treasurer of Vermilion county. The great growth that attended the company's inception resulted in the moving of the main offices from Danville to Peoria in 1914. Here, also, the company's prosperity continued unchecked and today it is rated as one of the firmest insurance companies in the middle west. It deals exclusively in health and accident policies. It has branch offices all over Illinois and Indiana and its surplus is more than $50,000. Mr. McCord, the founder, is now secretary-treasurer and general manager. The other officers are Frank L. Davis, Danville, Ill., president, and E. C. Ferguson, E. St. Louis, Ill., vice-president.

MARSH & McLENNAN

METHODS perfected by Marsh & McLennan for the solution of insurance problems of all kinds have made the name of this organization synonymous with satisfaction to thousands of clients wherever insurance is known and its importance appreciated by business leaders and property owners.

The success of this firm has been based on the thorough and comprehensive nature of its service. Excepting life insurance, there is scarcely a line of business, or a form of hazard that can be insured against, but what is served or protected by some department of this far-reaching organization. Service is based not on a theory of insurance but on the actual needs of the firm's clientele as revealed through years of constant contact and exhaustive investigation of the wide variety of needs that must be served. This is why Marsh & McLennan numbers among its clients many of the greatest commercial and industrial institutions of the Nation.

Industrial leaders who have large responsibilities will save time and money and get the maximum of protection by entrusting their insurance problems to this firm. Through its offices in seventeen of the great cities of the country, as well as its foreign branches, the firm is in an especially advantageous position to handle the huge risks involved in the operation of great enterprises. Connections established with the greatest insurance companies in the world, experience in determining the type and amount of protection needed for all classes of risks, and the proper premium to be charged, advice to clients for the removal or safeguarding of hazards, and for determining and protecting their legal rights and interests, facilities for handling settlements and adjustments, and an organization trained in the handling of every detail of the transaction from the inspection and appraisal of the property to the writing of the insurance through its many connections, and the settlement and collection of losses—these are the factors that enter into the firm's service and enable it to handle risks of any size or kind.

Business leaders and property owners owe it to themselves to use the comprehensive service this organization offers. No policy is too large or none too small to receive the thorough attention for which the name of the firm has become synonymous. Protection of property and assets by insuring against fire and marine loss, employers' liability and the many other forms of protection now offered to the public, is a duty that everyone owes to himself and his community. The past record and experience of the firm has been made a basis on which still more comprehensive service will be rendered in years to come.

The main office is at 175 W. Jackson blvd., Chicago. Branch offices are located at New York, Buffalo, Pittsburgh, Cleveland, San Francisco, Portland, Denver, Winnipeg, Columbus, Detroit, Duluth, Minneapolis, Seattle, Phoenix, Montreal and London, Eng.

N. L. PIOTROWSKI

N. L. PIOTROWSKI, attorney and president Great Lakes Insurance Co., was born in Poland, Sept. 15, 1861; s. of Simon and Johanna (Kopiewska) Piotrowski; studied in Berlin, Germany; came to America in 1882. Student, Notre Dame, Ind., and Valparaiso (Ind.) Univ. (1888). Married Theresa R. Maag, of Richmond, Ind., Sept. 27, 1893. Daughter, Angela. Prof. of Physics and Chemistry, St. Thomas Seminary, St. Paul, Minn., 1889-91; practiced law in Chicago since 1892; assistant Corporation Counsel, 1897-1902; candidate for State Treasurer, Democratic ticket, 1906; city atty. of Chicago, 1911-15; special war correspondent for the Chicago Herald and other papers, 1915-16, during which time he visited Poland, London, Paris, Rome, Petrograd, Vienna and the Balkan States; pres. Great Lakes Insurance Co. since 1917; pres. Polish Catholic Union of America since 1918. Mem. K. of C. Club: Union League. Office: 175 W. Jackson blvd.

LEWIS F. TUELLS

LEWIS F. TUELLS, vice president of the Liberty Mutual Insurance company, was born in Boston, May 19, 1884; the son of Eva (Rand) and Francis Tuells. He was educated in Boston schools. Feb. 21, 1907, he married Mabel Frances Dodge, of Boston. Children: Ruth Frances, Phoebe Dodge, Helen Rand. Mr. Tuells learned the rudiments of the insurance business in Boston and in 1919 came to Chicago to become vice president for the Liberty Mutual Insurance company.

DR. JOSEPH CLAR BECK

DR. J. C. BECK, physician and surgeon, was born in Bohemia, Sept. 26, 1870; s. of Elizabeth (Pollock) and Ignatz Beck; ed. in schs. of Prague and Catholic convent sch. in Holden, Mo.; Coll. of Phys. and Surg. (U. of I.) 1895. Married Carrie Stein. Children: Elsa, Philip and Joseph C., Jr. Began practicing in Chicago in 1895, limited practice to eye, ear, nose and throat. Prof. Otology and Laryngology, Chicago Eye, Ear, Nose and Throat Hosp. until 1915. Associate Prof. Otology and Rhino-Laryngology, Coll. of Phys. and Surg.; partner in North Chicago Hosp.; former surgeon at Cook Co. Hosp. and University Hosp. Mem. Am. Acad. Opthal. and Oto-Laryng., Am. Laryng. Rhinol and Otol. Soc., A. M. A., Ill. State Med. Soc., Chicago Roentgen Soc., Chicago Opthol. Soc., Chicago Pathol. Soc., German Med. Soc., Am. Med. Editors' Assn. Fellow, Coll. of Surg., Am. Oto. Soc. Republican. Mem. of Masons.

Clubs: Chicago Press, Buena Shore. Home: Webster Hotel. Office: 2551 N. Clark st. and 108 N. State st.

DR. BENJAMIN GRUSKIN

DR. BENJAMIN GRUSKIN, diag-nosis chemist, pathologist and bacteriologist and originator of the blood test for cancer, was born in Russia in 1878. He received his early education in European schools and then removed, with his parents, to America, settling in Pittsburgh. He studied medicine at University of Pittsburgh and medical dept. of University of Valparaiso. In 1910, he came to Chicago. Dr. Gruskin held the chair of serology at Loyola University for several years. In 1908, he married Mary Rosindale, of Pittsburgh. Children: George Leo and Edward. Dr. Gruskin is a director of laboratories for Mt. Sinai Hospital and a member of the American Medical Association and the Chicago Pathological Society, Chicago Chemical and Medicine Society of Am. His blood test for cancer has won wide recognition because of its efficacy. Dr. Gruskin's clubs are the North Shore Country Club and the Press Club. Home: 4300 Clarendon avenue. Office: 25 E. Washington street.

CHARLES PIEZ

AFTER Mr. Piez graduated at the School of Mines, Columbia University, he entered the employ of the Link-Belt Engineering Company, in Philadelphia. Seventeen years later (in 1906) after attaining the position of chief engineer and general manager of the Philadelphia works, he was elected president of the Link-Belt Company, a consolidation of three related companies, the Link-Belt Machinery Company (Chicago), the Ewart Manufacturing Company (Indianapolis), and the Link-Belt Engineering Company (Philadelphia).

Largely as a result of his fame as an organizer and manager of industry, Mr. Piez was selected Vice-President and General Manager of the United States Shipping Board Emergency Fleet Corporation.

As General Manager, and later as Director General, Mr. Piez advised upon and directed the expenditure of three billion dollars. He had control over 600,000 persons employed in the shipyards and fabricating plants, and in industries furnishing supplies to the Yards.

He has been instrumental in framing much of the labor legislation of the state of Illinois, having been a member of the Commission that drew the State Factory Act; was Chairman of the Workmen's Compensation Commission; and a member of the State Arbitration Board.

COMMERCE AND INDUSTRY IN CHICAGO

CHICAGO is already an accomplishment so extraordinary that its story and message can be adequately delivered without an excess of phraseology.

By the forty per cent of railway mileage of the United States concentrated here are served 40,000,000 people. The wholesale trade of this distributing center was estimated at $6,000,000,000 in 1921 and here is conspicuously the world's greatest market for livestock, grain and lumber, and here is held a commanding position in the distribution of general merchandise. As producer and distributor putting forth from its manufacturing zone annually, from more than 20,000 factories, goods valued at $6,500,000,000, it has the indispensable co-operation of banks with joint resources of nearly $3,500,000,000. This volume of products of the metropolitan industrial district, Chicago, has grown from that of the city of 1870, one year before the great fire, when the estimated output was worth $92,518,742. Here center the raw products of the Mississippi Valley—iron, copper, lead, zinc, petroleum, lumber, wool, hides, grain—and here the nation's constructive thought expresses itself in the 700 conventions a year that are held in Chicago.

Daily there move 2,500 through package cars to 1,800 points, with one transfer of service to more than 60,000 others. Here is developed manufacturing power unlimited—electricity and coal gas—and here a score of nationalities offer the labor of hand and brain.

Conditions of Chicago's growth heretofore promise indefinite expansion. This can be affected favorably or otherwise by its larger economic policies, and transportation is of course qualifying all. At this railroad center is laid in the case of many great lines the first or last rails of their system. Without these gigantic instruments of progress an empire of the West would not have been and Chicago would have continued a portage.

This great market and workshop finds constant stimulus in the rivalry of other advancing centers of population, trade and industry, not to speak of operation of forces expressed in problems resulting from the war. The business success of the Pageant of Progress of 1920 and 1921, considered with the distant background of the trade and sample fairs of Europe, counsels Chicago to make an organized effort to create periodic international fairs. Place and time are opportune.

A commercial museum, containing a permanent exhibit of goods, which find favor in Europe and which Chicago can supply, is another institution advocated by students of Chicago's foreign trade.

The statistical methods of the government permit the disclosure of only a meager portion of the export trade of Chicago, because exported goods are credited not to the place of origin but to the port of exit. Inquiries by the Chicago Association of Commerce lead to the conclusion that this city's foreign trade in 1920 may have been as great as $1,750,000,000, or possibly $2,000,000,000. In that year the enormous foreign trade of the United States amounted to $13,358,963,000, of which perhaps the very considerable portion of twenty per cent is to be credited to the Chicago district. One Chicago industry alone in 1920, that is the packing industry, exported not less than $1,160,000,000 worth of products and in the same year Chicago's grain exports reached the total of 285,000,000 bushels.

A new facility which may in time distinguish the Great Central Market as a point of export is a free port, such as is now in operation at Hamburg and Danzig. It is reasonably contended that such an institution would greatly stimulate Chicago's foreign trade and would be easy of establishment by virtue of the practical creation of Chicago as a seaport by the development of the Great Lakes-St. Lawrence waterway project. When Chicago is once connected with the Atlantic and the Gulf by deep sea ship services, additional steamship companies will establish offices here and it will be possible to book freight over any route and to any port of the world right here in Chicago, and that day consular and commercial representatives in the world will be active promoters of trade on this spot.

Two agencies of progress have sprung out of the requirements of business, and calculated to be of much service in the future as they have already proven to be in the short period of their existence, the Commercial Arbitration Court and the Advertisers' and Investors' Protective Bureau. Both services have been started for the general welfare by the Chicago Association of Commerce, the former designed to adjudicate business disputes without resort to the public courts, and the latter operating already with striking effect in the regulation of misrepresentative advertising and fraudulent investment securities.

The Commercial Arbitration Court has been acclaimed as one of the most unusual business undertakings ever assumed by a group of private citizens. The movement began in 1917 in an effort to promote the adjudication of commercial cases by voluntary tribunals very much after the Briths manner. Appropriate new legislation has been secured from the State of Illinois and the state supreme court has sustained the constitutionality of the act and passed on certain matters of procedure thereunder. The Commercial Arbitration Bureau was established May 4, 1921. The manager has already arbitrated a number of important cases, and a corps of 165 investigators has been formed, three trade experts from each of the fifty-five divisions of the Chicago Association of Commerce giving the litigants a wide range of selection of arbitrators.

Also unusual, effective, too, but little heard of, is the Advertisers' and Investors' Protective Bureau, the functions of which relate to and control in way of censorship, financial exploitation and commercial publicity, to the end that the offering and sale of fraudulent and hazardously speculative securities are prevented and misrepresentation in merchandise advertising is eliminated. The manager of the bureau, a special investigator for the secretary of state in administering the Illinois blue sky law, has in the past three years reviewed for the Illinois secretary proposed flotations of securities amounting to $660,000,000, approximately forty per cent of which was declined for approval for sale in this state. The bureau has also the unreserved co-operation of the Chicago newspapers in excluding undesirable advertising of every character.

A new and important service is found in the organization in 1921 by the Chicago Association of Commerce of the Interstate Merchants' Council, of which the first general convention was held in 1922. Twenty-six states are now represented in the growing membership and it is planned to hold conventions in Chicago twice a year.

148

FREDERICK S. OLIVER

FREDERICK S. OLIVER, realtor, was born in Buffalo, N. Y., 1867; s. of Frederick and Eliza J. Oliver; ed. in De Veaux Coll., 6 yrs.; Hobart Coll., Geneva, N. Y., 2 yrs. Married Miss J. G. Campbell of Henderson, Ky., 1908. In employ of Snow & Dickinson, real estate, 1886-93. Mem. of Oliver & Scott, 1893, succeeding to business of Snow & Dickinson. In 1904, the firm became Oliver & Co. of which Mr. Oliver has been the head since that time. Mem. of Chicago Real Estate Bd., Chicago Assn. of Commerce. Episcopalian. Republican. Clubs: Union League, Chicago Athletic, South Shore Country. Office: 203 S. Dearborn St. Home: 561 Surf St.

ANTHONY W. STANMEYER

ANTHONY W. STANMEYER, president of the W. C. Heinemann & Co., real estate and investment broker, was born in Dubuque, Iowa, April 18, 1869. He came to Chicago in 1881 and one year later entered the employ of Charles H. Slack, retail grocer. For ten years he was identified with Slack, advancing to the position of assistant manager. In 1892, he resigned to engage in the real estate and mortgage business and five years later he became manager of W. C. Heinemann & Co. He was elected vice-president in 1910 and in 1914 he purchased the Heinemann interests, and became president. Mr. Stanmeyer is an authority on tax problems. Formerly president of Kenmore Improvement Assn. and vice-president of Lake View Park and Boulevard Assn. President, Cook County Real Estate Board, 1920; re-elected in 1921. Director of Chicago Mortgage Bankers Assn. and Cook County Real Estate Board. Mr.

Stanmeyer is married and has three children: Alfred Edgar, John Richard and Geraldine Marie. Home: 6330 N. Paulina street. Office: 10 S. La Salle street.

JOHN SUMNER RUNNELLS

JOHN SUMNER RUNNELLS, chairman of bd. of Pullman Co., was born in Effingham, N. H., July 30, 1844; son of John and Huldah S. Runnells; grad. Amherst Coll., 1865; studied law Dover, N. H. Removed to Iowa, 1867, becoming pvt. sec. to governor; filled consular appointments in England, 1869-71; married Helen R. Baker in Des Moines, March 31, 1869; children: Mabel (Mrs. Robert I. Jankes), Lucy (Mrs. A. A. Jackson), Clive, Alice Rutherford (Mrs. William James, Jr.). Admitted to Iowa bar, 1871; practiced at Des Moines, 1871-87; U. S. Dist. Atty. for Iowa, 1881-85; removed to Chicago as gen. counsel of Pullman Co., 1887; vice pres. and gen. counsel same, 1911-21; chmn. of board, 1922; dir. Merchants Loan & Trust Co., Pullman Trust & Savings bank, Roseland State Savings bank, Guaranty Trust Co., National Biscuit Co.; chmn., Iowa State Rep. com., 1879 and 1880; mem. Rep. Nat. Com. from Iowa, 1880-84; del. Rep. Nat. Convention, 1880. Prominent as orator on patriotic and public occasions. Clubs: Chicago, University, Union, Chicago Literary, Fellowship, Onwentsia; University (New York). Home: 1515 N. State St. Office: Pullman Bldg.

STANDARD OIL COMPANY (INDIANA)

TO be the home of the greatest gasoline manufacturing and marketing organization in the world is an ambition worthy of the greatest of cities, for gasoline has come to be one of the greatest essentials of our modern life. Chicago has attained this ambition; the general offices of the Standard Oil Company (Indiana) are located at 910 South Michigan Avenue, and from there is marketed more gasoline than is distributed from any other point on the globe.

Just outside the municipal limits of Chicago, is Whiting, Ind., where is located the greatest of the company's refineries. The Whiting Works are said to comprise the finest, most complete petroleum refinery to be found anywhere. Other refineries, second only to Whiting, are located at Wood River, Ill., Sugar Creek, Mo., Casper, Wyo., Greybull, Wyo., Laramie, Wyo., and Florence, Colo.

General Office Building of Standard Oil Company (Indiana)

While the bulk of the products manufactured consists of gasoline, kerosene, and lubricating oils, everything having crude oil as a base, from petroleum ether to petroleum coke, is turned out of these huge plants.

While the manufactured products of the Standard Oil Company (Indiana) go to practically every country of the civilized world, the marketing activities of the company are largely concentrated in eleven middle western states: Illinois, Indiana, Michigan, Wisconsin, Minnesota, South Dakota, North Dakota, Kansas, Iowa, Missouri and Oklahoma. In all of these states it ranks among the largest taxpayers.

In distributing the products of its refineries, the Standard Oil Company (Indiana) utilizes 6,000 tank cars, besides large numbers of box cars for package goods. On the Great Lakes, it maintains a fleet of three large tankers and a powerful ocean-going tug. The contribution of this fleet toward making Chicago and the Calumet district a great port is shown by the fact that in the first ten and one-half months of 1919 this company shipped more gasoline from Whiting, by boat, than was exported in the twelve months of the preceding year, from the customs district of New York, and half as much as was exported from the United States, during the same period.

To make its products easily available throughout the territory it serves, nearly 4,000 bulk stations, more than 2,400 service stations and more than 6,000 tank wagons are maintained. In its sales and manufacturing departments more than 25,000 men and women are constantly employed.

In its manufacturing department, the company has set up an industrial democracy, wherein matters pertaining to wages, hours, working conditions, seniority and other matters of immediate interest to employees are passed on by a committee composed of representatives elected by the employees and appointed by the management. While the Board of Directors may veto the findings of the council, the employees may in turn appeal to the Department of Labor at Washington, and, by agreement, this decision is final.

The company has in operation a plan whereby employees who have performed a specific term of service, are retired on a liberal annuity, without cost to them. Employees who have been in service one year or more are entitled, if they so elect, to purchase stock in the company on terms which are most advantageous. The employee may subscribe for an amount not exceeding 20 per cent of his annual salary, and for every dollar subscribed, the company makes him a gift of fifty cents. This is invested in stock for his account at a price which is set at the beginning of the fiscal year.

In May, 1922, the ownership of the company was divided among stockholders, of which many were employees.

On this date (May, 1922) the management of the company centers in a board of directors of nine members: Col. Robert W. Stewart, chairman; Dr. William M. Burton, president; W. E. Warwick, vice president; B. Parks, vice president; E. G. Seubert, vice president and secretary-treasurer; Allan Jackson, vice president; R. H. McElroy, traffic manager; E. J. Bullock, director of purchases, and T. J. Thompson, general manager, sales department.

G. S. FERNALD

G. S. FERNALD, lawyer, was born in Otiseld, Maine, November 11, 1857; s. of Osborne and Hannah E. (Stockman) Fernald; descendant, Dr. Reginald Fernald, British naval surgeon, who was granted land on which Kittery Navy yard is located. Ed., Oxford Normal Inst., Paris, Me.; read law in office of Gen. Mattocks, Portland, Me. Married Gertrude W. Buckman, Portland, Sept. 24, 1878. Children: Frank Osborne, Robert Witham. Adm. to bar, 1882, and began practice at Brainerd, Minn.; city judge, 1 yr. and city atty., 1 yr.; atty., 1886-90, tax commr., 1890-5, N. P. Ry.; spl. counsel for receivers, same, 1893-6; mem. of legal staff of Pullman Co. since 1905 and general counsel since 1920. Mem. Am., Minn., Ill. and Chicago Bar Assns. Republican. Episcopalian. Clubs: Chicago, Exmoor Country, Minnesota, Town and Country (St. Paul). Home: Virginia Hotel. Office: 400 Pullman Bldg.

ALFRED S. AUSTRIAN

ALFRED S. AUSTRIAN, prominent Chicago lawyer, was born in Chicago, June 15, 1871; son of Solomon and Julia R. Austrian. He received his education in Chicago schools, later entering Harvard, where he received an A. B. degree in 1891. Married Mamie Rothschild, of Chicago, Oct. 1, 1901. Daughter, Margaret Fuller. Mr. Austrian was admitted to the Illinois bar in 1893 and has since engaged in practice at Chicago; member of firm of Mayer, Meyer, Austrian and Platt since 1905. Member of American, Illinois State and Chicago Bar Associations. Home: 53 E. Division St. Office: Suite 2010, 208 S. La Salle St.

EUGENE BRADLEY CLARK

EUGENE BRADLEY CLARK, president of Clark Equipment Co., was born in Washington, D. C., July 27, 1873; s. of Sylvia Anne (Nodine) and Ezra Westcote Clark. Father was chief of U. S. Revenue Marine service for 25 years. He was educated in pub. schs. of Washington; received M. E. degree from Cornell Univ. in 1894. Entered Westinghouse Electric Co., Pittsburgh. Later became asst. mgr. of Illinois Steel Co., Chicago. Next made pres. of Am. Sintering Co., Chicago; later of Clark Equipment Co., Buchanan, Mich., and Am. Ore Reclamation Co., New York. Twice married. First wife, Laura Wolfe, Pittsburgh. Children: Helen Cecil, Sylvia Anne, Eugene B., Jr., John M. Second wife, Mrs. Luella M. Coon, Darien, Conn. Mr. Clark installed first alternating current and first reversing motors in rolling mills of U. S. Holds patents on electric lifting magnets, electrical hoisting devices, methods of treating ore, etc. Mem. of Am. Iron and Steel Institute, Soc. of Automotive Engrs., and Am. Institute of Mining Engineers. Clubs: Chicago, University, Duquesne, Pittsburgh; Detroit Athletic, Youngstown, India House, New York. Office: 86 E. Randolph street. Homes: 60 Scott street, Chicago, and Buchanan, Mich.

THE INTERNATIONAL HARVESTER COMPANY

THE International Harvester Company was incorporated in 1902 under the laws of New Jersey, bringing together five well-known lines of implement manufacture—the McCormick, Deering, Champion, Plano and Milwaukee.

Originally the capitalization was $120,000,000, of which $60,000,000 was preferred stock and $60,000,000 common stock. In 1910 it was increased to $140,000,000 of which $60,000,000 was preferred stock and $80,000,000 common stock. Every dollar of this capitalization was represented by cash received in the treasury before the stock was issued against it, or by actual physical properties appraised with severe conservatism. Not a dollar was allowed for good will, patents, trademarks or shop rights. Thus the Company began, and still continues, without a drop of "water" in its capitalization.

The Company's present authorized capital is $230,000,000, of which $100,000,000 is preferred stock and $130,000,000 common. Of this total, $154,340,014 had been issued up to January 1, 1922, or $60,223,900 preferred and $94,116,114 common. The latest increase in capitalization was authorized in 1920, chiefly to meet the future requirements of the Employes' Extra Compensation and Stock Ownership Plan; of the $90,000,000 increase, $30,000,000 was for stock dividend purposes.

The purpose of the formation of the Harvester Company was to bring together the resources of capital, of manufacturing facilities and of men trained and experienced in the selling and handling of farm implements that were absolutely necessary to the development of America's foreign trade in farm machinery.

There had been some exploration of the foreign field by American farm implement manufacturers, but it was not until the Paris exposition of 1900 that the foreign field and the American manufacturer began fully to understand how much each needed the other. A considerable volume of business in American farming machinery had been worked up abroad, but it was chiefly done through jobbers who were interested only in quick cash returns and could furnish no competent service of instruction and repairs.

The real foreign field for one of America's greatest inventions lay among the millions of individual farmers who were still harvesting their crops by hand. The educating of these farmers away from their primitive customs and traditions meant enormous expense. So did the establishment of means of local distribution, of service to customers and of supplying repair parts. These tasks also required a large force of American-trained experts, skilled in the use, setting up and repair of farm machines, and in selling them along progressive, educational lines. There was also the important factor of much longer credits that must be extended in pioneering so large and remote a field. None of the constituent companies had money, manufacturing facilities or trained men enough to undertake these tasks alone.

How successfully the foreign requirements of the implement business were met by the Harvester Company, is shown by the fact that in 1902 the total foreign sales of the constituent companies amounted to about $10,000,000. In 1912, ten years later, the Harvester Company sold $51,000,000 worth of its products abroad, an increase of 410%. The General Agency at Omsk, Siberia, achieved the Company's banner sales record of 1912 with total sales of $3,184,325.

Up to and including 1916, the International Harvester Company's sales of farm implements and binder twine in foreign countries amounted to approximately $450,000,000. In that year 36,578 dealers in 38 foreign countries were selling Harvester products.

In the domestic business the Company has devoted its energies and resources to the improvement of both its goods and the means of their manufacture, and to the development of new machines to take the place of hand labor on the farms.

154

Up to the time the Company was formed the constituent concerns had produced only nine kinds of machines, all connected with harvesting. While other companies manufacture longer lines of some machines, the Harvester Company is now producing 54 classifications of machines, including all the essential implements of agriculture. One result of this policy has been to provide work all the year round for the selling organization, instead of goods that were commonly salable only in the brief harvest period. Another result is better continuity of operations at the factories, insuring more regular employment on the manufacturing side of the business.

Accompanying this development has been a steady improvement of the means and methods of distributing the Company's products and of promptly furnishing repair parts, as well as expert service in setting up and adjusting the machines. There are now 93 Harvester branch houses in the United States, each having a staff of experts and carrying adequate repair stocks.

From its formation the Company has given earnest attention to the development of sound and progressive policies affecting all its relations with its employes. In 1909 it organized an Employes' Benefit Association to protect employes and their families against the consequences of non-occupational accident and of illness and death. This Association is jointly administered by the management and the employes and is liberally supported by the Company. Up to January 1, 1922, it had allowed more than 59,000 claims, and had paid out total benefits of $4,722,753.

Medical attention for employes at all factories is provided by the Company without charge through a staff of full-time and part-time physicians, nurses and dentists.

A pension plan adopted in 1908 is entirely supported by the Company. Up to January 1, 1922, a total of 1,076 employes had been retired on pension and the total of pension payments was then $1,402,148.

The Harvester Industrial Council Plan, adopted in March, 1919, is in successful operation. It gives the employes an equal voice with the management in the shaping of all industrial policies, including wages, hours and working conditions.

After several years of experience with plans combining profit sharing and employe ownership of Company stock, under which about 8,000 employes became stockholders, the Extra Compensation and Stock Ownership Plan was adopted in 1920. Under this plan employes qualifying by continuity of service receive as extra compensation 60 per cent of the net earnings of each year above 7 per cent on the invested capital. Payments are made as nearly as possible half in stock and half in cash.

Chicago has been the most important center of American farm implement manufacturing ever since Cyrus Hall McCormick, inventor of the reaper, established his first factory here in 1847. It is the principal seat of operation of the Harvester Company, which maintains its general offices here and eight of its factories—the McCormick and Deering Works, with a binder twine mill at each, the Tractor Works, West Pullman Works, Weber Wagon Works, and the Wisconsin Steel Works at South Chicago. In normal times the Company's factory employes in Chicago average above 20,000.

The other Harvester plants in the United States are: the Milwaukee Works, making tractors, gas engines and cream separators; motor truck factories at Akron and Springfield, Ohio; P. & O. Plow Works at Canton, Ill.; Chattanooga Plow Works at Chattanooga, Tenn.; tillage implement factory at Auburn, N. Y.; implement factory at Rock Falls, Ill.; seeding machine factory at Richmond, Ind.; coiled spring factory at Springfield, Ohio; binder twine mills at Auburn, N. Y., and St. Paul, Minn. Construction work was begun in March, 1922, on a new motor truck factory at Fort Wayne, Indiana.

There are three factories operated by subsidiary companies in Canada—two at Hamilton, Ont., and one at Chatham, Ont. In Europe there are four implement factories operated by subsidiary companies. They are situated at Croix, France; Lubertzy, Russia; Neuss, Germany; and Norrkoping, Sweden. The three foreign binder twine plants are at Croix, Neuss and Norrkoping.

The executive officers of the Company are: President, Alexander Legge; Vice Presidents, Herbert F. Perkins, Addis E. McKinstry, Henry B. Utley; General Counsel, William D. McHugh; Secretary and Treasurer, George A. Ranney; Comptroller, William M. Reay.

ALEXANDER LEGGE

ALEXANDER LEGGE, president and director of the International Harvester company, was born in Dane county, Wisconsin, Jan. 13, 1866; son of Christina (Fraser) and Alexander Legge. He was educated in the public schools of Wisconsin and Nebraska. He is married to Katherine McMahon. His first work was farming and stockraising in Nebraska and Wyoming. In 1891 he entered the employ of the McCormick Harvesting Machine Co., working as collector and salesman out of the Omaha agency. He was made collection agent at Council Bluffs in 1894; general agent at Council Bluffs in 1894 and in 1899, manager of the collection department at Chicago. Mr. Legge, in 1903, was made assistant manager of domestic sales for International Harvester Co. of America; 1906, assistant general manager, International Harvester Co.; in 1913, general manager; in 1919, vice-president and general manager; in 1922, president. During the war Mr. Legge served as manager of Allied Purchasing Commission, vice-chairman of War Industries Board and commercial adviser to peace conference. Clubs: Commercial, Chicago Athletic, Illinois Athletic, Press, and Metropolitan (Washington). Home: Hinsdale, Ill. Office: 606 S. Michigan av.

THE LINK-BELT COMPANY

IN the early period of the development of modern agricultural machinery, much trouble was experienced with the transmission of power from one part to another with flat belts, especially where it was important to have the movements of the parts definitely timed with each other. Moisture from dew in the early mornings, the dryness of noon heat, the presence of dust, and varying weather conditions, made belts too tight or too loose and required frequent adjustment.

To overcome these difficulties William Dana Ewart, selling agricultural implements in Iowa, invented what is known all over the world as the Ewart Detachable Link-Belt, a chain made up of malleable iron links which can easily be detached, but which will not come apart in any operating position on the sprocket wheels. This gave a positive motion, and admitted of easy repair or adjustment in the field, and proved to be the salvation of the modern agricultural implement industry.

Mr. Ewart organized the Ewart Manufacturing Company, at Chicago, in 1875, for the purpose of manufacturing the chain and wheels, largely for the agricultural implement trade at that time; and in 1880 he organized the Link-Belt Machinery Company, at Chicago, to extend the field of operations of Link-Belt and wheels to power transmissions, elevators and conveyors, in the various industries.

In 1888 the New York office of the Link-Belt Machinery Company, and the firm of Burr and Dodge (which handled the Ewart Manufacturing Company's chains and wheels in Eastern and Southern territory, from Philadelphia), united to form the Link-Belt Engineering Company, with plant and main office at Philadelphia.

In 1906 these three related Companies, the Ewart Manufacturing Company, then located at Indianapolis, the Link-Belt Machinery Company, Chicago, and the Link-Belt Engineering Company, Philadelphia, consolidated as the Link-Belt Company, with Mr. Charles Piez as its president.

The field of manufacture was extended in the passing years to include a large variety of devices for handling materials in bulk or package, including besides general elevating and conveying machinery, complete equipments for handling and storing coal, coal tipples, coal washeries, sand and gravel washeries, locomotive cranes, electric hoists, portable loaders, traveling water intake screens, coal crushers, feeders, Peck Carriers, etc., etc., besides chain and wheel power transmissions for a large variety of speeds and conditions.

In 1921 the Link-Belt Company bought the H. W. Caldwell & Son Company plant and business, at Chicago, thus increasing its screw conveyor and power transmission lines, and adding machine-molded gears and other Caldwell specialties.

The Link-Belt Company now owns and operates two large plants in Chicago, three in Indianapolis, and three in Philadelphia; besides having branches in the principal cities of the United States, some of which are supplemented with machine shop equipment and warehouses; the Canadian branch has a regular manufacturing plant at Toronto, and warehouse and office at Montreal.

FINLEY P. MOUNT

FINLEY P. MOUNT, president of Advance-Rumely Co., was born in Montgomery Co., Ind., Nov. 26, 1866; son of Elizabeth S. (Pogue) Mount and Elijah C. Mount; ed. in Pub. Schs.; received B. S. and A. M. degrees from Wabash Coll., 1890. Married Henrietta Allen, June 9, 1896, in Denver, Col. Practiced law in Crawfordsville and Indianapolis from 1892 to 1915. In 1915, appointed by U. S. Dist. Court of Indiana as receiver for M. Rumely Co. and Rumely Products Co. Closed up receivership in a year. Assisted in formation of Advance-Rumely Co. to purchase the old Rumely Co., beginning business Jan. 1, 1916. Pres. and Dir. of Advance-Rumely Co. since organization. Pres. and managing director, Canadian Rumely Co., Ltd., a subsidiary. Mem. of Ex. Comm., of National Assn. of Farm Equipment Mfrs. Mem. bd. of trustees. Wabash Coll. since 1902. Clubs: Union League, Mid-Day, Indiana Soc. of Chicago; Columbia Club (Indianapolis). Offices: La Porte, Ind., and 701 Tower Bldg., Chicago. Home: Rumely Hotel, La Porte; 5492 S. Shore Drive, Chicago; Burk Lake, Mich.

THE HOLT MANUFACTURING COMPANY

IN the development of the agricultural, mine and forest wealth of the Pacific Coast, the name of Benjamin Holt stands in the forefront as the designer, inventor and builder of many new and important types of agricultural and road machinery.

Established in 1883 at Stockton, Calif., the Holt Manufacturing Company has since been constantly engaged in the manufacture of agricultural and road machinery. Its products have been used on every continent in the widest variety of work.

From the necessity for providing a surer traction for soft soils, Mr. Holt gave the world his master invention, the track-laying type of tractor, bearing his name and universally known by the Holt trademark "Caterpillar." The Stockton plant had been greatly enlarged and the prominence into which "Caterpillar" tractors came more than a decade ago necessitated the establishment of an eastern factory at Peoria, Ill., in 1909. The two Holt plants now comprise more than fifty acres of ground with an aggregate of over 5,000 employes and with a combined output per year of thousands of tractors, harvesters, trailers and other machinery.

With the outbreak of the war, great power and dependable traction were indispensable for heavy ordnance and supply transportation and in 1914 the Allied Governments adopted the "Caterpillar" exclusively for this type of work. Thousands of "Caterpillars" were used by the Allied Armies on every front, these tractors performing seemingly impossible tasks. The great fighting "tanks" were inspired by the performance of these tractors.

After continued tests, severe service in Mexico, "Caterpillar" tractors were adopted in 1917 by the United States for the great program of motorizing the field artillery, as well as for heavy military transportation. During the entire period of the war, the Peoria plant was devoted exclusively to the manufacture of "Caterpillars" for the needs of the United States and the Allied Governments.

Since the war, the leadership of the "Caterpillar" has been still further emphasized in every phase of industrial and agricultural tractive service. Its unequaled ability to travel, climb and pull in mud, loose sand, on the roughest grades and soils and across roadless country; its unfailing performance, its power and endurance for all soil conditions and for every climate have established the "Caterpillar" as a dependable, economical power for every phase of road making; for county, township, city and public work of every kind; for contracting and engineering construction, in oil field, logging and mining transportation, for snow removal, belt work and every other tractive service where power and endurance are at a premium.

159

W. J. O'BRIEN

W. J. O'BRIEN, President Sterling Midland Coal Company, general office, Fisher Building, Chicago.

INLAND STEEL COMPANY

THE SPIRIT of the Inland Steel company, manufacturing a great variety of steel products, is the spirit of striving to excel. Every step in every process through which the product passes is accompanied by a most rigid inspection.

The expression "good enough" is never used. Unless the product can leave each process in virtually perfect condition, it is not permitted to leave at all. So true is this that the motto of every Inland inspector is "When in Doubt Reject."

This, in a measure, is the key to the remarkable rise of the Inland Steel company from a modest steel works, with an annual production of only 10,000 tons, to one with a 1,000,000 ton production, owning great iron deposits, ships and factories. Organized in 1893, the company now is capitalized at $30,000,000 and represents one of the large investments in the steel industry.

During its first year, the company bought the equipment of the Chicago Rolling Mill Company for re-rolling rails and billets. In 1902, the Indiana Harbor Works was completed for the production of Basic Open Hearth Steel. The company now has its own ore and coal lands and has the necessary blast furnace and open hearth equipment for the production of 1,000,000 tons of ingots a year. The finished products are rails, bars, plates, structural shapes, sheet steel in black, blue annealed and galvanized finishes. Track accessories consist of bolts, spikes, nuts and splice bars.

The basis on which the Inland product is made is exact information and the basis of exact information is system. One would think that one blast furnace heat would be just like another—all the ore coming from the same mine, the coke from the same ovens, the limestone from the same quarries. And they are near enough like to make an average of considerable excellence. But average product is not what the Inland company is after—it wants every individual sheet or finished section to be perfect in itself; as near perfection as it can be made.

And this is how it is done: Every heat from the blast furnace is analyzed and its whole history written down. Then it is given a number, and that number follows every ladle of molten iron and every cast of pig iron from that heat.

Similarly every heat of every Open Hearth furnace is analyzed and numbered and that number is chalked on every ingot poured from that heat.

But that is only a beginning; for every bloom, slab and sheet bar rolled from that heat bears the heat number, and any incident in the progress of any of these offshoots from the original heat that throws suspicion on the quality of that steel leads to an immediate investigation of the behavior of every other child of the same father.

Not only in this negative way is the numbering system useful, but particularly, and in a larger way, is it of positive helpfulness. For the chemical and physical elements of each heat require a different treatment from every other heat.

The men largely responsible for the initiation of this policy by which both the company and the user are protected are the officers. It is also to their progressiveness that the company owes much of its success. They are L. E. Block, chairman of the board; P. D. Block, president; E. M. Adams, first vice president; E. J. Block, W. C. Carroll, H. C. Jones, J. W. Lees, C. R. Robinson, vice presidents; and W. D. Truesdale, treasurer. W. A. Maxwell, Gen. Supt. The directors are E. M. Adams, R. J. Beatty, E. J. Block, L. E. Block, P. D. Block, Samuel Deutsch, G. H. Jones, H. C. Jones, A. W. Thompson, D. P. Thompson and Gordon Batelle.

Main offices are at 38 S. Dearborn street, Chicago. Plants are located at Indiana Harbor, Ind., and Chicago Heights, Ill. There are branch offices in Milwaukee, St. Louis and St. Paul.

FREDERICK W. MATTHIESSEN

A BORN leader, Frederick W. Matthiessen ranks with the greatest of Illinois' sons. With Edward C. Hegeler, he created the zinc industry of America and laid the foundations for several other businesses. Mr. Matthiessen was the founder of the Western Clock company, which produces 3,000,000 clocks annually. He gave millions of dollars to improve the community life of La Salle, Illinois, and his donations are also responsible for the opening to the public of the beautiful Deer Park. A more complete account of the great career of Mr. Matthiessen will be found on the next page.

162

FREDERICK W. MATTHIESSEN

FREDERICK W. MATTHIESSEN was endowed with a rare creative ability. Making something that a country needed but did not have—thus reads the beginning of the story of his life. His creative urge impelled him to give up a promising career as an engineer in Germany to blaze new paths in America, in company with his friend and partner, Edward C. Hegeler. He knew that in order to succeed in business he must regard the rights and interest of his fellow man as well as his own. So in choosing zinc as the product for his labor, he chose the undeveloped material which the people wanted.

The same keen judgment made him select as a site for his industry La Salle, with its inexhaustible fuel, its ideal location on the banks of the Illinois, its proximity to the Illinois Central and Rock Island Railway lines. Another inducement was the fact that La Salle is contiguous to the ore fields of Wisconsin and Missouri and the world market at Chicago.

Thus came into being the zinc industry of America. Mr. Matthiessen's natural inventive ability and scientific training entered into the development of all the processes of the great industry.

For many years, he and Mr. Hegeler together carried on investigations and experiments leading to important discoveries which were embodied in patents on inventions, taken out jointly by both. He maintained and operated personally an experimental laboratory, in which he invented electrical smelting and rotary gas furnaces, upon which he was awarded patents and which are working great improvements in the smelting industry.

As the Matthiessen and Hegeler Zinc Works grew, Mr. Matthiessen also managed those large allied business relations, which included the buying of materials, the acquiring and developing of coal mines, the procuring or building of means of transportation, the sales of the product, the investment of surplus earnings and the selection of the field for enlargement. In time, his employees and associates constituted in themselves a city and the name of Matthiessen and Hegeler became synonymous with great energy and business acumen.

To provide a new outlet for his creative force, Mr. Matthiessen established the Western Clock Company, and the La Salle Tool Company and it is to his initiative and energy that these enterprises owe their success. From the Western Clock Company factories at La Salle and Peru, Ill., come each year three million clocks bearing the world famous name of Westclox.

His work in establishing the beautiful resort, Deer Park, and his example, influence and contributions were largely instrumental in stimulating the State of Illinois to establish the neighboring State park. Here is to be found the historical souvenir of Starved Rock.

The welfare of the people of La Salle who had assembled about him was with Mr. Matthiessen always his chief concern. He gave freely and con-

163

tinually to provide them with safe, attractive and well lighted streets, pure milk depots, healthful sewage disposal, sanitary hospitals, athletic fields and parks, schools, libraries, charity organizations and a well-directed community life. He also had a hand in the direction of the municipal affairs of La Salle, serving as president of the school board and mayor for a number of years.

Through his kind acts of repeatedly acquiring and cancelling public obligations for large sums, both the municipality and the school authorities were able to increase their revenues and meet the rising cost of the higher type of municipal life and education.

He literally gave away hundreds of thousands of dollars so that he might better the lives of the people of his community.

Frederick W. Matthiessen was born a leader. Rare self-control, overflowing vitality, vision and perception, keen farsightedness, strength of character. breadth of sympathy, determination of purpose, inexhaustible geniality and serenity of temper, tact and skill in dealing with people—all these were his in a superior measure.

Among the brilliant and able leaders that Illinois has contributed to the world, none deserves a more prominent place than Frederick W. Matthiessen.

GOLDSMITH BROS. SMELTING & REFINING CO.

THE Goldsmith Smelting and Refining Company has played a leading part in the copper and lead industry of America for nearly seventy-five years. The company was founded in 1861 by Marcus Goldsmith in Cincinnati. In 1865 the plant was moved to Lexington, Ky., and in 1884 to Chicago.

Upon the death of Marcus Goldsmith, the control of the firm passed into the hands of his sons, Moses and Simon. Under their direction, the organization has become international in scope. It has branches in Canada, as well as in the United States and its capitalization has passed $1,500,000, making it one of the largest smelting companies in the world.

Present officers are Moses Goldsmith, president; Simon Goldsmith, vice president; and L. Adelsdorf, treasurer. Directors are Moses Goldsmith, Simon Goldsmith, L. Adelsdorf, S. Adelsdorf, Kenneth McKenzie, E. J. Mayer, Melvin M. Goldsmith, H. J. Eisendrath.

The company's general offices are located in the Heyworth building, Chicago, and 20 John street, New York. Its factories are in Chicago, Brooklyn and New York.

WALTER DOUGLAS MAIN

WALTER DOUGLAS MAIN, president of the General Explosives Company, was born in Portland, Maine, April 9, 1880; s. of Mary Jane (Whiteley) and John Main; received ed. in pub. schs. of Detroit, Mich. Married Alice Erdman in Chicago, in 1903. Mr. Main was associated with the New Jersey Zinc Company from 1899 to 1915. He engaged in manufacturing Sulphuric Acid and other chemicals in 1915. He organized the General Explosives Company in 1916 and now devotes all time to the manufacture of dynamite and other explosives. Mr. Main is a liberal patron of music and art. Clubs: Chicago Athletic, Skokie Country, Bob O'Link Golf, Chicago Yacht, City, Cliff Dwellers Home: 531 Roscoe st. Office: 7 S. Dearborn st.

CRANE CO.

FROM a modest concern, founded in 1855 by Richard Teller Crane, the Crane Co. has developed into the largest manufacturer of valves and fittings in the world and has acquired extensive interests in plumbers' enamelware and sanitary pottery.

It has factories at Chicago and Bridgeport, Conn., and seventy-four branch stores and warehouses in other cities of the United States. Through Crane, Limited, a subsidiary, it has a manufacturing plant and warehouse in Montreal and nine branch stores in Canada.

The company, since its organization, has been engaged in the manufacture of and sale of steamfitters' and plumbers' supplies and all necessary apparatus for the control of and conveyance of steam, water, oil, gas or air. It also manufactures sanitary appliances, heating apparatus, mill supplies and kindred articles.

It is capitalized at $65,000,000, of which $15,000,000 is in preferred stock. The company's subsidiaries are the Crane Export Corporation of New York; Campagnie Crane, Paris, France; Crane-Bennett, Ltd., London, Eng.; Crane Limited, Montreal; Canadian Potteries, Ltd., St. Johns, Que.; Crane Enamelware Company, Chattanooga, Tenn.; and the Crane Co. (of Minnesota), St. Paul. It is also affiliated with the Mutual Potteries Company, of Trenton, N. J.

Officers of the Crane Co. are R. T. Crane, Jr., president; J. B. Berryman, first vice-president; A. D. Mac Gill, vice-president; C. A. G. Wayman, vice-president; E. H. Raymond, vice-president; W. J. Clark, vice-president; H. P. Bishop, secretary; and P. T. Kelly, treasurer.

The directorate is composed of J. B. Berryman, W. A. Beville, W. J. Clark, J. H. Collier, C. R. Crane, II, H. P. Crane, R. T. Crane, Jr., A. F. Gartz, Jr., P. T. Kelly, A. D. Mac Gill, J. A. Murphy, E. H. Raymond, R. B. Stiles and C. A. G. Wayman.

The main offices are at 836 South Michigan avenue.

ROBERT BREWSTER

ROBERT BREWSTER, ceramic manufacturer, was born in London in 1845. The sudden death of his father took him from college and put in his hands the task of taking care of his mother, brother, and sister.

Visions of being an architect faded, and he took a position in a manufacturing jewelry house. His proficiency in drawing proved no advantage to him in this business, so he studied the precious metals, their alloys and adaptability; and his eldest son has carried on this work and has provided the dental profession with the finest alloys ever produced. In 1903, he established himself in the United States and exhibited his manufactures of steel, porcelain, and rubber, at the World's Fair. Mr. Brewster helped forward the artistic side of dentistry, and encouraged the use of porcelain for filling cavities in decayed teeth. He was one of the first in America to manufacture porcelain for filling cavities in natural teeth. The Brewster Porcelain was so largely in demand that it represented 85 per cent of the entire amount used. By one of his inventions, he has enabled persons who have to wear artificial teeth to obtain, for the first time, a thorough mastication of food. As a diversion he has also patented a target for golf, which, taken together with his instruction book for golf beginners, has made it possible for a beginner to learn the game in less than one-fourth of the time usually taken. His knowledge of mechanics has also helped to make the automobile speedometer the nearly perfect instrument it is today. He resides in Palos Park.

COL. ROBERT W. STEWART

WHEN Col. Robert W. Stewart became chairman of the board of directors and executive head of the Standard Oil Company (Indiana), he introduced a new fashion in business, which has won both the business man and the consumer. His first official act was to banish secrecy, except when necessary to the consummation of plans still in the development stage, and bring the public closer in the company's affairs. He encouraged publicity and had the company's advertisements so arranged that they treated more of its affairs than its products. Frankness, plainness, directness of manner and a habit of thinking clear through a problem are a few of Col. Stewart's characteristics. Under his direction, the Standard Oil Company (Indiana) has "enfranchised" its workers, given them a voice in its affairs and allowed them to become partners. The story of Col. Stewart's connection with the Standard Oil Company (Indiana) will be found on the next page.

"BOB" STEWART AND STANDARD OIL

THE STANDARD OIL COMPANY (Indiana) of today is not the Standard Oil Company of a decade ago. Today it does business in its shirt sleeves, out in the open where everybody can see it, because Col. Robert W. Stewart, chairman of the board of directors and executive head, brought with him from the Dakota plains a spirit of western directness, democracy and frankness which he infused into the business administration of one of the greatest industrial organizations in the world.

Born near Cedar Rapids, Iowa, in 1867, young Bob Stewart, after completing his education at Yale, went to the Dakotas where he punched cattle, did a little newspaper work and a number of other things while waiting for the Dakota folks to d.scover that they had in their midst a regular lawyer, attorney and counselor. They hesitated for a little while, but finally capitulated, and before the Spanish-American war came along to interrupt his career he was one of the successful young attorneys of the Northwest. The Roosevelt ranch was not far from his home, and like his famous neighbor he felt the urge to action and became a Rough Rider, returning a major in that organization. At the request of the governor of South Dakota he accepted a colonelcy and undertook with success the reorganization of the national guard of that state.

Returning to the law, Col. Stewart soon established himself as one of the leading lawyers of the state, and his work attracted the attention of the Standard Oil Company (Indiana). He was invited to join the company's legal department and accepted. Almost at once, he was made general attorney, and in a few years was elected general counsel and a director. When in 1919 a complete reorganization of the company was effected, Col. Stewart was made chairman of the board and executive head of the organization. Immediately, the ultra-conservative Standard Oil Company (Indiana) went into its shirt sleeves.

Things began to happen. The directors went into the refineries, and into the sales department, met and talked man-fashion with the rank and file of employes. They got into intimate touch with the viewpoint of the men and in turn gave the employes an opportunity to get the viewpoint of the management. Every member of the great organization was given to understand that the door to the office of the chairman of the board was open to them at all times.

Meetings were held where the affairs of the company were talked over fully and frankly until the men knew more about the company's business than many of the stockholders. An organized industrial relations plan was put into effect whereby men elected by the employes from among their number had a large voice in deciding all questions relating to the hours of labor, wages, and other questions of interest to the workers. The annuity plan, in operation for a number of years, was reorganized. An opportunity to buy stock in the company on very favorable terms was inaugurated and nearly 8,000 of the men and women became part owners in the business. An employes' magazine, which is a real employes' magazine and not a medium for preachments, was started. When all industry was disturbed by strikes and lockouts, harmony reigned in the ranks of the Standard Oil Company (Indiana). These are but a few of the things which Col. Stewart did to make the Standard Oil Company (Indiana) a leader in the industrial life of the country.

Believing the public was entitled to know something of the company's policies, practices and ideals, Col. Stewart began telling the company's "business secrets," largely through paid advertisements. These featured the company and its methods rather than the products the company made to sell.

A new attitude was shown newspaper men seeking information about the company. They were given every opportunity to get into the office and were told frankly what they wanted to know if the information they asked for was available.

"A permanent attitude of secrecy implies that a company has policies of such a character as to make secrecy necessary," wrote Col. Stewart in a recent magazine article. "A well-managed company has no such policy, and secrecy is unnecessary except when it relates to plans still in the stage of development.

"When I was called to head this company, I put this idea into practice, even though it was, in a way, a reversal of established policy. For example, I found that when newspaper men came to find out something about the affairs of the company, the impression was given that these affairs were essentially private, even though the interest of the public might be obvious, and further inference was given that the curiosity of the press was something to be resented. The result, undoubtedly, was unfavorable. I knew that we had nothing to conceal, therefore when publicity came I welcomed instead of resenting it. In this way we gained the positive advantage of getting the real facts before the public instead of gross distortions which was so likely to be our portion under the old order."

This is the spirit of directness, democracy, frankness which Col. Robert W. Stewart, chief executive of the greatest gasoline marketing organization in the world, director in the Continental and Commercial National Bank, Chicago, and the National City Bank, New York, is introducing into the business world. It is a spirit which is certain to have a marked influence upon the industrial and commercial life of tomorrow.

THE AMERICAN SEATING COMPANY

THE AMERICAN SEATING COMPANY does not assume or pretend that the primary purpose of business is not financial gain. However, it does believe that it is the duty of business men to merit the profit by excellence of service rendered impartially to user, distributor and producer.

The company has branch offices in the following cities: New York, Boston, Philadelphia, Pittsburgh, Buffalo, Cleveland, Cincinnati, Detroit, Indianapolis, St. Louis, Memphis, Jacksonville, Fort Worth, Kansas City, Des Moines and Minneapolis, and distributing jobbers in all other territories of the United States and foreign countries.

The company was founded in 1899 and each year has seen the sales augmented as the result of its idealistic yet practical policy. Mr. Thomas M. Boyd is the president and guiding spirit of the company, which is capitalized at $4,000,000. The company's factory at Grand Rapids, manufacturing school desks and theatre chairs, is not only the largest in the "Furniture City," but has developed into one of the show factories of the country. It is visited annually by educators and others interested in inspecting the highest development of production facilities and methods, and of factory morale.

In addition to the manufacture of school desks and theatre seating the company operates a plant at Manitowoc, Wisconsin, devoted exclusively to the building of church pews, sanctuary furniture and general church interior work. In this plant are produced real works of art in wood sculpture. Most of the elaborate cathedrals and churches of the country are decorated with these carved wood altars, pulpits, statuary, panellings, rood beams, choir stalls and other fitments for sanctuary and nave.

170

MATTHIESSEN & HEGELER ZINC COMPANY

IT is now more than sixty years since two industrious and determined young men, having resolved to seek their fortune in America, left their native land and, after spending a few years investigating the various ore properties with a view to making zinc, finally came to La Salle, Ill.

Many were the difficulties and obstacles encountered by these two pioneers in this industry, yet with a spirit of determination and enterprise that is seldom encountered, they established what was later to become one of the largest zinc plants in the world.

The two pioneers, Frederick W. Matthiessen and Edward C. Hegeler, selected La Salle because of the abundance of coal underlying the surface there. It requires about two tons of coal to smelt one ton of zinc ore, consequently the practice is followed of bringing the zinc to the coal. Zinc ore had been discovered at Mineral Point, Wis., and in the search for coal La Salle was found to be the nearest point where the fuel could be obtained. Another reason for locating there was La Salle's favorable position in regard to the market. Railroads were few and mileage short in those days and the canal was the great highway of commerce.

Writing of the opening of plant, Mr. Matthiessen stated: "The first shovelful of dirt was turned in December, 1858. We had a furnace running successfully when the civil war broke out; there being no sale for spelter after the outbreak of hostilities, we ceased temporarily, but began operations again when in 1862 or 1863, a lively demand arose for zinc in the manufacture of arms and cartridges. During the cessation of manufacturing, we had been making experiments so that when we started again, we did so with decidedly improved methods. Our means were limited and we were very careful in our expenditures. We spent no money that was not absolutely necessary."

During the years that followed, the story of the Matthiessen & Hegeler Zinc Company is one of continual progress. In 1882, the manufacture of sulphuric acid as a by-product was begun, the company being the pioneer in this branch of the industry in the United States. At the present time, eighty-five tank cars, of twenty and thirty-ton capacity, are required to distribute the product to the customers in various lines of manufacture.

The plant has been greatly enlarged from time to time and today it covers sixty acres of land. The company was the first in America to roll sheet zinc and continued alone in this field until 1876.

In 1871 the firm was incorporated under its present name. Since the death of Mr. Matthiessen and Mr. Hegeler, control has passed to Joseph Brennemann, who now serves in the capacity of president. The other officers are E. Roth, vice president; Edward H. Carus, secretary, and H. C. Nichol, treasurer. The directors beside the aforementioned officers are Lester H. Strawn, Ralph H. Matthiessen and F. O. Wetmore.

171

KELLOGG SWITCHBOARD AND SUPPLY CO.

"ONCE upon a time," as the fairy stories begin, a man went into a drugstore and found a telephone on the wall. There were only a few in town, and everyone thought them wonderful. That was only a few years ago, comparatively speaking, and in the memory of a good many of us today.

It is appropriate to begin our story "Once upon a time," because the inventing, perfecting, manufacturing and distributing of the telephone far surpasses the most absorbing fairy story ever written. Just a few years ago, there were few telephones anywhere. In Chicago, for instance, there was not half enough to supply the business needs of the town, and crude were the instruments of those days. The telephone on the farm was unknown.

The growth and development of the telephone system, as we know it in Chicago, and its perfection, in spite of criticisms, its part in, and connection with other telephone systems throughout the country, is an accomplishment ofttimes not appreciated.

But in the early days the manufacturer could not begin to supply the demand for quantity production and types of apparatus.

So to satisfy this increased and increasing demand for telephone service, groups of men about thirty years ago started the Independent telephone, its manufacture and distribution and, today, these systems are found throughout the country. Their growth and magnitude today is of even greater interest and wonder, because of the obstacles and struggles which these Independent telephone men had to overcome in the production of a standard line of telephones and switchboards of the highest type to supply the Independent manager who believed in giving a telephone service of his own responsibility and ideal, and independent of any other organization.

Few people realize that in Chicago, we have one of the first factories that produced Independent telephones and switchboards. Milo G. Kellogg founded the Kellogg Switchboard and Supply Company, rented a school building and hired a few men in Highland Park in 1897 to build the first large Independent switchboard which was successfully installed in St. Louis and kept in operation many years. The Kellogg Company shortly after moved to Congress and Green Streets, requiring, several times, changes to larger quarters until in 1915, it moved to its present factory building on Adams and Aberdeen Streets, which contains over fourteen acres of floor space and is one of the largest factories and most up-to-date for the production of telephone equipment in the world.

Since the first shipment of telephones from this organization, the name "Kellogg" has had a good deal to do with the progress of the telephone industry. Free to develop telephone engineering along the lines that people's demand indicated as the best type of telephone service, the Kellogg Company has been a strong aid to the Independent telephone men who are working to give a better service, not only in larger cities, but in the small towns and in the country.

Largely through continuous and dependable efforts of the Kellogg Company, telephone managers have been furnished equipment of the very latest type.

Those who remember the crude and limited telephone service prior to 1897, which was the best offered to the public at the end of 20 years of development, and compare it with the more modern service brought about by Independent telephony, will appreciate the service rendered by this Chicago organization.

172

The Kellogg Company originated and made available economical party line systems for the small town telephone users, as well as metropolitan exchanges. Twenty years ago, the Kellogg Company produced the Kellogg transmitter which was the first real Independent product, and today it is considered a standard instrument and is practically without change. There are now more than 3,000,000 in service. The Kellogg Company produced the first real unbreakable desk telephone and designed the first receiver without the outside binding posts from which we used to receive electric shocks, and Kellogg receiver shells as now made are practically unbreakable.

Today in this country, there are over seven hundred Kellogg switchboards in use in the larger towns and cities, and many thousands of magneto boards in the smaller towns and villages, giving a service acknowledged the best available anywhere with a low first cost and great saving in maintenance.

The Kellogg Company has been in the front rank in producing equipment of the very latest types and to meet the latest demands, but has been free, as stated, to follow the requirements of the public, unhampered by excessive standardization. The Kellogg Service switchboard in the largest size exchange has every advantage of any system now in use, doing away with all of the disadvantages, handicaps and expensive operation of other types.

The Kellogg Company believes in furnishing the very best apparatus based on public demand, and at the lowest cost consistent with sound business principles. The history of the growth and success of the Kellogg Company brings out the wisdom of this policy. Kellogg telephones and switchboards are standard and can be used with any operating system.

In the Kellogg factory on the West Side are maintained standard stocks of telephones and switchboards, available for immediate or prompt shipments, whether for Chicago, or Troy, Ohio or the Argentine, or the farthest point on the globe. Many important cities in South America and abroad are Kellogg equipped.

On every Kellogg advertisement appears the words, "Use is the test." Kellogg users believe in it.

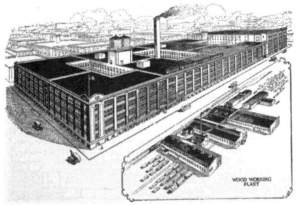

KELLOGG SWITCHBOARD & SUPPLY COMPANY, CHICAGO

BENJAMIN F. MIESSNER

BENJAMIN FRANKLIN MIESSNER, president of the Miessner Inventions Corporation and director of phonographic research laboratory for Brunswick-Balke-Collender Co., was born in Huntingburg, Ind.; s. of Mary (Reutepohler) and Charles Miessner; ed. in Huntingburg schs., U. S. Naval Electrical Sch., Brooklyn, N. Y., 1912; Harvard Univ., 1912; Purdue Univ., 1916. Married Eleanor Marguerite Schulz, Buffalo, N. Y., 1916. Children: Jane Eleanor, Mary Elizabeth. Radio operator and later chief, U. S. Naval Radio Station, Washington, 1908-11; radio engineer, associated with John Hays Hammond, Jr., 1911-12; assistant to Fritz Lowenstein, consulting radio engineer, New York; expert radio aide to Navy Department, 1916-17; radio research work for Emil J. Simon, New York, 1917-20; director of laboratories, Brunswick-Balke-Collender Co. since 1920. Mr. Miessner has contributed a number of highly important radio, airplane and phonographic conventions. With D. Van Nostrand, he is the author of "Radio Dynamics." Mem. Am. Physical Soc., Am. Soc. for Advancement of Science. Clubs: Purdue (Chicago). Home: 5937 Magnolia av. Office: 623 S. Wabash av.

174

AUTOMATIC ELECTRIC COMPANY

THIRTY years ago, A. B. Strowger, an amateur inventor, decided to create a telephone system that would operate without "Hello girls." Today the Automatic Telephone he dreamed of is being adopted throughout this country, and America will bid farewell to its telephone operators as soon as this modern equipment can be installed.

Prompted primarily by a business loss, the blame for which was laid to a telephone operator's mistake, Strowger worked over his crude plans and models and dreamed of the time when telephone users would no longer have to endure wrong numbers, and slow connections.

This was more than thirty years ago. One day Strowger met the one man who could make this dream come true—Joseph Harris, a Chicago business man. Young and daring, Mr. Harris examined the home-made model, and was interested.

Mr. Harris induced a leading firm of electrical contractors in the East to investigate the possibilities of this idea, which was already being called the "Automatic Telephone" and the man chosen to make the study was A. E. Keith.

Mr. Keith came, he saw, and was conquered by the idea. He plunged at once into the task of overcoming the enormous technical difficulties that stood in the way of making Strowger's dream a reality. For months he worked with incredible concentration and gradually with the help of a staff of engineers the apparatus destined to make telephoning perfect took shape.

Meanwhile, Mr. Harris with equal devotion to purpose, was marshalling capital and building a manufacturing and selling organization for this creation. This organization grew and expanded. Affiliated companies were established abroad, and today the manufacture of Automatic Telephone equipment has become one of the world's great industries, commanding thousands of men and millions of capital.

Engineers and experts from Europe have come to America to study this Automatic Telephone system. Foreign governments have adopted it in their networks. Exchanges have been and are being built in Great Britain, France, Germany, Australia, Austria, Canada, India. Cities like Havana, Honolulu, Manila, Harbin (Manchuria), Sydney (Australia), Simla (India) are now using the dial.

Year after year the fame of the Automatic Telephone has spread and still those who have created and developed it, look forward to the day when it will be used universally. The greatest telephone operating organizations in all parts of the United States have announced that just as soon as possible, the Dial is going to take the place of the telephone girl, first in the larger cities, New York, Chicago, Philadelphia, Detroit, Boston, Cleveland and San Francisco, and later in the smaller centers.

Mr. Harris was president of Automatic Electric Company from 1901 until June, 1919. Since that time, he has been continuing his activities as chairman of the board of directors. Harmon A. Harris, his son, who for many years was active in promoting the sale of Automatic equipment, is now vice-president and general manager. Other officers are A. F. Adams, president, and H. L. Gary, vice-president and treasurer.

JOHN CONRADES WAHL

JOHN CONRADES WAHL, inventor and first vice president of Wahl Co., was born on a farm near Morrisonville, Feb. 7, 1876; s. of Mary (Meister) and Conrad Wahl. Twenty-eight years later he was building his epoch marking adding and subtracting attachment to the Remington Typewriter, so that those machines were ready for use and sale in 1907. The interim until incorporation of the Wahl Adding Machine Co. had brought him 8 years of intensive shop experience at Peoria, St. Louis, Chicago. In 1915 Wahl Co. took over a controlling interest in the Eversharp Mechanical Pencil which had been marketed by a corporation at Bloomington. Besides some dozens of patents and applications bearing on pencils, fountain pens and their production, Mr. Wahl enlarged the mechanical resources of the Adding Machine by two dozen patents before its outright sale to the Remington Co. in 1920. He was married to June Estabrook in 1897, at Taylorville. They have one son, J. Estabrook. Mr. Wahl was awarded the John Scott Legacy's medal and premium by City of Philadelphia in 1915. Same year, he won the Industrial Medal of the Panama-Pacific Exposition at San Francisco. Office: 1800 Roscoe St.

BRUNSWICK-BALKE-COLLENDER COMPANY

B RUNSWICK-BALKE-COLLANDER COMPANY, one of the most widely diversified manufacturing concerns in the country, was founded in 1845 by John M. Brunswick in Cincinnati. At its inception, the company manufactured only billiard tables and a few of the incidentals.

In 1859, Mr. Brunswick formed a partnership with his brother, and the firm was operated under the name of Brunswick Brothers, with branch houses in St. Louis and Chicago.

This was followed by the entry into the company of Julius Balke, of Cincinnati. With the new addition, the corporate name was again changed, this time to J. M. Brunswick and Balke Company. In 1872, it was incorporated under the same name and in 1880, it was consolidated with the H. W. Collender Company, of New York and Stamford, Conn.

Capital stock was then increased to $1,500,000. The rising volume of business necessitated in 1907 an increase in capital to $12,000,000, of which $6,000,000 was preferred stock and the balance common stock. At about the same time, the company started the manufacture of hard rubber goods and billiard table cushions. The manufacture of phonographs was added in 1914 and automobile tires in 1917.

But the figures tell only a half of the company's story. Its growth to a $12,000,000 corporation, manufacturing three distinct sets of products, did not come overnight. It came, first, through manufacture of a product that was unexcelled in America; second the company's confidence in the superiority in its product; third, a keen selling force and fourth, application of conservative business principles.

As it forged ahead in the manufacture of billiard tables, cues and balls, so is it gaining recognition in the manufacture of automobile tires and phonographs.

Through its gifts, the educational and recreational benefits of billiards have been taught to Americans and the United States has wrested practically all of the billiard championships from Europe. Under its direction, many of the championship billiard and pocket-billiard events have been staged in America.

The company has manufacturing plants at Chicago, Muskegon, Mich.; Dubuque, Ia.; Rockford, Ill.; Long Island City, L. I.; Jersey City, N. J.; Knoxville, Tenn.; Toronto, Ont.; Buenos Aires and Paris, France. It also has branch houses in all of the leading cities of the United States.

The executive force consists of B. E. Bensinger, Chicago, president; B. H. Brunswick, Cincinnati first vice-president; Julius Balke, Chicago, second vice-president; H. F. Davenport, Chicago, secretary; J. C. Schank, Chicago, treasurer and P. L. Deutsch, Chicago, assistant secretary and assistant treasurer.

The concern has always been a closed corporation, as the common stock has been held almost exclusively by the heirs of the founders, their relations and the officers and employees.

THOMAS CHARLES RUSSELL

THOMAS CHARLES RUSSELL, president of the Russell Electric company, was born in Midland, South Dakota, in 1887. His preparatory education was received in the public schools of Evanston, Illinois, High School at Paw Paw, Michigan, later entering the Liberal Arts College of Northwestern University, where he was graduated in 1911, with the degree of B. S. In 1916, he was married to Mabel L. Chittick, of Oak Park, Ill. Children: Thomas Charles, Jr., and Howard Chittick. Following his graduation from Northwestern, Mr. Russell decided to engage in the electrical business, which had always fascinated him. He organized the Russell Electric company, manufacturing "Hold Heat" appliances. The company's products have enjoyed a wide sale. Mr. Russell is a Republican. Member of Psi Kappa Psi fraternity. His home is in Evanston. Office: 340 W. Huron street.

178

WESTERN CLOCK COMPANY

IN 1886, a Connecticut clockmaker drifted into La Salle, Ill. He came only with an idea, a quick, accurate, low-priced method of assembling clock wheels. Added to this he had a stanch faith in it. He believed in the value of his idea and was looking about for others who would believe with him. He thought best to try it on the adventurous spirits of the middle West.

Once in La Salle, he organized a company for the manufacture of alarm clocks by means of his new process. His associates were chiefly workingmen, unaccustomed to the financial management of manufacturing concerns. He himself was not a practical clockmaker. He had specialized mainly on wheels.

Combine inexperience in manufacturing and ignorance of finances and the enterprise is almost certain to go the way of other failures.

The group of workingmen found that the business of running the affairs of the plant was not all that they had hoped. Most of them were glad to sell out their stock at a very low figure; some even gave away their holdings to be relieved of a financial liability.

This is a brief sketch of the events that preceded the organization of the Western Clock Company. The stock of the defunct company was taken over by a group of men who had not only the necessary training in watchmaking but also a sufficient amount of cash. They also had faith in their ability to work out problems.

And so the factory started up again. One store in La Salle used to sell the entire factory output; then production was increased, and fifty clocks were turned out each day. At this time the little band of clockmakers set two hundred clocks a day as their ultimate ambition.

With the improvement in production, with strong financial support, with years of manufacturing experience to guide it, the young concern soon began its steady climb to the top. The youngest clock company in America, the only one west of the Hudson river, yet it is the largest manufacturer of alarm clocks in the world.

The Western Clock Company today employs more than two thousand people and its daily output is fifteen thousand clocks. Its clocks are well known and admired in Canada, South America, South Africa, Australia, Mexico, Great Britain and Japan as they are in the United States.

Its auxiliary companies are the Western Clock Manufacturing Company, of New York City, which is located at 109 Lafayette St., and the Western Clock Company, 10 S. Wabash Ave., Chicago. Its Canadian sales headquarters and factory are at Peterborough. Besides its La Salle plant, the company maintains another Illinois plant, this one in Peru. The company's offices are in La Salle and its main plant is in Peru, Illinois.

179

CHARLES ARTHUR TILT

CHARLES ARTHUR TILT, president of Diamont T. Motor Car Co., was born in Chicago, June 28, 1877; s. of Sarah Bowes (Thompson) and Joseph Edward Tilt. Received ed. in Chicago Pub. Schs. In 1896 he began his business career in his father's shoe factory. Later he was made salesman and in 1901 he was acting gen. mgr. In 1903 he become mgr. of a large stock farm at Beloit, Wis., but remained here only a year. He then became sales mgr. for Mr. Knight, inventor of Knight Silent Motor for autos. The year following (1905) he began business for himself as builder of passenger cars. In 1910 he built his first Diamond T. Truck which since become universally famous. Married Agnes Josephine Morgan in Chicago, Nov. 5, 1902. Children: Margaret and Mary. Clubs: Chicago Athletic, Chicago Yacht, Edgewater Golf. Office: 4517 W. 26th St. Home: 2064 Pratt Blvd.

DIAMOND T MOTOR CAR COMPANY

THE Diamond T Motor Car Company has been in the business of manufacturing high grade passenger cars and commercial motor trucks continuously since 1905. About the year 1911, the manufacture of passenger cars was discontinued and the concern devoted entirely to the manufacture of motor trucks. This company was the first to exhibit a 1½-2 ton worm drive truck, the exhibition being made in Chicago in 1913.

Up to 1915, C. A. Tilt, the president of the present company, was the sole proprietor of the business, but in November of that year the company was incorporated, and the business which had been confined to Chicago and the adjacent territory, was considerably extended by the execution of contracts with automobile distributors in the larger centers throughout the country, and the Diamond T Motor Car Company became a national concern. Its business grew rapidly until early in the year 1917 it became necessary to take steps to provide for greater production. Early in 1917, plans were drawn for the erection of a new factory building and the company moved into the new plant (its present location) in May of that year.

The new plant covered approximately ten acres, including double switch-tracks. loading platform, and over 100,000 square feet floor space devoted to assembly and allied departments. It also provided a machine shop, test, paint, and service departments, and a power plant equipped with high pressure boilers, and an adequate administration building.

The plant was designed according to the ideas of the company's officials and laid out especially for the systematic and progressive assembly of heavy truck units in quantity.

It thus came about that when in the later months of 1917 the Government started an investigation to ascertain what plants were available for quantity production of standardized Class B military trucks, this company was in an unusually favored position to accept and properly take care of contracts for the production of these Government models. In November, 1917, the War Department sent a representative to inspect and report on the condition and facilities available in the plant. As a result of the report made by this inspector and the fairness of the company's bids, contracts were awarded for over 1,200 Class B standardized military trucks. An additional contract for 2,000 trucks was awarded, but was cancelled on the signing of the armistice.

During the war, the company supplied the War and Navy Departments with considerable quantities of its regular standard models of Diamond T trucks, and in the meantime, continued its regular commercial production.

To provide for its growing business, an addition to the plant was built to permit of the extension of the machine shop and the installation of automatic machinery, and for the purpose of confining its manufacturing operations within its own plant property and to permit of thorough testing, of the trucks before shipment, the company also constructed a concrete testing track of one-third mile in length.

An additional building of 56,000 square feet was also constructed to take care of special equipment, testing and painting departments, so that at the present time the company occupies a plant area of about thirteen acres, with approximately 200,000 feet under roof.

The company's success and progress has been based largely upon the fact that for seventeen years it has been operated under one management carrying into actual practice ideals of standardization and of service that have always proven of first importance to truck users.

No radical changes have at any time been made in design, although the company's production has continually kept pace with the improvement in engine and other unit design. "Service" has been the watchword, and it is the company's firmly established policy to enter no field of distribution in which service cannot be adequately rendered to the truck operator.

CHARLES S. RIEMAN

WHEN, at the age of eighteen, Charles S. Rieman came to Chicago, he had no idea he would become president of the largest automobile company in the city—the Elgin Motor Car Corporation—in addition to controlling three other large successful companies.

He was only a boy, with neither friends nor money, but he brought with him something that is worth infinitely more—an unshakable belief that if he would think long enough and hard enough and work long enough and hard enough, he could accomplish anything he wished.

His indefatigable energy, plus his willingness to think hard and work hard, is directly responsible for the remarkable growth of the Elgin Motor Car Corporation. Starting in a humble way, in less than four years, Mr. Rieman built up this company until it became the largest manufacturer of motor cars in the country's second city.

Charles S. Rieman was born Sept. 5, 1878, at Monticello, Ill. His mother's family, the Bonds, descended from English, Welsh and French forbears, were prominent patriots in revolutionary days and later pioneers in the development of the Middle West.

Bond county, Ill., was named after Shadrach Bond, first governor of Illinois and his grandfather's uncle. Other ancestors took an active part in making early history of Illinois and were prominent in the development of the Illinois Central Railroad as well as other enterprises in the state.

On his father's side Mr. Rieman's ancestry dates back to sturdy old Baron von Riemann of Berlin, prominent in German political and financial affairs of his day.

Mr. Rieman is an earnest and hard working supporter of movements for civic improvement. A living exemplification of Chicago's "I Will" spirit, he has visions of a bigger and more beautiful Chicago and contributes liberally of his time and money to make those dreams come true.

Active management of a large motor car corporation, coupled with the duties involved in the control of three other large companies, would be more than most men would care to undertake. But not so with Mr. Rieman.

In recognition of Mr. Rieman's activities in advancing Chicago's interests in aircraft, he was elected president of the Chicago Aeronautical Bureau, an organization formed to make Chicago first in the manufacture of aircraft and in the operation of air transportation lines. With Mr. Rieman's resourcefulness and driving power directed to the problem, Chicago seems destined to become the dominating center of aircraft activities in America.

Men who know Charles S. Rieman, still a comparatively young man, predict that what he has accomplished is only the beginning of a great career. Yet, with all his success, he is the same quiet, unassuming individual as when he came to Chicago seeking a position. He has never forgotten his early struggles and is always willing to lend a helping hand to the other fellow.

Mr. Rieman, who is a Shriner and 32nd Degree Mason, a member of the Society of Automotive Engineers and a charter member of the Aero Club of America, is also a member of the following clubs: South Shore Country; Chicago Yacht; Hamilton Club; Illinois Athletic; Olympic Fields Country.

WESTERN WAREHOUSING COMPANY

WESTERN WAREHOUSING COMPANY PLANT
Polk Street Terminal, Pennsylvania System

LOCATED in downtown Chicago is a mammoth establishment that is coming to be known nationally as one of the big traffic assets of this city. For a long time Chicago has been recognized by manufacturers as a logical distributing center for their products, and they have always been keenly alive to any facility developed here that will permit them to get their products to their customers in Chicago and the Middle West with a minimum of cost.

This facility is now provided in the immense plant of the Western Warehousing Company at the Pennsylvania Railroad's Polk street freight terminal. Half a million square feet of floor space is available here for merchants and manufacturers maintaining stocks in Chicago.

Some idea of its size may be gained when one realizes that beneath the structure there is track space for 360 cars, 18 tracks of 20 cars each. It is operated in conjunction with the Polk street freight terminal of the Pennsylvania System—upon the edge of the "Loop." The warehouse and freight station are served by thirty-six electric elevators, varying in capacity from 5 to 10 tons. Electric tractors provide inter-warehouse and station rapid transit and prompt service to customers.

It has a direct connection with the Chicago Tunnel, and in addition to this outgoing service, reshipments are made over the Pennsylvania System or any other System, East or West, without necessity of trucking. The insurance rate on contents is very low.

It was to reduce distribution costs that the plant of the Western Warehousing Company was constructed. It is no longer necessary for out-of-town manufacturers to rent off-track space and attend to the detail of distribution, with their heavy overhead costs. Forward-looking manufacturers simply establish their sales representative in a loop office and have him spend his time making sales. The stocks from which the sales representative draws for immediate delivery to his Chicago customers or for reshipment to out-of-town buyers are consigned in carloads to the warehouse company, received on its 44-car capacity tracks at the Pennsylvania freight station, stored on its spacious floors, and delivered or reshipped on the orders of the sales representative.

The economy consists in the fact that merchandise is here stored and handled on a per-package basis, and a manufacturer pays for space only as he uses it, instead of for a portion of leased space often only partially occupied.

Officers of the Western Warehousing Company are: J. G. Rodgers, Chicago, president; William Hodgdon, Chicago, vice-president; J. J. Turner, Pittsburgh, vice-president; S. H. Church, Pittsburgh, secretary; T. H. B. McKnight, Pittsburgh, treasurer; J. W. Orr, Pittsburgh, auditor; Wilson V. Little, Chicago, superintendent. Directors are: J. G. Rodgers, William Hodgdon, J. J. Turner, W. H. Johnson, T. H. B. McKnight.

EDWARD C. HEGELER

NOTABLE among Illinois leaders was Edward C. Hegeler, who, with Frederick C. Matthiessen, established the first zinc works in America. Through his unceasing efforts, La Salle, Ill., has grown from a sprawling village to a model little city. His benefactions opened new paths for the study of monist, psychological and theological problems. In 1887, Mr. Hegeler founded the Open Court Publishing Co., an institution devoted to the discussion of religious and psychological problems, and in 1890, he launched a quarterly, "The Monist." In 1910, he died. A more complete story of Mr. Hegeler's life will be found on the next page.

184

EDWARD C. HEGELER

DEEPLY stamped on the pages of Illinois history is the name of Edward C. Hegeler, manufacturer, scientist, philanthropist and inventor. His record of achievements to help found on the rolling savannas of Illinois a great educational and industrial commonwealth extended over a half-century. Death wrote "Finis" on his career in 1910.

Mr. Hegeler was born in Bremen, Germany, in 1835. In his education, he specialized in mining and mechanical engineering at the University of Bremen. The university welded a strong friendship between Mr. Hegeler and Frederick W. Matthiessen, a fellow student, that lasted until their deaths.

One little incident or contact has been known to alter a man's life. In the case of Mr. Matthiessen and Mr. Hegeler, it was the letters from friends, telling of the great natural resources of America that were still unplumbed, that caused them to abandon plans for careers in Germany. In 1857, after a tour of the continent, they sailed from England and landed in Boston in March. While they were debating as to which section of the country afforded the most opportunities for mining engineers, they learned of Friedensville, Pa. Here a zinc factory had been built, but it stood idle because the owners had been unable to manufacture zinc. Mr. Matthiessen and Mr. Hegeler, stepped in and with the same furnace succeeded in producing spelter, then pioneer work in America, for previously the metal had been imported from Europe.

Hard pressed for funds by the depression of 1856, which still persisted in 1857, the owners of the Friedensville work refused to put any more money into the enterprise. Neither did Mr. Matthiessen and Mr. Hegeler feel justified in risking their own capital, mainly because they had no confidence in the mine. Their suspicion of the mine's value was confirmed eight years later, when it actually gave out.

Followed a year or two of roving for the two students, during which they investigated the zinc possibilities of several middle west states. In Wisconsin, they found suitable ore. In Illinois, they found an abundance of coal. They decided that it would be more profitable to bring the ore to the coal, as it requires two tons of coal for the production of one ton of zinc, and so they settled at the base of their coal supply, which was La Salle, Illinois. Here they started the famous Matthiessen and Hegeler Zinc Works.

The works began on a small scale, but in a comparatively short time the working force was increased from a few employees to about 1,000 men and the modest plant developed into one of the most modernly equipped smelters in the Middle West. Today, the Matthiessen and Hegeler Zinc Company mines its own coal for producing zinc and its zinc and numerous by-products, including sulphuric acid, the manufacture of which was started in 1882, are used not only in the United States but also in many remote quarters of the world.

Mr. Hegeler's cheerfulness permeated the institution and won for him the esteem of his workers. Capable management, unfaltering enterprise and a spirit of justice marked the business career of Hegeler. He carefully systematized the firm in all departments, avoiding needless expenditures of time, material and labor.

His personality was that of a man of great force. He was ever ready to aid the distressed, to watch over the interests of the unfortunate and to accord the laborer his full hire. Mr. Hegeler held memberships in a number of famous organizations, including the American Institute of Mining Engineers, the Chicago Press Club and the Art Institute of Chicago.

Unlike the average engineer, who is only concerned with the science of materialism, Mr. Hegeler engaged in a deep study of religious and psychological problems of the day. In 1887, he founded the Open Court Publishing Company, which has opened up new vistas of thought to students of religion and science and which has provided an outlet for their beliefs. Dr. Paul Carus, noted publicist and son-in-law of Mr. Hegeler, was placed at the head of the company, and he still retains that post.

The purpose of this institution is the free and full discussion of the religious and psychological questions on the principle that the scientific world-conception should be applied to religion. Mr. Hegeler believed in science, but he wished to preserve the religious spirit with all its serious endeavor, and in this sense he pleaded for the establishment of a religion of science and a science of religion. Dualism he rejected as an unscientific and untenable view and accepted monism upon the basis of exact science. For the discussion of the more recondite and weightier problems of science and religion, he founded a quarterly, "The Monist," in October, 1890.

Although a very wealthy man, Mr. Hegeler lived quietly and simply and he was one who looked upon himself as a trustee holding his worldly possessions for the best benefit of all.

Among the numerous contributions he made to the world were important scientific discoveries and improvements, the result of investigations and experiments by himself and his associate, Mr. Matthiessen. Many of their discoveries were embodied in patents for inventions taken out jointly in the names of both.

CENTURY RUBBER WORKS

THE record of the Century Rubber Works, manufacturing "Century Cord" and "Century Fabric" tires, is in high mileage figures. The company's tires have come to be known throughout the nation for their longevity, for their ruggedness, for their durability and ability to stand up under the most exacting of usages. Yet the tires possess a certain lightness that makes for speed.

Three plys, and sometimes more, of the best rubber fabric that South America affords go into the making of a single tire. For trucks, the Century Rubber Works manufactures a heavy duty pneumatic tire that is seldom equalled in service.

The company has enjoyed a steady climb in business since its organization in 1912. Receipts for 1921 were $2,750,000. The rise in business has necessitated the establishment of branch houses at St. Paul, Minneapolis, Milwaukee, Los Angeles, Kansas City and Pittsburg and it is planning to open several more branches in the next year.

Charles J. Venn is president and treasurer and to him and George W. Wheatley, vice president, and Henry L. Venn, secretary, goes a large measure of the credit for the company's success. General offices and main plant are located at 54th avenue and 18th street, Cicero.

CHARLES DICKINSON

CHARLES DICKINSON, seed merchant and aviator, was born in Chicago, May 28, 1858; s. of Albert F. and Ann Eliza (Anthony) Dickinson; ed. Chicago High Sch., Chicago, Med. Coll., Harvey Med. Coll.; m. Chicago, Sept. 29, 1897, Marie I. Boyd (widow). Children: William T., Margaret F., Henry J., Louis M. and Gordon. In 1872, joined brother, Albert Dickinson, in their father's business; incorporated 1888 as Albert Dickinson Co., wholesale grass and field seeds, of which he was vice pres. until he retired in 1920, to make flying his work and play. He had two of the first phonographs in Chicago, 1889-90; had one of first automobiles, 1897. Made first flight as passenger with Graham White at Belmont Park, L. I., N. Y., in 1910. Made "solo" flight Feb., 1921, when 63 years old. Broke air record with five persons, Chicago to New York, Nov. 25, 1921, with Eddie Stinson as pilot—non-stop in same day. Author of pages on "Aircraft" and "Good of Humankind," in "Economist" of Chicago. Vice pres. and trustee Chicago Acad. Sci., Iroquois Mem. Hosp.; member Chicago Board of Trade since 1879, N. Y. Prod. Exchange, Minneapolis C. of C., Duluth Bd. of Trade, St. Louis C. of C. Mem. Soc. of Friends (Quakers). Mem. Citizens' Assn. of Chicago. Mem. Chicago Assn. Commerce. Clubs: Union League, South Shore Country Club, Chicago Athletic, Aero Club of Ill. (pres. 7th term), Adventurers, New York Club, Railway Transportation, Lotos, Aero Club of America (New York). Residence: Union League Club and Blackstone Hotel.

C. S. PETERSON

CHARLES S. PETERSON, head of the third largest printing company west
of New York, is one of the few Americans of Swedish extraction who hold
that much-coveted decoration, Nordstjerneorden (The Order of the North
Star). It was presented to him in 1920 by King Gustaf of Sweden in recognition
of his great contributions for the advancement of Swedish art and literature in the
United States. The annual Swedish-American Art Exhibitions, held in the
Swedish Club of Chicago, were inaugurated by Mr. Peterson. His aid has also
enabled the Swedish-American Foundation to have translated into English the best
of modern Swedish literature.

[A more complete story of Mr. Peterson's career will be found on the opposite page.]

PETERSON LINOTYPING CO.

CHAS. S. PETERSON, one of the leading Swedish-American citizens in Chicago, was born in Daglosen, Sweden, August 29, 1873. After attending the Jacob Collegiate School in Stockholm, Mr. Peterson at the age of 14 came to Chicago, where he was first employed on the Swedish weekly newspaper, "Hemlandet." In 1888, he went West, and returned to Chicago in 1895.

In 1899 he organized the Peterson Linotyping Company. Before long the company had developed into the largest concern of its kind in the West. This position it still maintains in spite of the keen competition in that particular field. In 1908 Mr. Peterson acquired an interest in the Regan Printing House at 523-537 Plymouth place. Finally, in 1915, he bought the entire Regan Printing plant and the G. D. Steere bindery, together with the building in which these concerns were located, thereby becoming the sole owner of one of the largest printing and bindery establishments in Chicago, and employing 800 persons. At present it is the third largest printing house west of New York. Mr. Peterson has erected an eleven-story white tile building to house his printing plants.

In 1913 Mr. Peterson was appointed a member of the Board of Education by Mayor Carter H. Harrison, and in 1915 he was reappointed by Mayor William Hale Thompson. He was elected chairman of one of the board's most important committees, the Committee on Finance, which position he held for five years.

As president of the Swedish Club for twelve successive years, Mr. Peterson performed a work that reflects great honor upon his mother country, not only in Chicago but in the United States. The annual Swedish-American Art Exhibitions, the tenth of which was held in December, 1921, were inaugurated by Mr. Peterson. At these exhibitions, Swedish-American artists from all over the country have been represented, a number of prizes awarded, and many paintings sold.

Mr. Peterson was one of the organizers of the Swedish Choral Club of Chicago and is its president. In 1920 he took the club with its one hundred members for a tour of Sweden. He also sent an exhibit of Swedish-American art to Sweden and contributed the entire cost of the exhibit. He is a member of the Chicago Art Institute, the Chicago Athletic Association, the Press Club, the South Shore Country Club, the Lincoln Club, Bankers' Club, Hamilton Club, Cliff Dwellers, Arts Club, Municipal Art League, the Swedish Club, the Norske Klub, and is an honorary member of the Swedish National Association of Chicago and honorary president of the Swedish Glee Club.

In the American-Scandinavian Foundation, which has its headquarters in New York, Mr. Peterson is a trustee. His aid has enabled the Foundation to have translated into English the best of modern Swedish literature. Mr. Peterson is vice president of the Swedish Chamber of Commerce of the United States and chairman of its Advisory Committee for Chicago and the West.

During the war, Mr. Peterson raised a company of the Volunteer Training Corps (Company M, 1st Regiment), and was its captain.

In 1920, on the occasion of the Swedish Choral Club's memorable trip through Sweden, Mr. Peterson was decorated by King Gustaf with Nordstjerneorden (The Order of the North Star).

Mr. Peterson financed the Master School of the Bush Conservatory. He has taken a prominent part in charitable work, being co-chairman with Judge Olson in the Augustana Hospital drive, chairman of the drive for the Denver Sanatorium, and is at present chairman of the drive to raise $200,000 for the Swedish Societies Old Peoples' Home in Evanston.

NELSON BLACKWELL UPDIKE

NELSON BLACKWELL UPDIKE, grain merchant and publisher of Omaha, Neb., Bee, was born in Pennington, N. J., Dec. 2, 1871; son of Mary (Stout) and Edward Updike; ed. in Harvard, Neb., pub. schs. At 18, he became asst. cashier of Union State Bank of Harvard. Later being made cashier. He married Metta Babcock, June 12, 1895. Children: Hazel Updike Reasoner, Nelson Blackwell, Jr. After his marriage Mr. Updike purchased a grain elevator at Eldorado, Neb., and in a few years owned a string of country elevators. Moved offices to Omaha in 1899, incorporating the Updike Grain Company. Corporation was dissolved in 1917 and Mr. Updike became sole owner of the business. In 1920 he bought the Omaha Bee Publishing Co. He is president of Standard Timber Co., and Updike Grain Co. of Chicago; secy. of Woods-Updike Land Co., director of Updike Lumber and Coal Co. Vice-president, Nebraska div., Council of State of Great Lakes-St. Lawrence Tydewater Assn. Member Advisory Board of the War Finance Corporation. Clubs: Omaha, Omaha Athletic, Omaha Country, Chicago Athletic. Office: 625 Omaha Grain Exchange, 140 W. Van Buren St., Chicago. Home: 3614 Jackson St., Omaha.

190

BUTLER AND PAPER

ON October 9, 1871, the only newspaper issued in Chicago was the Daily Journal. It was literally published in the midst of the great Chicago fire. From the Butler Paper Company, the Journal secured a supply of print paper which had not been damaged, fortunately, and thus its famous "extra" was made possible and its record of continuous publication remained unbroken.

"Butler" has always meant paper—when it was needed, as it was needed and the kind that was needed.

"Butler" has always meant service—dependable, faithful, understanding service—the kind of service that supplies a need promptly, properly and efficiently.

"Butler" is a name that is closely associated with the production and distribution of paper in the United States. Early in the 19th century, Zebediah Butler, and his son Zebediah, Jr., operated a paper mill in Vermont. It was there that Oliver Morris Butler learned his trade, and there that J. W. Butler was born. In 1841, Oliver Morris Butler established the first paper mill west of Pittsburgh, at St. Charles, Ill. In 1844, the house of Butler was established in Chicago, with J. W. Butler in charge. From that concern has grown the Butler Paper Corporations which, as is seen, touches the entire history of successful paper making and paper distribution in the United States.

The growth of the Butler institution rests upon two fundamentals—quality and service. Butler paper is standardized. It is produced by masters of their craft. Whether it be ordinary news print or the finest of bond paper, it has to conform to Butler standards. Butler service is stabilized. Whether your requirements be a small quantity or a large one, Butler service is at your command and you will be supplied with equal quickness and thoroughness.

Having been through all its years so closely allied with "the fourth estate," the Butler institution takes pleasure in expressing its good will toward its friends of the journalistic profession and assures them of its hearty co-operation in meeting any and all of their needs in paper.

AMERICAN PRINTING INK CO.

WITHIN the confines of Chicago is to be found one of the most modern printing ink plants in the world. It is the plant of the American Printing Ink Company and is located at 2314-24 West Kinzie street.

The American Printing Ink Company, running normally, can produce in its "black" department a quarter of a million pounds of black ink a week. In an emergency, this output can be tripled. The chemical, experimental and research department is kept going at an annual expense mounting into the thousands.

The color department, as is the case with the black department, is equipped with the latest improved machinery. The mills are all of standard size, water cooled—separate motor for each mill—direct connection. Not a belt or pulley is to be found in the plant.

The company came into being in 1897. Today its products go to every country where printing inks are used.

191

WILLIAM HENRY FRENCH

WILLIAM HENRY FRENCH, president of Barnhart Brothers & Spindler, type founders, was born in Greggsville, Ill., May 14, 1850; son of Harriet Newell (Hoyt) and Nathan French. He was educated in Greggsville schools and in Cornell University. In 1896, he married Olive Helen Walter, Chicago. Children: Hazel French Robertson, Walter Hoyt, Vincent Thorne. Mr. French was Chicago agent for Associated Press from 1873 to 1881 and assistant general manager in New York from 1881 to 1884. He was secretary and treasurer of Oak Ranch, Benkleman, Neb., from 1885 to 1911 and secretary of Barnhart Brothers & Spindler from 1887 to 1911, since which time he has been president. He is also secretary and treasurer of Oak Ranch Co., secretary and treasurer of West Suburban Hospital, Oak Park; and director of Transportation Bank, Chicago. Member of Delta Upsilon and Cornell Alumni of New York and Chicago. Clubs: Oak Park Country, Westward Ho Golf, Union League, Executives, City, of Chicago; and City, of New York. Home: 221 S. East av., Oak Park. Office: 719 S. Dearborn street, Chicago.

192

W. F. HALL PRINTING COMPANY

ON January 23, 1893, there was organized and came into being on Plymouth Court, Chicago, what was destined to later become the World's Greatest Printing Plant of Catalogs and Magazines.

From this small beginning the company soon built up a substantial business, which, from its inception over twenty-eight years ago, has continued without interruption to keep pace in the production of high class work in larger volume and at satisfactory prices with each succeeding year.

After eleven years, the company had outgrown its quarters on Plymouth Court, and led the march for a larger location to the new North Central District, in the leasing of a seven-story and basement mill construction building at Kingsbury and Superior Streets, erected and adapted to its special needs. Two years later, the business required an increase in manufacturing space, and a duplicate building adjoining was leased; three years later, the company purchased the adjoining ground and erected a building of its own next adjoining the leased structures at Townsend and Superior Streets. This building and the leased

ROBERT M. EASTMAN

structures form one complete plant. The company also owns a tract of land fronting 340 feet—an entire block—on Chicago Avenue, 130 feet on Townsend and 130 feet on Kingsbury Street, which will be used for further expansion. Today it is generally conceded that W. F. Hall Printing Company is the largest and most up-to-date printing establishment in the world, devoted exclusively to magazine and catalog printing and binding.

The constant development of its physical resources is indicative of the substantial progress of the company, which, steadily increasing in prestige throughout its existence, has placed this organization in a position of leadership where it can and does choose the character of work it handles. It now confines its operations exclusively to the largest and most extensive classes of printing.

Its plant possesses every facility for handling the largest jobs of mail order

EDWIN M. COLVIN

193

catalogs and magazine printing. Approximately 2,000 employees are required for its operation, and it produces on an average of 350,000 pieces of printed matter per day. Those familiar with printing processes will form a conception and value of their equipment from the statement that they own and operate practically to capacity thirty-six of the latest type rotary presses with a capacity of printing over 5,000,000 16-page signatures per day, and thirty-three cylinder presses, thirteen of the latter being equipped to print two colors at once. In binding, covering, trimming and mailing machinery, its equipment is of equal magnitude and productive capacity.

The company is controlled and actively managed by Robert M. Eastman, President, and Edwin M. Colvin, Vice-President, both of whom have large financial interests in the business. These executives have been identified with the business from its inception, and since the death of Mr. W. F. Hall in 1908 they have been in complete charge. Their ability to continue the business successfully and to guide it to even greater success and proportions in the future is best evidenced by its growth under their management, as heretofore outlined.

The executives have surrounded themselves with a highly intensified organization with a view to securing the greatest efficiency and economy of operation and the highest quality of workmanship obtainable. All workmen are thoroughly trained in their particular line, and throughout the entire history of the company, its employees, both skilled and unskilled, have proven themselves exceptionally loyal and reliable.

CHICAGO ROLLER COMPANY

THE Chicago Roller Company has served printing shops and newspapers of the middle west for more than twenty years and has acquired a reputation for being one of the most efficient printers' roller manufacturers in the country.

The company was founded in 1898 by George E. Crane. The superiority of its printers' rollers, compositions, padding glues and pressroom pastes soon become patent to printing firms. The business rapidly expanded, forcing the company to take up larger quarters at 554-570 West Harrison street, Chicago, its present location.

To take care of its fast growing eastern trade, the company opened a plant at 1432-1438 Hamilton ave., Cleveland, O.

George E. Crane is president and treasurer of the company. His associate officers are James Rowe, vice president, and H. A. Bresemann, secretary.

SAM'L BINGHAM'S SON MFG. CO.

SAM'L BINGHAM'S SON MFG. CO. has the distinction of being the largest printer's roller concern in the United States. It was started by Samuel Bingham, in New York City, in 1849.

The company has branch factories and offices in Kansas City, Mo., Des Moines, Minneapolis, Pittsburgh, Indianapolis, St. Louis, Dallas, Atlanta, Cleveland and Springfield, O. The main offices and plant are at 636 Sherman St., Chicago.

THE GOSS PRINTING PRESS COMPANY

THE present state of mechanical perfection as represented in the Goss "High Speed" Straightline Newspaper Press is the result of 35 years of ceaseless effort on the part of one organization.

The daily turning out of thousands of copies of newspapers, printed, folded and even counted in bundles, is often taken for granted. We no more marvel at one machine that can complete 72,000 newspapers per hour than we do when we pick up a telephone receiver and chat with a friend a thousand miles away.

A group of practical printers and experienced business men organized the Goss Printing Press Company of Chicago in 1885 for the purpose of building printing presses. The start was made with a press printing four-page and eight-page newspapers with a capacity of 6,000 papers per hour. But it speaks well for the high grade workmanship and the splendid design of these first machines that most of them are still in operation and daily serving some small newspaper. Shortly after came the perfection of presses in two, three, four or more decks, printing from the same number of rolls of paper at one end and with the folding mechanism on the other and the webs of paper traveling between the two ends in a straightline. This became a patented feature that gave great popularity to the Goss press. The Goss "Straightline" Press was soon found in every state in the Union and in many foreign countries. At that time the maximum number of papers that could be completed by any press in an hour was 24,000.

In 1910 the Goss Printing Press Company's engineers invented the "High Speed" folding mechanism which made it possible to print 36,000 papers per hour, or an increase of 50 per cent of that of any other folder then constructed.

The company has offices in New York City and London. Officers of the company are George A. Eddy, president; M. L. Redfield, vice-president; M. W. Brueshaber, second vice-president; G. C. Abbott, secretary; H. Fankboner, treasurer.

THE GOSS "HIGH SPEED STRAIGHTLINE" OCTUPLE PRESS

195

CHARLES R. MURRAY

THE great growth of the Barnhart Brothers & Spindler, one of the largest type-making organizations in the world, has come under the leadership of Charles R. Murray, general manager and treasurer. In 1911 he initiated the plan of reorganization by which the manufacturing departments were separated from the Chicago local selling organization.

Mr. Murray has been with Barnhart Brothers & Spindler for more than thirty-four years. In fact, he was never with any other concern. He started with the organization in a minor capacity and by dint of hard work advanced himself to his present position.

Mr. Murray's father was with Barnhart Brothers & Spindler before him, as superintendent of the foundry, and the advice he gave his son was to get a job with the right people and stick to it. This was advice in which he himself believed, as he had held only two jobs in his life. The story of the rise of Barnhart Brothers & Spindler will be found on the next page.

196

BARNHART BROTHERS & SPINDLER

BARNHART BROTHERS & SPINDLER has inaugurated a new policy in the development of type designs, borders and decorative material for typography. Abandoning the once universal type foundry practice of designing such products within the foundry—where the work usually was handled by mechanics—Barnhart Brothers & Spindler now searches the art world for designs.

Ample testimony as to the wisdom of this policy can be found in the growth of the company, which in the past six years has trebled its business. The oldest type foundry in the country without change of name, the company was founded in 1868 and re-incorporated in 1911, with a capital of $3,000,000. Its officers today are W. H. French, president; Charles R. Murray, general manager and treasurer, and E. W. Conable, secretary.

The unparalleled rise of advertising has created an able class of letter and decorative designers in this country, who produce special work to order for large advertisers. They are producing typographic work of new and original tendencies, embodying character of the best periods and adapted to modern requirements.

The type foundry must exercise keen judgment in the selection of the designer and his designs. That the Barnhart Brothers & Spindler foundry affords this ability is evidenced in the fact that its productions of recent years have enjoyed great vogue. Its newer type faces have the added distinction of having been produced by artists of established reputation among advertising professionals and prominent printing craftsmen.

With its present foundry at Monroe and Throop streets, Chicago, for its nucleus, Barnhart Brothers & Spindler has developed into a world-wide commercial organization, with nine branches and many dealers in this country and throughout the world.

The company's sales have doubled the past four years and trebled during the past six years. This is largely the result of the firm's progressive policy in increasing the variety and extent of its manufactured products and by enlargement of the selling organization.

Its products include superior copper-mixed type, borders, ornaments and brass rules, steel chases, brass galleys, leads and slugs, saw-trimmers, metal furnaces, and divers other specialties and tools for printers.

A universal demand has sprung up for the products of Barnhart Brothers & Spindler. Markets have been organized in Canada, England, India, Australia, New Zealand, China, Japan, France, Egypt, Ireland, Philippines, South and Central America, Africa, Mexico, West and East Indies, and still further trade outlets are to be developed.

Its Sales and Service houses are located in Chicago, Washington, D. C., St. Louis, Kansas City, Dallas, Omaha, St. Paul, Seattle, and Vancouver, B. C., Canada.

The company is also a merchant for many other manufacturers of printing plant equipment, its branch houses and dealer organization serving as the marketing channel for a complete line of presses and printers machinery of all kinds, steel and wood cabinet outfits, printing and binding materials and supplies.

CONGRESS HOTEL AND ANNEX

YOU cannot enter the Congress hotel, Chicago's famous hostelry, without sensing an atmosphere as welcome as it is intriguing. You relax. The inner man expands. Care vanishes. In the witching hour before dinner, you feel an invisible bond of union between you and the other guests about you.

It is inevitable. The inclusive hospitality of this world-famous hotel endears him who visits it for the first as unfailingly as the veteran guest. That intangible something cannot be bought; it is given everyone who regards the Congress as his Chicago home.

JOHN BURKE
Managing Director

Mention of the Congress stirs visions of Peacock Alley, the most-widely known hotel promenade in America. In the celebrities who trod it, in the air of camaraderie that hangs over it and in the splendor of its settings, it is faintly reminiscent of the leading casinos on the Riviera. It is truly cosmopolitan. It is the one place in Chicago where the world makes its rendezvous.

The richness of its furnishings and settings does not detract from the atmosphere of real hospitality and homelike comfort and content which seem to be indigenous to the Congress hotel. There is no affected service; it is unobtrusive, quiet and considerate. That intangible something which makes for a closer union of guests cannot be purchased.

The Congress is also distinguished for four of its rooms, the Pompeian room, the Elizabethan room and Louis XVI room, and the gold room. These are all beautiful spots to conjure with. The composite art of Pompeii on the arc of the Bay of Naples and in the shadow of Vesuvius has been faithfully reproduced in the Pompeian Room and seems to share in style the majestic columns of the Temple of Apollo, tinted blood red and gold. It is all reminiscent of the fierce tribal wars of Pompeii and the sad eruption of Mt. Vesuvius. in which a whole countryside was laid to waste and thousands killed.

Mrs. Honore Palmer was recently heard to say that in beauty and breadth of concept the Elizabethan room was unexcelled by anything of its kind in Europe. Coming from Mrs. Palmer, this stands as a high testimonial to the Congress hotel and the designers of the room, as Mrs. Palmer not only holds an enviable place in the social domain but is also recognized as one of the ablest art critics in the country. The Elizabethan room is a veritable Hatfield House, but glorified larger and much more habitable. The walls are richly paneled and beautifully wood carved. The lofty ceiling is beamed and supported by great pilasters. This room contains many costly tapestries and paintings and a large library, which includes many rare and interesting books, is provided for the edification of the guests.

The lobby is not only striking for its wealth of mosaic work, paintings and great spherical electroliers, but also for its splendid spaciousness and harmony of architectural proportions. Peacock Alley, which begins at the southern end of the main lobby, is of Roman design in Italian white marble and is three hundred feet long. One of the famous paintings which adorn the wall of Peacock Alley is the beautiful "Blindman's Bluff" by Achille Fould.

Another of the rooms for which the Congress is noted is the Gold room, which, with its elaborate decorations, represents one of the finest banquet and ball rooms in the country. It has a capacity of 650 covers. The Gold room is so ventilated that the temperature can be maintained at any degree to suit the party. For after-theater dinner parties there is the Pompeian Grill, which in its Pompeian colors and designs is next to the famous Pompeian room. In the grill, every effort is made to give absolutely perfect service.

But it has not been its splendor alone that has made the Congress one of America's famous hostelries. The efficiency of the organization that mans the hotel, an organization carefully selected and trained by John Burke, managing director of the hotel, has had no little part.

In an institution the size of the Congress, it is seldom possible for the president to leave his executive duties to greet every incoming guest. But, however, in the organization which he has provided to perform this service, there is reflected the close personal interest the president has in all the hotel's guests.

THE GOLD ROOM
199

LOUIS XVI ROOM

THE POMPEIAN GRILL.

200

THE ELIZABETHAN ROOM

It is true that to the desk clerks, managers, waiters and bellboys is deputized the task of establishing an air of hospitality and making the surroundings more conducive to contentment. It is also true that on the shoulders of the house manager rests the responsibility. But it is also true, and quite patent by now, that no set of clever rules or tricks can make an organization function smoothly. It must have unit spirit—an esprit de corps that discharges its work expeditiously, wisely and with a view to making the guest feel comfortable. Such unit spirit is to be found in the group of Congress employes.

There is a wide difference in acting genial and polite and actually being genial and polite. Hotel employes of the former category have a tendency to overplay their feigned emotions and making the guest uncomfortable. This is overcome at the Congress by the manner in which the employes are chosen.

The arrangement of furnishings, tapestry and colorings in the rooms, each of which is equipped with the latest conveniences, is all designed to make them restful. The Congress hotel has the largest floor space devoted to public use of any hotel in the world.

The Congress is located at Congress street and Michigan avenue, thus giving the benefit of pleasant lake breezes without the disadvantage of sudden climatic disadvantages. The hotel is also within easy reach of all the leading theaters, clubs, stores and points of interest in the loop.

The problem of housing between 1,000 and 1,500 guests each night seems to have been more than adequately met by the management.

The Congress hotel was opened for the World's Fair. As its fame grew, an annex was erected and today the hotel has 960 rooms. The greatest number of persons taken care of in a night was 2,200 during the Republican convention of 1920.

H. L. Kaufman is president of the Congress Hotel and John Burke managing director. The board of directors is made up of John Irwin, James Irwin, G. D. Edwards, John Burke, U. L. Kaufman, H. L. Kaufman and E. J. Hudson.

CHICAGO BEACH HOTEL OF TODAY

MORE than a quarter of a century ago, Warren Leland founded the Chicago Beach Hotel. A few years after the opening of this hotel, the property was taken over by the late John G. Hately. Then came expansion and development. Mr. Hately's directive genius, coupled with the vision and support of Mr. John B. G. Lester, formerly vice-president and now president of the Chicago Beach Hotel, were instrumental in moulding this property into one of the great hotel institutions of the day.

On the death of Mr. Hately, in 1921, Mr. Lester succeeded him as president of the Chicago Beach Hotel. As Secretary of the Foreign Department of the Panama Pacific Exposition held in San Francisco in 1914, Mr. Lester was appointed by the United States Government as special commissioner to visit South Africa early in that year in order to interest the South African Government in the Exposition. Mr. Lester reached England on his return from South Africa as war was declared and became engaged in the organization of supplies made by Great Britain to her Allies, eventually being appointed Director of Allies' Supplies at the British Ministry of Munitions. He was decorated by the British, Belgian, Italian and Russian governments.

In 1919, he returned to America at the request of Mr. Hately to supervise the erection and organization of the new East Building, being appointed vice president on his arrival. Since the completion of the East Building, Mr. Lester has carried through the entire reorganization of the hotel staff which included the appointing of Mr. A. G. Pulver as General Manager. He is now considering and working out preliminary plans for the further development of the fourteen acres owned by the company. This building program will be proceeded with as the new lake boulevard, now under construction in accordance with the City Beautiful Plan, is completed.

MR. JOHN B. G. LESTER
President Chicago Beach Hotel

Originally built to contain 380 rooms, the Chicago Beach Hotel, through the addition of the new East Building, has almost tripled its accommodations and now provides a total of 980 rooms. All rooms have outside exposures. Eight hundred are with bath; some are single, others are arranged in suites of two, three, four and five rooms; all are comfortable and luxuriously furnished.

The hotel property covers 14 acres of land, the eastern and northern portion of which slopes smoothly and evenly into the refreshing waters of Lake Michigan.

On the hotel's private bathing beach stands the hotel's Bath House equipped with lockers, dressing rooms, service booths, a refreshment-dispensing Casino and many other conveniences and comforts for the guests of the hotel.

Guests of the Chicago Beach Hotel never find it necessary to leave the hotel premises when they wish to indulge in outdoor pleasures. The private properties of the hotel offer facilities for bathing, sailing, rowing, tennis, skating and other sports of the open, including golf on the newly installed 9-hole putting course.

The surrounding districts, however, are not without their appeal. Flanking the Chicago Beach Hotel on the south is beautiful East End Park, while on the west Hyde Park Boulevard winds its broad green-girdled way through the shaded parkways of Chicago's exclusive south side residential and hotel district.

Nearby is Chicago University, which attracts to this exclusive district refined and cultured residents. Adjacent, too, is Jackson Park, chosen for its beauty as the city's logical showroom for the great World's Fair. Picturesque evidences of that historical event still exist in this park of a thousand acres, and never seem to lose their interest although surrounded with such delightfully distracting influences as rolling golf courses, sheltered playgrounds, bridle paths, lagoons and other haunts of pleasure.

The turmoil, dirt and confusion of Chicago's industrial and business sections are many miles removed in point of distance, yet conveniently near in the matter of time. The man with offices in the Loop who makes the Chicago Beach Hotel his home, travels to and from his business headquarters inside of ten minutes. Illinois Central express trains, without a doubt the most efficient transportation service in the city, furnish this ten minutes' service at practically any time of day or night. All through trains on this line also stop at a station just a block from the hotel, while those of the Pennsylvania, Rock Island, Nickel Plate, and New York Central Lines take on and discharge passengers at the Englewood station, only a few minutes away.

In addition to the beauties of environment, the facilities for outdoor recreation and the conveniences of transportation, the Chicago Beach Hotel also has many exceptional advantages in accommodations, cuisine and service. Spaciousness and luxury are characteristic of its lobbies, lounging rooms, sun porches and corridors. Rooms, both single and en suite, are decorated and furnished in quiet good taste and provide genuine homelike comfort and luxury. The cuisine—far-famed for its excellence—meets the exacting requirements of the most discriminating. And the delightful view of the lake through the great windows of the dining rooms adds much to the charm and satisfaction of dining at the Chicago Beach Hotel. Then, too, there is the matter of service. The management of the Chicago Beach Hotel, realizing how much real service means to the hotel guest, has developed a system of personal attention which functions smoothly and unobtrusively. Service at this hotel is not a matter of surrounding guests with ever-present attendants. On the contrary they are secluded from all annoying intrusions. Yet their slightest wish finds response in immediate careful attention. This knack of getting things done at the time guests want them done is strikingly characteristic of this great hotel.

Volumes could be written on the advantages to be gained by living at the Chicago Beach Hotel. The fact alone that many men in the higher walks of life, famous professional men, jurists and national figures have selected it as the ideal place to make their home is evidence of the high esteem which the Chicago Beach Hotel enjoys in the minds of thinking people.

CLARENCE SAUNDERS.

The story of Clarence Saunders' rise from a Tennessee farm boy to the presidency of the Piggly Wiggly stores, a $5,000,000 corporation, will be found on the next page.

204

PIGGLY WIGGLY STORES

THE Piggly Wiggly store idea "just happened" out of the brain of Clarence Saunders while he was toiling for another in a Memphis store five years ago. Today that idea has expanded into a corporation doing a $5,000,000-a-month business and which embraces 600 stores all over the country.

Piggly Wigglies are the cafeterias of the grocery business, where everyone does his own shopping. The staff of each store includes only a combination cashier and manager.

Clarence Saunders, the business genius, who with one fell blow overthrew all the deeply entrenched traditions of the retail grocery business, celebrated his fortieth birthday on August 9, 1921. And he still drives ahead with irresistible energy.

Two weeks after the Piggly Wiggly "idea" had entered his mind, Mr. Saunders had resigned as manager of the grocery department of a Memphis store and had launched into business for himself. That was in September, 1916. The bizarreness of the venture struck Memphis as humorous. But the laughing ceased when the people found themselves buying all their groceries at the Piggly Wiggly store.

They bought because Piggly could undersell the other stores for the reason it did not have the item of labor to figure with in setting prices, the service was efficient and the goods were of the best.

And Mr. Saunders found he had sold in the first six months three times the amount of the old store in that location. The old store had done $34,500 of business at an expense of fifteen per cent, while the new store did $114,000 business at a cost of three per cent.

Then came Mr. Saunders' resolution to expand the business. One after another, stores were opened in Memphis until the number reached thirty-five. "Memphis is just as good a barometer of the fancies and likes of America as any other city. What Memphis likes, undoubtedly other cities would like," Mr. Saunders reasoned and he broadened his expansion plans to include every major city in the United States.

The success of this move is attested to by the fact that today there are 600 stores in operation. Today, also, the facilities of the Piggly Wiggly corporation include a big refrigerator factory in Memphis.

Piggly Wiggly is really an adventure into psychology. The big advantage in the self-serve plan—and Mr. Saunders says it is an advantage—is that persons who see goods temptingly displayed on all the shelves they have to pass will buy more.

"They are constantly looking for the goods they have planned to buy," says Mr. Saunders, "and while looking for them and picking them out they see something else that they would like, and buy that too. We not only save in clerk hire but our sales per customer are larger than they otherwise would be."

205

These are the three axioms for business success, according to Mr. Saunders:

1.—Know what you are trying to do.

2.—Know how to do it.

3.—Go ahead.

"What is the use of wasting time?" Mr. Saunders asks. "If you have an idea and know that it is a good one, why not go ahead and put it into execution right away? What is the use of living to a ripe old age if you haven't accomplished something when you get there? I would rather die young and do something than live to be old and do nothing.

"And yet I don't mean that a man should shoot ahead wildly and not try to examine his ideas. I am constantly turning things over in my mind to see whether there can be any possible flaws in the methods that I am setting out to use. But once you are sure of yourself, why put off the execution of your plan? Your ideas and plans will grow as you begin to practice them."

In building his organization, Mr. Saunders left nothing to chance. Everything was laid out in black and white so that there could be no mistake. The arrangement of every store the country over is the same, with a place for every bar of laundry soap and bottle of ketchup. Everything is mapped out for the store manager in a little book, from placating irritated customers to limiting the number of keys to the Piggly Wiggly Stores.

A shopping tour at a Piggly Wiggly store begins at the outside of the building. The stores are always painted blue, brown and yellow. The color scheme goes with Piggly Wiggly just as red goes with the five- and ten-cent store. The windows of the store are not taken up with a display; the display is in the interior of the store itself.

Everything is arranged for convenience. The shelves are so placed that the goods can easily be reached. The heaviest goods are the last the customer has to handle. As many as 185 customers can be handled in one hour. A Piggly Wiggly store employs from two to five men, depending on the volume of the business.

The chain store plan of merchandising will ultimately become the leading method of food distribution, although the regular type of retail grocer will always have a place in the field, according to Mr. Saunders.

In the metropolitan districts, where chains are most flourishing, they have within a few years advanced from serving 12 per cent of the food distribution to fully one-half, Mr. Saunders said.

Mr. Saunders sees one opportunity for saving by the chain stores in the possibility of eliminating services of salesmen from the manufacturer through concentrated buying by one executive for a great number of stores.

One of the plans Mr. Saunders has under consideration is a chain of stores that will sell goods for nine cents and less. They will not be five- and ten-cent stores, but stores where the odd pennies will be caught.

JOHN V. FARWELL COMPANY

B Y STEADFAST adherence to honorable business principles, the John V. Farwell Wholesale Dry Goods Company has withstood the great fire, panics and changes, both mercantile and political, for over 70 years and today it is recognized as one of the leaders in its business.

To the late John V. Farwell, and the late Charles B., and their children does the company owe its stability. Today, its voluminous stocks are constantly kept at the highest point of completeness; its salesmen reach every part of the country and its buyers, by importing direct and by contracting for the production or part production of many mills, are able to avail themselves of every opportunity offered by the marts of the world in obtaining merchandise of quality.

The nucleus for the John V. Farwell Company was built in 1850 when the late John V. Farwell, Sr., became a member of the firm of Cooley, Wadsworth and Company. The firm name was changed to Cooley, Farwell and Company. The sales swelled that year from $100,000 to $300,000. This necessitated larger quarters and the business moved from South Water street to 42, 44 and 46 Wabash avenue, where the John V. Farwell Company had its inception. Later, the location was moved to 102-6 Wabash avenue, where a fire in 1870 destroyed the building, forcing the company to move a few doors south on Wabash avenue. Like many others, the Farwell Company was hard hit by the great fire of 1871. However, a fresh start was made on Monroe street, where the company erected a six-story building. The steady growth of the business resulted in the company erecting its present quarters, a six-story building, occupying the block between Monroe and Adams streets on the west side of Market street and fronting the Chicago River.

In 1891, the business was incorporated under the laws of Illinois as the John V. Farwell Company. When the late John V. Farwell retired, his sons took over control of the company. The careers of Charles B. Farwell as merchant, congressman and senator and John V. Farwell as merchant, are known to all in the central west.

Back of the company's progress covering so many years has been fair dealing with customers, employees and sources of supply. The company today is selling to many retail dry goods merchants who have bought from this house continuously for half a century. When a merchant receives an acceptance of a future delivery order from the Farwell firm, he knows the goods will be delivered as the contract specifies.

Buying offices are now established in New York, Liverpool, Paris, Yokohoma and Chemnitz, Germany.

The officers of the company are John V. Farwell, president; Arthur L. Farwell, first vice-president; Herbert M. Anning, second vice-president; Charles M. McLeod, third vice-president; Francis C. Farwell, treasurer; and Frank F. Ferry, secretary. Directors are John V. Farwell, Arthur L. Farwell, Herbert M. Anning, Charles M. McLeod, Francis C. Farwell, Albert D. Farwell, Frank Farwell Ferry, John A. Yates, Farwell Winston, Walter Farwell, Frederick E. French, Edwin T. Fogarty, Ellis McDonald and Frederick O. Streich.

BLUM'S, INC.

WHEN Harry H. Blum entered the ladies' wearing apparel business, he had already learned what every merchant should know, but which many do not, that the three chief fundamentals of business, whether in the time of Carthaginians or at present, are intelligence, work and quality of the product offered.

Long study of the successes and failures of the trade convinced him that all the artifices used to evade these three fundamentals ended usually in disaster.

HARRY H. BLUM

At the time he opened his first shop in 1910 in the Congress hotel, he already possessed two of these requisites—intelligence and the willingness to work—and his next task was to find goods and styles that would outdo in excellence, durability and modishness those of his rivals. Herculean task, as he was competing against some of the greatest modistes in the world.

He bought the best material he could obtain and he surrounded himself with salesmen and women who were such in every meaning of the term. No detail was overlooked by Mr. Blum in the development of his business.

208

The wisdom of bringing the best to his clientele is reflected in the rapid strides taken by the business. Larger quarters soon became imperative and a second shop was opened in the Congress hotel.

The working force has been increased to 400 men and women.

Also, it should be said in passing, that the volume of business increased some thousands per cent over the 1910 figure.

All this because its owner knew the elemental requirements of business and saw to it that they were faithfully adhered to. Today he has come to be known as a leader in inaugurating new styles in ladies' apparel and his clientele not only numbers leading women of Chicago but also from all parts of the middle west.

In 1920, to meet the increasing demand for additional space, Mr. Blum purchased from the Michigan Avenue Company the building and a 150-year lease on the ground at 624-30 S. Michigan Av. The figure involved in the transaction is said to be in the neighborhood of $1,000,000. Mr. Blum now has under construction a seven-story addition. The building fronts eighty feet on Michigan avenue, and has a depth of 173 ft.

Mr. Blum was born in New York City in 1876; In 1880, he removed, with his parents to Chicago, where he was educated. Mr. Blum's clubs are the Idlewild Country and the City Club of Chicago. He resides at 1226 Hyde Park Blvd. His office is in the Blum Building.

THE BLUM BUILDING

A. STARR BEST

CHICAGO first knew the store of A. Starr Best twenty years ago. At that time, it was purposely restricted to apparel for the infant and child, for it was felt that only through specialized service could that degree of perfection be maintained which should be inherent in all the merchandise of the store.

Guided by this policy, the store has grown. The increase of its physical size has been marked by move after move to larger headquarters, until today it owns and occupies the building at Randolph and Wabash. The store has expanded conservatively. Departments were added only after thorough and competent preparation had been made to serve an enlarged clientele.

After a score of years, this is still a store of specialized service, now meeting the needs of men of all ages. From the looms and the finer shops of Europe come choice fabrics and garments embodying the standard of correctness typified by this store. Buyers are in the markets of the world, collecting the merchandise which is to reflect in discrimination in what it offers to its patrons.

CAPPER & CAPPER

BY making business more than merely business, by making it an opportunity to contribute to civilization and enrich the experience of all and an adventure in human service, Capper & Capper has made its name synonymous with the utmost in men's furnishings.

Its record of sartorial achievements is high. It is the medium by which the best the Old World as well as America affords in clothes is brought to the youth of the Middle West: linen from Ireland; tweeds from England; silks from Japan; hats from Italy. It deals in everything worn by the well-dressed man, except his shoes.

The clientele of Capper & Capper represents the best of manhood of the Middle West. It has two Chicago stores, Michigan avenue and Monroe and in the Hotel Sherman; and branch stores in Detroit, Milwaukee, Minneapolis and St. Paul. Capper, Son & Co., Ltd., are its London representatives.

Mr. George H. Capper, V. Pres., gives his business views in the following few sentences: "To express good feeling toward your fellow man in the beauties of the scarf or the style of the hat which you sell him, or in the qualities of the shirt which you make for him, or in clothing a little better and finer and more adequate, or in a golf ball that gives him 'fifteen yards more' is one of the privileges and pleasures and profits of being in business.

"The hour of successful selfishness is passing. The man, the business or the nation that seeks to serve itself alone is being challenged to show cause why its further existence should be tolerated. The world war was a gigantic and successful challenge of selfish exploitation. The world peace, now at hand, brings with it a new order, a new point of view, a new set of values, a new sense of responsibilities and of opportunities.

"Now, much more than ever before, business is more than merely business."

FRANK CRAWFORD LETTS

FRANK CRAWFORD LETTS, president of the Western Grocer Co. and The National Grocer Co., was born in Magnolia, Ill., 1861. Ed. in pub. schs. Married in 1897, Cora Perkins, daughter of late U. S. Senator Perkins. Children: Fred Clayton, Herma Leona (Mrs. Frank E. Weeks), Courtney Louise (Mrs. Wellesley Stilwell), Hollis. Began as clerk in store at Afton, Ia., 1876-8. Employed by A. T. Stewart & Co., dry goods, Chicago, 1878-81. In retail dry goods business in Marshalltown, Ia., 4 years; wholesale groceries, Marshalltown, 1885, as the Letts-Fletcher Company; 1898, president, Western Grocer Co., operating 12 wholesale grocery houses; president, Nat. Grocer Co., operating 15 wholesale grocery houses in Mich., Ill., and Ind. Director, Pacific-American Fisheries, Puget Sound. Chairman, Board of Directors, Durand-McNeil-Horner Co., Chicago. Republican. Colonel on staffs of Governors Jackson, Drake and Shaw, of Iowa. Mason. Clubs: Chicago, Mid-Day, Industrial, Casino, Old Elm, Shore Acres. Home: 1100 Lake Shore Drive. Office: 208 S. La Salle St., Chicago.

HENRY HAVEN WINDSOR

HENRY HAVEN WINDSOR, editor, was born in Mitchell, Ia., Nov. 13, 1859; s. of Rev. William (D. D.) and Harriet Butler (Holmes) Windsor; ed. Ia. Coll. Married, Marengo, Ill., June 25, 1889, Lina B. Jackson. Son, Henry Haven, Jr. Was city editor Times-Republican, Marshalltown, Ia., 1879-80; pvt. sec. to officials N. P. Ry., St. Paul, 1881-82; sec. Chicago City Ry. Co., 1883-91; founder, editor and pres. Street Railway Review, 1892-1901; founder, 1901, and since editor and pres. Popular Mechanics magazine. Republican. Congregationalist. Clubs: Press, Chicago Athletic, South Shore Country, Chicago Yacht, National Press (Washington, D. C.); University, Evanston, Ill.; Atlantic Yacht; Camden (Me.) Yacht; mem. first board of dirs. of the Hamilton Club. Homes: 1120 Forrest av., Evanston, Ill.; Camden, Me.; Daytona Beach, Fla. Office: 6 N. Michigan av., Chicago.

STEELE-WEDELES COMPANY

THE STEELE-WEDELES COMPANY, distributors and packers of Savoy Super-Quality Foods, one of America's largest and best equipped wholesale grocers, handle a complete line of general groceries for the home, club, restaurant, and hotel trade. Their development and expansion of the business is due to studying what the public wants and to satisfying its needs through the change of time.

It is interesting to know that Chicago consumes immense quantities of canned foods. Its population being so cosmopolitan there is a wide and discriminating range of taste for all varieties of foods. But wherever the finest products are desired the request invariably calls for Savoy Brand.

A survey made by disinterested parties for statistical purposes revealed the fact that more Savoy canned and packaged Foods are used in this market than any other. Therefore in addition to being known as the best, they are also the best known.

The housewife cheerfully accepts food products from her grocer when they bear the Savoy label and the chef or steward at your favorite club or restaurant is assured of positive success in preparing the dinner when Savoy foods are used. Savoy Products dominate in their field. We often see "Savoy" specified on the menu cards of the best dining rooms.

Be content when you see the above mark on foods. It stands for super-quality and guarantees your complete satisfaction. Every Savoy product is marketed under that policy—an insurance that you secure the best value for the price you pay.

SAVOY FOODS MUST SATISFY OR BACK GOES THE PRICE YOU PAID.

ALEXANDER IRWIN

A LEXANDER IRWIN, member of the firm of Irwin Brothers, one of the country's largest provision companies, was born in 1858, in Ireland, the son of Olivia (Clark) and John Irwin. He received his education in the public schools of Ireland and Chicago. In 1900, he was married to Mary D. Dobson, of Chicago. With the aid of his brothers, John and James C., he established Irwin Brothers' Company, purveyors to hotels, clubs and restaurants, specializing in the highest grade meats of all kinds. Because of the appealing quality of its provisions and the magnetic personality of its directors, the company steadily moved forward. Today, its sales forces cover Chicago, the middle west, southwest, as far east as Buffalo and Pittsburgh and as far northwest as the Dakotas. Mr. Irwin is a member of the following clubs: South Shore, Beverly Country, Old Town and Illinois Athletic. Home: 4801 Grand blvd. Office: 807 S. State street.

LOTT HOTEL COMPANY

PICTURESQUELY ranged along Chicago's famous Lake Shore Drive, removed from the noise and grime of the business districts, the Webster and Parkway hotels immediately overlook Lake Michigan and the velvet lawned beauty spots of Lincoln park. Winter or summer, guests will find these ideal surroundings conducive alike to quiet comfort and pleasantly varied recreation.

CHARLES H. LOTT
President Lott Hotel Company

Wave-flecked beaches — with facilities for bathing, sailing and rowing—rolling golf courses, shaded playgrounds, tennis courts and winding bridle paths all tend in season to tempt the idle fancy of the guests.

There is an intensely human and enjoyable side of life at the Webster and Parkway hotels; life that supplies more than the mere comforts and conveniences of perfect modern appointments and service. And then what a genuine pleasure it is to sense in the environment that perfect harmony of surroundings which makes for solid contentment!

Then, too, there is the cuisine—exceptional cuisine—food in the savor of which one's sense of taste fairly revels. Table d'hote dinners are featured at both hotels at attractive prices, with also an a la carte service provided.

To the creative and administrative genius of Charles H. Lott do these two hotels owe their existence. Mr. Lott was born in Thornville, Ohio, January 28, 1876, son of Lorena J. and George W. Lott. After receiving all the education that Thornville afforded, he decided to investigate the business possibilities of the Pacific Coast. Here he received the training in the rudiments in the hotel business that later made him one of the leading hotel directors of the country.

The year 1909 will always remain indelibly stamped in the mind of Mr. Lott, for it was in this year that he was married to Cora A. Lichlyter in San Francisco and came to Chicago. He operated as a private owner of hotels from 1909 to 1914. The latter year saw the incorporation of the Lott Hotel Company. In 1916, the Parkway Hotel was erected and in 1916 an addition was completed, giving it a capacity of 400 rooms, each bedroom with a bath, and a restaurant with a seating capacity of 800 persons.

The erection of the Webster hotel was begun in 1919 and the following year it was ready for occupancy. In June, 1922, Mr. Lott started construction of the Belden Hotel, two blocks north of the Webster Hotel on Lincoln Park West.

These three hotels will put under Mr. Lott's jurisdiction 1,450 rooms facing Lincoln Park. Six hundred and fifty of these rooms will be in the Belden Hotel, which will be operated as an apartment hotel, with an electrically equipped kitchenette in each apartment.

Mr. Lott is president and treasurer of the Lott Hotel Company, Webster

PARKWAY HOTEL
Lincoln Park West at Garfield

Hotel Company and the Belden Hotel Company and a director of the Century Trust & Savings Bank. He is a member of the Hamilton Club, Ridgemoor Country Club and Chicago Yacht Club.

The Lott company has a capitalization of $3,000,000, fully paid. The officers are Mr. Lott; Cora A. Lott, vice president, and Earl S. Lott, secretary. The directorate is composed of the following: Charles H. Lott, Cora A. Lott, Earl S. Lott, D. H. McGilvrey, J. Rice Brown, William A. Eichler, John F. Burns, T. J. Magner, and John W. Fowler.

Mr. Lott epitomizes the whole business in this terse statement: "The hotel man who succeeds is invariably the one who makes his hotel as nearly approaching the ideal home as possible."

Mr. Lott continued: "In writing of the Parkway and Webster hotels, I am anxious for you to remember that they are far more than mere stopping places—places to eat and sleep; they are the last word in hotel creations. They contain every improvement, every device designed for home comfort, good service and an atmosphere of taste and refinement surrounding, so pleasing to those desiring accommodations of a superior standard of excellence.

"The designers of the Parkway and Webster hotels have accomplished in the two buildings, as is evidenced by their skill and taste, an abode of superior quality and comfort.

"The Webster and Parkway hotels, therefore, strive to reckon with people of good homes who find it convenient to close their houses for an indefinite period, and to whom the thought of dispensing with home comforts, good service and cuisine has ever been a hardship."

WEBSTER HOTEL
Lincoln Park West at Webster

215

DR. A. RALPH JOHNSTONE

DR. A. RALPH JOHNSTONE, director of the Lakeside hospital, was born in Owen Sound, Ontario, Dec. 18, 1865; the son of Marian (Cherry) and James H. Johnstone. His education was received in Canadian schools and in the Medical Department of the University of Illinois, where he also took up post-graduate work. On June 30, 1897, Johnstone married Muriel Richardson, of Chicago. Son, Richardson. Dr. Johnstone became a member of the staff of Lakeside hospital and by dint of hard work and sheer ability he was rapidly promoted. He now is President and surgeon-in-chief. He is also medical director of the National Bureau of Analysis. Dr. Johnstone served as chairman of the Chicago Draft Board No. 4 during the war. Member of Mont Joye Commandery, Masons. Member of Chicago, Illinois and American Medical Associations. Home: 3735 Lake Park av. Office: 3410 Rhodes av.

DR. LAWRENCE HOWARD ROBLEE

LAWRENCE H. ROBLEE, physician and surgeon, was born in Minneapolis, May 22, 1888; s. of Alma L. (Partridge) and Rev. Henry Scott Roblee. Ed. in Benton Harbor schs. and Univ. of Mich., 1912. He then joined resident staff of Metropolitan Hospital; Dept. of Pub. Charities, New York City; clinical asst. in Urology, Post Graduate Med. Coll., New York City. Clinical asst., Central Free Dispensary, Chicago; consulting Urologist, Illinois Masonic Hospital. Served as surgeon, 7th Reg., U. S. Engineers; Urologist, Base Hospital No. 66, A. E. F.; surgeon, Camp Covington, A. E. F.; div. Urologist, 2nd div., A. E. F.; A. of F., Germany; commissioned major, Med. Corps, U. S. A. Mem. Am. Medical Assn.; Am. Institute of Homeopathy; Ill. and Chicago Medical Socs.; Ill. and Chicago Homeopathic Socs. Mem. of Alumni Assn., Univ. of Mich.; S. A. R. Clubs: Hamilton, So-

journers, Glen Oaks Country. Abdallah Shrine, A. O. O. M. S. Army No. 1, Consistory, Illinois Commandery, Columbia Chapter, Legion Lodge, A. F. & A. M., Chicago. Home: Hotel Melbourne. Office: 25 E. Washington st.

YELLOW CAB COMPANY

A TREMENDOUS business that was built on the Golden Rule—that is what they say of the Yellow Cab Company. A little more than seven years ago, the only Yellow Cab was in the imagination of John Hertz. Today Chicago has 1,800 real Yellow Cabs and there are Yellow Cabs in every city in the United States.

John Hertz made his dream come true and in making it real, he made every one of his associates rich and made better wages and better working conditions for every man who worked for his company.

Courtesy is the answer to the question of Yellow Cab's success. The whole fabric of the business is based on courtesy. The cabs are built to give constant and comfortable service. That is courtesy.

The drivers are selected carefully for their cheerful kindliness as well as for their ability and integrity, so that there is small chance of a customer's complaint against one for discourtesy.

Chauffeurs are taught the things that passengers like—little attentions, like opening doors, tucking robes about riders in cold weather, opening windows on fine days, cheerful greetings and pleasant "thank yous."

The idea of courtesy extends even to pedestrians and the drivers of other cars on the streets. Yellow Cab drivers show a uniform respect for the rights of others. They do not wilfully block crossings. They slow down to allow other cars a chance to get in and out of traffic. They respect the rules of the road and the city ordinances and they are setting an example of courtesy that makes driving safer and more comfortable.

The idea of universal courtesy was born in John Hertz' brain and so permeates the entire industry that it isn't unusual for the officials of the company to expect Yellow Cab drivers to go any length in courteous treatment of people, whether they are cab-riders or not.

Besides the idea of courtesy, John Hertz believes in charging just as little for his cab service as the profit side of the ledger will stand.

Yellow Cab was the first transportation company to reduce its fares to the pre-war level and now its fares are lower than they ever were, with the prospect that they will be lowered still further at a future date.

Men who are well treated by their company can't help being cheerful and courteous. That is the idea behind the Yellow Cab Company. Almost every employe is a stockholder in the corporation and thereby has a direct financial interest in its welfare, outside of his wage. Every man at the wheel in a Yellow cab has a financial interest in that cab and the welfare of the passengers it carries.

Lost business hurts him. Accidents, which cost money, hurt his dividends. That is another reason why he is courteous.

But the real reason for the kindliness and courtesy of the Yellow Cab is that John Hertz is kindly and courteous and his men just naturally inherit it.

217

BENJAMIN HARRISON BUNN

A T THE age of 32, Benjamin Harrison Bunn is the president of a company with a large volume of business. The Bunn Package Tying Machine, which he began during his spare time while a student at the University of Illinois, and which became his life work, is now making his fortune. This machine is enjoying a world-wide sale, because business men have found that by its use they are able to cut in half what otherwise would be the cost of package tying. Bunn's machine ties packages at high speed with unfailing accuracy, it is economical and efficient. A more complete story of this remarkable inventor and his machine will be found on the next page.

218

B. H. BUNN COMPANY

WORKING out an idea suggested to him by his father has made Benjamin Harrison Bunn the inventor of a package-tying machine and the head of The B. H. Bunn Company manufacturing these machines. Mr. Bunn, Sr., while working in the Chicago Post Office conceived the idea of a machine to tie packages of mail. He conveyed this idea to his son, who, during his leisure time and while at the University of Illinois, worked out the idea. The result of his work is a package-tying machine now in use in several hundred lines of business.

Mr. Bunn was born in De Smet, South Dakota, Oct. 16, 1887; son of Mary M. (Murdock) and Romanzo Norton Bunn. He received his education in Chicago Public schools, R. T. Crane Technical High school and the University of Illinois. After he left the university, Mr. Bunn brought with him to his home in Chicago such materials as he had been able to manufacture and continued developing his idea for a tying machine. In the garret of his home, he manufactured his own drill press and procured a small lathe, both of which he operated by hand power.

His first actual tests began in 1909; the following year he obtained approval from the postoffice department for a series of practical demonstrations in the Chicago postoffice. From this time on, he was engaged alternately in testing and correcting mechanical faults and making trips to Eastern cities to exhibit to government officials and business men.

Late in 1911, two Chicago business houses purchased machines from Bunn, using them in tying mail for dispatch to the postoffice. The Canadian government became interested in the invention and also purchased machines.

The sale of fifty machines to the United States put Mr. Bunn's business on a paying basis. These machines were divided between the postoffice department and new bureaus created by war activities. The American Tobacco Company purchased twenty machines which they have installed in one room in their plant at Louisville, Kentucky. These machines do the work of forty girls and have been in operation over a year.

Demands arose from various industries for machines for a great variety of purposes, resulting in the development of various models, all of which have received the inventor's personal attention. A large field now opening for these machines is in tying candy boxes and ice cream cartons, these being tied two ways in one operation and in one and one-half seconds of time.

Business men throughout the world have found that the Bunn tying machine will tie packages at high speed with unfailing accuracy. It is economical and efficient. It ties each package in the same way, wrapping the string around tightly each time and insuring a non-slip knot. There is no wasting of string. The machines are now in use in several hundred lines of business.

The B. H. Bunn company was incorporated in 1922, with Benjamin Harrison Bunn, president; Harry E. Bunn, vice president and Romanzo N. Bunn secretary and treasurer. The main plant is in Chicago.

ROBERT WOOLSTON HUNT

THE John Fritz medal, the highest honor an engineer can attain in America, has been awarded to Robert Woolston Hunt, head of the R. W. Hunt and Co., the largest inspection and consulting engineering company in the world. The Fritz medal was awarded to Mr. Hunt for his signal services in advancing the development of the Bessemer Process for the manufacture of steel. Also in recognition of his great scientific contributions, the American Institute of Mining and Metallurgical Engineers has hanging in its quarters in New York a portrait of Mr. Hunt by Emil Fuchs, famous artist. A more complete story of Mr. Hunt's career will be found on the next page.

ROBERT WOOLSTON HUNT

HIS great contributions to the development of the Bessemer process for making steel have won for Robert Woolston Hunt the John Fritz medal and the first Hunt Medal. Mr. Hunt is head of Robert W. Hunt and Co., the largest inspecting engineering company in the world.

Mr. Hunt was born in Fallsington, Bucks County, Pa., Dec. 9, 1838, son of Martha L. (Woolston) and Dr. R. A. Hunt. Because of Dr. Hunt's failing health, he moved to Covington, Ky., where he died in March, 1855. His son continued Dr. Hunt's drug business for two years, but impaired health compelled him also to relinquish it. He moved to Pottsville, Pa., where he entered the iron rolling mill of John Burnish & Company, whose senior partner, T. W. Yardley, was his cousin. In 1859, he entered the analytical laboratory of Booth, Garrett & Reese in Philadelphia. In 1860, he was employed by Wood, Morrell & Co., then lessees of the Cambria Iron Works at Johnstown, Pa., and established a laboratory for them.

In 1861, he assisted in organizing the Elmira Rolling Mill, Elmira, N. Y., which had been erected by his cousin, Col. Yardley.

In the fall of that year he entered the army and was stationed at Harrisburg, Pa. Following his being mustered out of service, he returned to the Cambria Iron Company, and in 1865, was sent to Wyandotte, Mich., where the Kelly Pneumatic Process Co. erected a plant.

At Wyandotte, Mr. Hunt made many experiments in the then unexplored field of American Bessemer steel. Mr. Hunt remained in charge of the Wyandotte Works until 1866, when he returned to Johnstown because the Cambria Co. was then intending to erect a Bessemer plant. The plant was not completed until 1871. In the meantime, he had charge of the rolling into rails at Cambria of steel ingots, made at the Pennsylvania Co.'s plant at Steelton, for the Pennsylvania R. R., these rails being the first ones produced on a commercial order in America.

At the new Cambria Bessemer plant an elaborate system of bottom casting was developed and introduced. This was covered by letters patent, issued to Mr. Hunt, John E. Fry, and A. L. Holley.

In 1866, Mr. Hunt married Miss Eleanor Clark of Ecourse, Mich.

Mr. Hunt quit the Cambria Co. in 1873, and later in the year became superintendent of the Bessemer Steel plant of John A. Griswold & Co., Troy, N. Y. Later the firms of John A. Griswold & Co. and E. Corning & Co. were consolidated under the name of the Albany & Rensselaer Steel & Iron Company.

In 1886, the company was changed to the Troy Iron and Steel Co. While operating the Troy Works, Mr. Hunt was successful in making many grades of steel in the Bessemer converter, which had not been previously produced in America.

In the development of such special steels, Mr. Hunt, together with Dr. August Wendell, the chemist of the works, developed several special processes, which they covered by letters patent.

In 1883, Mr. Hunt was president of the American Institute of Mining Engineers, and in 1891 was president of the American Society of Mechanical Engineers. In 1906, he was again elected president of the American Institute of Mining Engineers. In 1893 he was president of the Western Society of Engineers. In 1912 he was president of the American Society for Testing Materials, and in 1914 was made American vice president of the International Association for Testing Materials. He is also a member of many other engineering societies.

In 1888, Mr. Hunt removed to Chicago, where he established the firm of Robert W. Hunt & Co., inspecting and consulting engineers, which firm is the largest organization of its kind in the world. It is now composed of Robert W. Hunt, J. J. Cone, and D. W. McNaugher.

ARTHUR EUGENE MAYO

A. E. MAYO, pres. of Mayo Federated Colleges, was born in Presho, N. Y., May 7, 1884; s. of Teresa (Jordan) and Timothy Adelbert Mayo; ed. in N. Y. pub. schs.; LL. B. degree from Ill. Coll. of Law, 1911, and LL. M. degree, 1912; Ph. B., De Paul Univ., 1916. Married Josephine Carlson, 1918, Chicago; Mr. Mayo was admitted to Ill. bar in 1911; dist. mgr. for Protected Home Circle in Ohio and Pennsylvania, 1908-10; began practice of law in Chicago in 1911; secy. Ill. Coll. of Law, 1911-15; dean, De Paul Univ., Coll. of Comm., 1915-18, pres. Mayo Coll. of Comm., 1919-20; pres. Mayo Federated Colleges since 1920. Mem. Am., Ill. & Chicago Bar Assn.; Ill. Soc. of Press Writers; Chicago Assn. of Comm., Elks, P. H. C., N. P. L. Club: Ill. Athletic. Office: 431 S. Dearborn St. Home: 1506 N. Highland Avenue.

DR. ANDRE L. STAPLER

DR. ANDRE L. STAPLER, with offices at 1002 Wilson av., is one of the leaders in the American movement to throttle that dread malady, cancer. Through his affiliation with the American Society for the Control of Cancer, he has lent his knowledge and the resources at his command to efforts to circumvent the spread of the disease, and mortality records show that his assistance has been of great avail. In his capacity as attending surgeon to the Lake View hospital, Chicago General hospital and the Lehigh Valley Railroad hospital, he has treated hundreds of cases of cancer. Dr. Stapler was born in Hamilton, Ontario, educated in the public schools there and received his M. D. degree at Columbia University. At one time he served as assistant professor of surgery at Valparaiso University. Dr. Stapler is a member of the American Medical Association, Illinois and Chicago Medical Societies, Mississippi Valley Medical Association and American Society for the Advancement of Science and Research. His wife's maiden name is Helen Gates. He resides at Parkway hotel.

ADOLPH SPIELMANN

ADOLPH SPIELMANN, president and treasurer of The Tablet and Ticket Company, was born in Germany, March 18, 1871; s. of Katharine (Fuchs) and Peter Spielmann. In 1872, he removed to Chicago and was educated in public high schools of the city and in Metropolitan Business College. He married Bertha M. Willson, July 20, 1892, Chicago. Son, Willson A. After leaving school, in 1890, Mr. Spielmann entered the employ of the Bank of Commerce. The following year he became a member of the office force of The Tablet & Ticket Co., and, in recognition of his faithful service, the company advanced him from one position to another until he was made president. Mr. Spielmann is director Chicago National League Ball Club, 32° Mason and Shriner. Clubs: Chicago Athletic (director), Chicago Yacht, Skokie Country. Home: Webster Hotel. Office: 1015 W. Adams St.

223

DR. ISAAC DONALDSON RAWLINGS

DR. ISAAC D. RAWLINGS, state director of public health, was born in Carrollton, Ill., 1869. Ed. in pub. schs. of Jacksonville, Ill., and Ill. Coll. and N. U. Med. Col. He studied for 2 yrs. in universities of Europe and then began practice of medicine in Chicago in 1895. Ill. Coll. conferred on him degree of Master of Science. Dr. Rawlings has held various positions on faculty of N. U. In 1895 he was made superintendent of Chicago Isolation Hosp. In 1904 he was named chief inspector for Chicago Health Department and in 1918 ass't chief of Bureau of Med. Insp. He waived appointment to state epidemiologist in 1915. During influenza epidemic of 1918, Dr. Rawlings was appointed acting ass't surgeon in U. S. Pub. Health Serv. He was completing 22d year in Chicago Health Dept. when he was named state director of pub. health in 1921. Mem. Am. Ill., Chicago Health Assns., Am. Pub. Health Assn., Mason. Club: Press. He is married and has one son.

JOHN DILL ROBERTSON

JOHN DILL ROBERTSON, former health commissioner of City of Chicago, was born in Indiana Co., Pa., March 8, 1871; s. of Thomas Sanderson and Melinda M. (McCurdy) Robertson. M. D. Bennett Medical Coll., Chicago, 1896; interne Cook County Hosp., 1896-7. Married Bessie M. Foote of Victor, Colo., June 15, 1899; one son, Thomas Sanderson. President of Bennett Med. Coll. (Loyola Univ.), 1905-15, and prof. practice of surgery at Bennett since 1905. Surgeon and chief Jefferson Park Polyclinic Hosp., 1904-15; attending surgeon to Cook County Hosp., 1898-1913. Health commr. City of Chicago from April 26, 1915, to 1922. Mem. of A. M. A., Ill. State Med. Soc., Chicago Med. Soc. Club: Hamilton. Office: 7 W. Madison st. Home: 3435 W. Monroe st.

CHICAGO AS A HEALTH CENTER

A VIGOROUS future is promised Chicago by its sanitary progress in the past fifty years. The death rate of 1921 was not much more than half as high as that of 1871, when it was 20.87, having fallen from 25 per thousand. The baby death rate is about one-third of that of the Great Fire. Men enjoy greater longevity today. The death rate of children from one to four is about one-fourth that of 1871, of typhoid fever about one-fiftieth, of consumption about one-fourth, while smallpox and cholera, a great menace half a century ago, no longer cause deaths.

In the past fifty years, science has made great advances, embracing introduction of the germ theory of disease, the X-Ray and application of the microscope and laboratory. Vaccines, anti-toxins and serums have been discovered and come into use. Surgery has taken the greatest steps forward in medicine, but no branch has lagged completely.

And what will the next fifty years hold for Chicago? The far-seeing say there will be an increase in the number of great hospitals and their aggregate bed capacity; from all over the world will come graduate and undergraduate students for research and clinical work, and post-graduate schools inviting medical practitioners from everywhere will spread the advances of medicines in hundreds of localities. Chicago is the home of the American Medical Association and the College of Surgeons, and place of issue of their journals.

The advances of that new day will have proceeded from the sanitary efforts of our ancestors of the seventies, when the high death rates of the forties and fifties had dropped because of better drainage, better sewerage and garbage disposal and better control of contagion. Just after the fire, the then city of 300,000 had 306 physicians, five medical colleges, with a registration of 300, and there were ten hospitals, with a capacity of 1,000 or more beds.

The fire destroyed six hospitals, leaving only 650 beds available after the conflagration. A few days after the fire, all relief work was concentrated by the Relief and Aid. One hundred and seven persons died in the fire. In spite of these casualties and exposure of homeless, Chicago's death rate was lower in October of 1871 than in the same month of 1870, 1872 or 1873.

The genius for organization born out of the great disaster soon showed itself in public health work. Public sentiment backed efforts for improvement of the city's health in a degree never known before. Much of the money left at the end of the relief period was used to endow beds in hospitals. The city ordered the removal of all slaughter houses from the district bounded by Fullerton avenue, Western avenue, Thirty-first street and the lake, and a law was drafted to prohibit the keeping of more than three cows in a city lot.

Chicago hospitals today are licensed by the health department, numbering 75, with 6,676 beds available. This does not include homes, asylums and places for convalescents. Chicago has six medical colleges, attended by 1,736 students and has at least four post-graduate schools, with many students each year. Besides, there are a few schools teaching certain medical subjects to graduates.

In the past six years, notable reductions have been made in Chicago's death rate, the department of health reports. The death rate from scarlet fever has been reduced 75 per cent; the death rate from typhoid fever, 90 per cent, and deaths from tuberculosis, 50 per cent.

The department of health is far from satisfied with the reduction in diphtheria. One version puts the blame for the high death rate on parents who do not avail themselves of the known and approved agencies that Chicago affords. The commissioner of health has appointed a diphtheria commission to co-operate in an intensive campaign against this dangerous disease of childhood.

225

PETER MICHAEL HOFFMAN

PETER MICHAEL HOFFMAN, coroner of Cook County, was born Desplaines, Ill., March 22, 1863; s. of Michael and Annette (Nimsgarn), Hoffman; ed. in pub. schs, of Desplaines and bus. coll. in Chicago. Married Emma May Peet, in Desplaines, 1889. Children: Edith, Nettie, Rae, Marguerite, Evelyn, Gordon H. Mr. Hoffman began career in grocery business and later was chief clerk and cashier for C. & N. W. Ry., 17 years; mem. of bd. of Co. Commrs. of Cook County, 1898-1904; coroner of Cook County since 1904. Served as mem. bd. of trustees, Village of Desplaines, for 3 yrs. (pres. 2 yrs.); chmn. of bd. of ed. of school district No. 64, Cook County, 1898-1917. Republican. Office: 500 County Bldg., Chicago. Home: Desplaines.

S. C. POSTLEWAIT

S. C. POSTLEWAIT, president of firm of undertakers bearing his name, was born in Newton, Hamilton, Pa., April 23, 1846. At 14, he started serving 3 yr. apprenticeship in office of Altoona Tribune; during this time, he enlisted in Pa. Vol. Inf., being honorably discharged in 1865. He returned to Altoona but, losing almost everything in a fire, he came west. After a few months in Chicago, joined the Freeport Bulletin. In 1868, he established Lee County Democrat, Dixon, and published it until the Chicago fire. Then Mr. Postlewait entered employ of Rand, McNally & Co. Later, he became salesman for a leading casket manufacturing company, which eventually resulted in his engaging in undertaking business. Postlewait Co. now has offices in Chicago, Oak Park, and Berwyn. Other officers of firm are: O. Allen Postlewait, vice-pres.; Henry F. Unser, secy.-treas. Mr. Postlewait is a life member of the Press Club of Chicago.

WESLEY MEMORIAL HOSPITAL

IN 1888, a group of Chicago's forward looking citizens banded together for the purpose of mitigating the suffering of the sick and destitute of the city. The result of their work was the incorporation of the Wesley Memorial Hospital.

Wesley Memorial hospital, which now cares for more than 7,000 patients annually, was founded in four rooms, provided by the Missionary Training School. On Thanksgiving Day, 1888, it received its first patient, a woman. Larger quarters became imperative the following year and a house near Pine and Ohio streets was rented. This soon proved inadequate, too, and a second house was purchased. Later the present site of the hospital was donated by William Deering and a brick building accommodating thirty patients was erected. Here the hospital carried on its work until 1891 when the present edifice costing $237,000 was built, largely through the zealous effort and contributions of William Deering, Norman W. Harris, Gustavus F. Swift, James B. Hobbs, and R. D. Sheppard. In the spring of 1906, a gift from Norman W. Harris made possible the erection of the Harris Home for Nurses, located on Dearborn, one block north of the hospital.

The plans of the founders of the hospital were completed in 1910 with the construction of a large addition, which contains, besides offices and class rooms, ten suites, thirty-two rooms, a new obstetrical department and an enlarged operating department.

The $1,000,000 gift from Mr. James Deering in memory of his father, William Deering, and sister, Abby Deering Howe, has greatly enlarged the hospital's possibilities for good. The income alone from the benefaction may be used and its employment is wisely directed into the channel of aid to the sick poor only.

The hospital's affairs are guided by the following officers: Perley Lowe, president; George W. Dixon, vice president; Edwin L. Wagner, secretary; M. Haddon McLean, treasurer; E. S. Gilmore, superintendent; J. L. Anderson, D. D., chaplain.

THE AMERICAN LABORATORIES

THE American Laboratories, 25 E. Washington St., under the direction of Dr. Marshal D. Molay, is rated high by Chicago doctors by virtue of its years of most satisfactory service. The laboratories are thoroughly equipped and recent rebuilding has made them one of the most modern in America. They have spacious rooms for chemistry, bacteriology, pathology and serology, large consultation rooms and offices.

They are fully prepared to carry out any investigations of a chemical, serological, pathological, bacteriological or sanitary nature. The X-ray department is complete in every detail and includes every known accessory for making accurate radiographs in any position, including the stereoscopic method and the Sweete for localization. The electro-therapy room is equipped with apparatus for treating high blood pressure, skin diseases and many other ailments.

Dr. Molay, the director, became head of the staff of the American Laboratories after years of study in leading European schools. He was graduated from Loyola University in 1912, with B. S. and M. D. degrees. He attended the University of Berlin and Vienna and became affiliated for a time with the University of London. Dr. Molay then was associated with Prof. Maximillian Herzog, and after several years of this association he took charge of the American Laboratories. Dr. Molay, in addition, is president of Speedografik Service Co. and secretary of Atlas Incubator Co. He is a member of the American and Chicago Medical Associations, Ill. State Med. Society, Chicago Optimist Club (ex-pres.), Executives Club; Mason and Shriner. He resides at 4815 Christiana Ave.

227

FRANK G. SOULE

FRANK G. SOULE, president of the National Bureau of Analysis, has found the answer to the question, Why Do People Die Too Young? He has found that people do not die; they kill themselves by neglect of the most delicate and yet overworked organs of the body—the liver and kidneys.

By the founding of the National Bureau of Analysis, Mr. Soule has saved hundreds of persons from premature death by forewarning them of improper conditions discovered through his bureau's careful examination of the urine. The analyzing is done by a body of scientists, under direction of some of Chicago's leading doctors. The clientele of the bureau today numbers many of the men and women in the forefront of business, art, science and literature.

Mr. Soule has also achieved national fame for his philanthropic and public welfare work. It was through his unceasing endeavors that the Juvenile Court Law was passed in Illinois and a new era ushered in in the reformation of delinquent boys.

He was born in Raymond, Wis., March 17, 1858; son of Caroline (Gookins) and Rev. John B. L. Soule. He is the nephew of Gideon Lane Soule, for 50 years principal of Phillips Exeter Academy. In 1886, Mr. Soule received A. M. degree from Blackburn College. He married Helene J. Shipman, June 12, 1886, Chicago. Children: Mrs. Marguerite Hamilton, Helen S., Lynette S. Home: 742 Columbian av., Oak Park. Office: 209 S. State st.

THE SALVATION ARMY

THE Salvation Army, a religious body, organized along military lines, was founded by Gen. William Booth in London, in 1865; its announced purpose being to reach and save the non-church goers of that day. It began work under the name of the Christian Mission and the military feature of its work was a later development. Today it is at work in more than 70 countries, employs 40 languages in its evangelistic work and publishes religious literature, the circulation of which exceeds one and one quarter million copies weekly.

The International Headquarters of the Army is at London and for governmental purposes the earth is divided into Territories, each of these in charge of a Commissioner. There are three Territories in the United States, viz., the Eastern, with headquarters in New York City; the Central, with headquarters in Chicago and the Western, with headquarters in San Francissco.

The Central Territory is under the direction of Commissioner William Peart with Colonel Sidney Gauntlett as Chief Secretary and includes 15 central states. It is divided into ten Divisions, each in charge of a Divisional Commander.

There are also Departmental Heads, having charge of the Social work of the organization. The Social Department is divided into Men's Social and Women's Social. The former includes Men's Hotels, Industrial Homes, Prison Work, and all forms of social endeavor for men. The Women's Social includes Rescue and Maternity Homes, Hospitals, Young Women's Boarding Homes and all forms of social work having to do with women.

There is also a Young Peoples Department, a Property Department, a Finance Department, a Field Department, which assumes control of the officers and workers, and a Special Efforts Department which has charge of financial campaigns and all matters which are of an unusual nature.

There is an Editorial and Trade Department. The former publishes the Central War Cry, a weekly publication with a circulation of eighty thousand copies.

Each Territory also has its West Point, or Training College where selected Candidates become Cadets and receive instruction along Salvation Army lines. There is a ten months' course in the Training College and this is followed by two years' work in the Field or institution before the Army issues a commission.

The Army begins its distinction among people at the Penitent Form, from which come virtually all of the Salvation Army workers. The first step is prisoner or convert. Conversion in the Salvation Army hall does not mean an acceptance of the Army doctrines and all who find them good and do accept are termed Recruits. After three months' probation a recruit becomes a Soldier Later if found worthy he may become a Local Officer, either as a Bandsman, or in one of the various Sergeant positions. This applies in both the Junior and Senior Corps.

The soldier who shows a leaning toward officership and is capable is encouraged to become a Candidate for the Training College and on entry to the college is ranked a Cadet. Leaving the college he or she becomes a Probationary Lieutenant or Captain. At the end of the field training and the completion of the correspondence course a commission is given and he leaves the probationary class.

The Salvation Army in the Central Territory maintains a Territorial Headquarters in Chicago at 108 North Dearborn steet, but is now in the process of changing to a new headquarters at State and Superior street. Communications for any department should be addressed to Commissioner Peart if speed in delivery is desired. Heads of Departments are as follows: Field Dept., Col. John T. Fynn; Finance Dept., Brig. Frank K. Robertson; Property Dept., Brig. John R. Wiseman; Young Peoples Dept., Maj. Walter Peacock; Training College, Col. Alfred Chandler; Editorial and Trade Depts., Lieut. Colonel Fletcher Agnew; Special Efforts Dept., Staff Capt. A. E. Marpurg; Women's Social Dept., Brig. Annie Cowden; Men's Social Dept., Brig. David Miller.

DR. MARK WHITE

SCIENCE has found a way to curb goiter and hay fever without the use of the surgical instrument. And for this discovery credit is due Dr. Mark White, Chicago physician, who gave to the world a serum made from the blood of a goat affected with para-thyroidism.

Long study convinced Dr. White that surgical removal of a part or whole of the thyroid gland is usually contra-indicated on account of the high mortality and that it does not establish normal function of the gland, or give dependable, complete or permanent results. In 1904, after leaving the University of Pennsylvania, he set about to find a way to circumvent this and first observed his new therapy. It was first tested out carefully on a large number of animals as to its therapeutic value and for the past fifteen years, both the originator and many leading medical observers have given it to hundreds of persons affected with hay fever, decided goitrous thyroids, and those which showed nervous and metabolic disturbances due to the inefficiency of the thyroid gland. The results obtained in most instances have been good and permanent and often follow only one treatment.

"It has been concluded that the therapeutic effect of the serum is to establish a normal function of the thyroid and harmonize the ductless gland," Dr. White said. "I have found that when my serum was injected into a human or animal, health usually followed, and the thyroid, when enlarged, reduced to normal size and function and the heart, mental and nervous complications disappearing permanently.

"Aside from marring one's appearance, the abnormal functioning thyroid gland can bring a multitude of other ailments often not recognized by the physician or laity. It is imperative that this organ having a blood supply equal to the brain (all of the blood in the body passes through the thyroid every sixty minutes). This vast amount of blood would not be necessary if the organ did not have so many functions to perform and the fact must not be overlooked that the thyroid gland secretes for the blood six of the seventeen elements and is often abnormal without enlargement.

"There is available only a limited amount of the serum and should be used in all cases of thyroidism or goiter for permanent reduction and function of the thyroid gland."

Dr. White was born in Winchester, Tenn., Jan. 15, 1879, son of Nannie (Ransom) and Mark H. White. He was educated in Tennessee, Pennsylvania, Colorado, Missouri and Illinois. He holds degrees of Science, Doctor of Medicine, Doctor of Veterinary Medicine and Doctor of Public Health. In 1922, he was married to Pauline Porter, only daughter of the late Washington Porter. They reside at 4043 Lake Park ave. Dr. White's office is at 30 N. Michigan ave.

CHARITY WORK OF THE ROMAN CATHOLIC CHURCH IN CHICAGO

EVERY now and then newspapers publish tidings of bequests, small or large, made by persons of different creeds in their last will and testament to the Associated Catholic Charities of the Chicago archdiocese or to some of the various individual Catholic charitable institutions conducted in Chicago and vicinity.

Such acts bring to light the fact that the quiet, extensive and systematic works of charity, which, under the direction of Archbishop George W. Mundelein, are conducted by the Catholic church in our midst, though little known or advertised among the vast masses of our people, are more and more recognized and appreciated as time goes on.

Through the zealous service of many thousands of nuns who have given up their entire lives to help and minister to the helpless, needy, unfortunate and suffering, through the co-operation of more than 1,000 priests and by the aid of a vast force of men and women of the Catholic laity, Archbishop Mundelein has made the works of charity in Chicago and vicinity stand out among the greatest achievements of the Catholic church in this country.

There is no form of human misery for which, in accordance with the Archbishop's plans, provision is lacking in the work of charity. Every phase of human misery is provided with some remedy or alleviation. While organized originally to give attention and to respond to the needs of their own co-religionists, the Catholic institutions and associations of charity, in their ministrations, take in all needy, irrespective of creed, race or color, in accordance with the spirit of its founder.

Helpless babes, who have been cruelly abandoned by their own parents, or infants, bereft of them by death or other causes even before they could know or feel a mother's love, are provided with homes in the infant asylums and foundling homes which are in charge of nuns. And just as homes are provided for the helpless who are on the threshold of life, so, too, are furnished retreats and homes for the aged people who are on the threshold of death, all in charge of those who consecrate their lives to that service.

Orphan asylums, industrial and training schools for dependent children, and schools where half orphans are cared for are maintained for boys and girls who are reared therein to become useful and worthy members of society. The boys and girls receive a thorough education and are also trained in trades, arts and industries to equip them to become independent, industrious members of society.

Hospitals for the cure and treatment of every form of physical ailment are maintained, as are various free dispensaries. There are day nurseries, homes for working girls, boys, and for adults in different parts of the city, all under Catholic auspices.

To all these institutions are welcomed not only the members of the Catholic religion but those of every form of faith and even those without any faith at all. The sisters in the institutions they conduct and the brothers in those which they manage make no distinction of persons, or nationality, or color, or creed, for their Christianity embraces them all.

In the work of charity of the Catholic church in Chicago and vicinity is not only the labor to assuage the physical distempers, but also the service to reclaim victims of moral ailments. The redemption and shelter of erring girls and women is conducted by nuns who are especially trained and who devote their entire lives to that service.

Unification and co-ordination of all charity dispensing bodies under the head of the Associated Catholic Charities of the Chicago archdiocese, in the management of which trained business men give their time and services without pay, is one of the important works originated and inaugurated by Archbishop Mundelein, which are proving such a success that they are being emulated outside of Chicago. In every one of the 344 churches, under the jurisdiction of Archbishop Mundelein, the people contribute and co-operate to help the poor, needy and suffering. From the central charity bureau, which the association maintains at the Holy Cross Mission, Desplaines and Randolph Sts., goes out food, clothing, financial and other aid into every nook and corner of Chicago and vicinity from which comes a call for help or a sound of distress. Families or people in need and distress, whose plight is made known to any of the priests, nuns, lay people or directly to the central office, are given help regardless of who or what they are if their distress is discovered.

Thousands of men give of their time and service every day and evening to further the work of charity as members of the Society of St. Vincent De Paul, by visiting the poor, helping them and by notifying the central charity bureau. Employment agencies are maintained to furnish work free of any fees to those who apply, and innumerable other activities are maintained to reach every possible need, ill and distemper of human society, in accordance with the teachings and spirit of the founder of the Catholic church.

There are many organizations of Catholic men and women directly and indirectly laboring in the cause of Catholic charities, with special fields of their endeavors planned for them. Some work within their parishes, while others extend beyond them. Among those which under the encouragement of Archbishop Mundelein have grown in great numbers is the Holy Name Society, which in a practical way does social welfare work, including the helping of boys through the big brother movement, giving free legal aid and advice and working for the improvement of conditions of the youth in the congested and poor districts. One of the activities of the Holy Name Society is to weed out cursing, swearing and the taking of the name of God in vain among the youths as well as grownups and by cultivating respect for law, authority and religion. There are a number of women organizations which are engaged in the service of social welfare under Catholic auspices.

In all the works of charity which Archbishop Mundelein directs and in the various associations and groups taking part in them, his first representative and most active co-worker is the auxiliary bishop of the Archdiocese of Chicago, the Right Reverend Edward F. Hoban, who, born and raised in Chicago, has intimate and personal knowledge of the needs, wants and requirements of this great city and its vicinity from a religious and charitable standpoint.

DR. LOYAL DEXTER ROGERS

LOYAL DEXTER ROGERS, A. M., M. D., LL. D., was born in Licking Co.
O., Dec. 10, 1856. His early education was acquired in country schools. He
worked on the farm during vacations until 1882, when he completed a seven-
year classical course at Denison Univ. at Granville, O., receiving the degree A. B.,
and later A. M. In 1884 he received the M. D. degree from Hahnemann Medical
Coll., Chicago, and in 1896 from Rush Medical Coll. He received the LL. D.
degree from Ill. Coll. of Law, Dept. of De Paul Univ. in 1905. He did post
graduate work in Europe in 1896, 1909 and 1910. He was Attending Surgeon for
two terms at Cook Co. Hospital, Chicago; Dean and Professor of Clinical Surgery, National Medical Univ., 20 years; Editor of the "People's Health Journal"
20 years; Editor of the "Panpath," a medical weekly, for several years. Since
1917 he has been editor of "The North American Journal of Homeopathy." He
is the author of several books "The Homeopathic Guide," 1893; "Asepsis, or
Surgical Cleanliness," 1900; "The Twelve-toed Baby Mystery," 1914; "Auto-
Hemic Therapy," 1916 and 1917; "Homeopathic Quizz Cards," 1921.

Much of his time is engaged in teaching Auto-Hemic Therapy, which he
originated in 1910.

Auto-Hemic Therapy consists of giving the patient a remedy made from a
small quantity of his or her own blood without the use of drugs or bacteria.
Over 400 physicians have tested it out in some 50,000 cases. The results obtained are well-nigh miraculous. He resides at 546 Surf St., Chicago.

JOHN ALFONZO WESENER

JOHN ALFONZO WESENER, president of The Columbus Laboratories, was born in Saginaw, Mich., March 14, 1865; son of Hugo and Bertha (Winguth) Wesener; ed. in Pub. Schs. of Saginaw and Owosso, Mich.; Mich. Agrl. Coll., 1886; Ph. C., Univ. of Mich., 1888; M. D. Coll. Phys. and Surg., Chicago, 1894; married Delilah Patty in Owosso, March 2, 1891. He began practice as chemist in Chicago, 1889. Prof. of Chem., Univ. of Ill., 1892-1902; Prof. of Chem., Am. Dental Coll., Dental Dept. of Northwestern Univ., 1893 and 1894. Held chair of Chem. in Chicago Coll. of Pharmacy, 1892-1894. Pres. Columbus Laboratories. Mem. of Cook Co. Coroner's staff of Toxicologists. Mem. A. M. A., Chicago Med. Soc., Physicians' Club, Am. Chem. Soc., Soc. of Chem. Industry; fellow Acad. of Med.; mem. of Military Order of Ill. Commandery of Loyal Legions. Club: Chicago Athletic. Protestant. Home: 4608 Malden St. Office: 1406, 31 N. State St.

OSTEOPATHY

OSTEOPATHY may be looked upon both as a discovery and a development. Andrew Taylor Still, a civil war surgeon, seems to have begun the practice of Osteopathy in 1874. As early as 1858, he expressed himself, however, as having lost faith in drugs as curative agents.

The first college of Osteopathy was established in 1892 at Kirksville, Missouri. Dr. Still had been practicing the new method for some years and his fame had grown until he was no longer able to care for all the people who came to him for help. He had enlisted the help of his sons after giving them his personal training. The demand grew beyond their efforts and a college was founded. This school grew so rapidly that within five years more than five hundred students were enrolled.

The phenomenal success of this college led to the founding of other institutions; colleges, hospitals, sanitaria, and the A. T. Still Research Institute.

Now there are seven colleges recognized by the Associated Colleges of Osteopathy and by the American Osteopathic Association, as follows: The Chicago College of Osteopathy, 5250 Ellis Ave., Chicago, Ill.; The American School of Osteopathy, Kirksville, Mo.; Kansas City College of Osteopathy and Surgery, Kansas City, Mo.; Des Moines-Still College of Osteopathy, Des Moines; College of Osteopathic Physicians and Surgeons, Los Angeles; Philadelphia College of Osteopathy, Philadelphia; Massachusetts College of Osteopathy, Boston.

Among the hospitals and sanitaria, are the following: Still-Hildreth Osteopathic Sanitarium, Macon, Mo. (nervous and mental cases); Delaware Springs Sanitarium, Delaware Springs, Ohio; Dufur Osteopathic Hospital, Philadelphia; The Laughlin Hospital, Kirksville, Mo.; Detroit Osteopathic Hospital, Detroit; Rose Valley Sanitarium, Media, Pa.; The Moore Sanitarium, Portland, Ore.; Asheville Osteopathic Sanitarium, Asheville, N. C.; Liberty Hospital, St. Louis; Des Moines General Hospital, Des Moines; Chicago Osteopathic Hospital, 5250 Ellis Ave., Chicago; Ottari, Asheville, N. C.; The Howell Sanitarium, Orlando, Fla.; Wayne-Leanard Sanitarium, Atlantic City, N. J.; Southwestern Osteopathic Sanitarium, Blackwell, Okla.; Chico Hot Springs, Emigrant Mont.; The Gamble Osteopathic Sanitarium, Salt Lake City; Osteopathic Hospital of Philadelphia; Terrace Springs Sanitarium, Richmond, Va.; Crane Sanitarium, Richmond, Ind.

The A. T. Still Research Institute is an endowed organization which is devoted to investigating Osteopathy from a laboratory view point. Its research work is under the general charge of Dr. Louise Burns, Los Angeles.

Today there are upwards of six thousand Osteopathic physicians practicing in the United States, Canada and European countries. There are also representative practitioners in parts of Asia, Africa, South America and Australia.

While Osteopathy has achieved legal recognition in practically every State in the Union, its greatest recognition has come from gratified patients, many of whom have been restored to health after failing in their search in many other directions. It may be said that the Osteopathic records of success and its reputation have been reared on the failures of other systems of treatment and diagnosis.

The early successes of Osteopathy were won largely in the field of chronic disease and with patients who had tried about everything else in the therapeutic world. But during the great influenza epidemic of 1918, Osteopathic physicians made such a wonderful record, that Osteopathy achieved at a bound the most widespread recognition in the treatment of this acute malady together with the treatment of the pneumonia which so often followed its onset.

Dr. George W. Riley of New York City collected the statistics of the Osteopathic profession with reference to this epidemic. Out of 110,122 cases of "flu" reported, there were 257 deaths, a mortality of ¼ of 1 per cent. The medical death rate was forty times as high. Out of 6,350 cases of epidemic pneumonia reported, there were 635 deaths, a mortality of only 10 per cent. The medical rate was three times as high. These figures were collected with the greatest care under responsible direction.

The Chicago College of Osteopathy has achieved an enviable reputation. It occupies a large building, together with the hospital, at 5250 Ellis Ave. It conducts a large Clinic where all types of cases, except communicable diseases, are treated. These include all classes of chronic diseases, surgical, obstetrical, eye, ear, nose and throat, gynecological, orthopedic and skin cases, in addition to the general cases which come to the Clinic from all parts of the city. The Chicago College has legal recognition in every State in the Union.

The Illinois Osteopathic Association at 27 E. Monroe St., is the representative body of the Osteopathic profession for its State.

Nationally the profession is represented by the American Osteopathic Association at 623 S. Wabash Ave., Chicago.

* * * * *

Osteopathy is the science of healing by adjustment of the body tissues through the application of natural laws. It was the first school of practice to recognize the relation of body mechanism to health. The osteopathic physician is trained through four separate school years of nine months each, in all branches necessary for correct diagnosis and in all the subjects which are universally recognized as a part of a professional education.

DR. I. R. WILLITS

DR. I. R. WILLITS, well known Chicago physician, was born at Keithsburg, Ill., February 4, 1882, son of Elizabeth (Kassion) and Ire Willits. He was educated in the public and high school of Keithsburg and the University of Illinois. On May 1, 1922, he was married to Gertrude Elsel. Dr. Willits came to Chicago, from Keithsburg, in 1905. He is a member of the Elks—Korashion Lodge. He resides at the Parkway Hotel, 2100 Lincoln Park W. His offices are at 530 N. Clark street, Chicago.

236

BUILDING—THE KEY TO PROSPERITY

NEXT to farming, local prosperity depends upon building activity. The reason is plain. Building is the country's second largest industry. It employs millions of workers directly, millions more to make the materials going into building, and hundreds of thousands in lumbering, quarrying and mining. It spurs activity in other lines—in transportation and in making and distributing machinery and furnishings for new buildings. The wages of these millions are used to buy food, clothing and other supplies that make business for farmers, storekeepers, wholesalers and manufacturers.

Everyone knows that a building shortage exists. One way to restore prosperity then is by a lively resumption of building. Materials and labor now are plentiful. Costs are lower. Cement will serve as a good example because it goes into nearly all building. It is used for making concrete for many buildings and almost exclusively for foundations of everything from chicken coops to skyscrapers.

For every ton of cement, 1¼ tons of raw materials and coal must be mined, shipped, assembled, dried, ground, weighed, mixed and then fused at about 3,000 degrees to a hard "clinker." This "clinker" must then be ground again, this time to a powder so fine that 78 per cent will pass through a sieve having 40,000 holes per square inch. To make cement, one literally must "tear down a mountain and put it through a sieve." And yet, cement sells at the mill for about $9 per ton! These facts caused the U. S. Geological Survey in a review of the cement industry a few years ago to say that "one could not scrape the free sand from the gutter for much less cost per barrel."

Prices Have Steadily Declined.

Portland cement has been made only about 50 years in America. U. S. production has grown from 42,000 barrels in 1880 to over 100,000,000 barrels in 1920. Several companies now ship more cement in one day than the entire yearly output of the industry in 1880. Prices declined as production went up, with lowest prices naturally in big markets near big mills. The average mill price in 1880 was $3 per barrel. Geological Survey figures give the average price for 1921 as $1.87 per barrel. Price reductions in some sections made late in 1921 and early in 1922 will doubtless cause 1922 figures to show a still further reduction. Prices per barrel to users naturally differ from net mill prices in that they must include:

(1) Refundable charge for package of 40 cents to 60 cents per barrel (4 sacks).

(2) Freight from mill to destination ranging from twenty-five cents to a dollar or more.

(3) Cost to dealer of unloading, hauling, warehousing, reloading and delivery to customer.

(4) Dealer's profit.

Of these items the charge for sacks is refunded in full for all sacks returned in good or repairable condition. By this "sack return" privilege, the cement industry enables cement users of America to save many millions of dollars a year merely by being careful in the handling of the 400,000,000 sacks in which cement is shipped to them. Of course, this privilege adds heavily to the accounting and management cost for manufacturers, besides the cost of cleaning and mending the many millions of sacks.

237

WILLIAM J. SINEK

WILLIAM J. SINEK, contractor, was born in Terre Haute, Ind., 1877, son of I. and F. (Winfield) Sinek. Educated in Public Schools; unmarried. Came to Chicago in 1891. Member of firm of Blome Sinek Co., (General Contractors). Member Building Construction Employers' Association, Chicago Association of Commerce. Aside from being Exalted Ruler of Chicago Lodge of Elks for third term, Mr. Sinek is also president for the third time of the Big Bros., Inc., an organization devoted to the betterment of boys of Chicago. He is a member of the Chicago Yacht Club, Edgewater Golf Club, Illinois Athletic Club, Bankers Club of New York, and Chicago Equestrian Association. Home: 7214 Sheridan Road. Office: 712 City Hall Square Bldg.

The cost of making cement is made up principally of labor, freight rates, coal and limestone, and the chief element in the cost of coal and limestone is labor. An investigation of the costs of one of the largest cement plants in the United States discloses the fact that its cost of coal at mines in February, 1922, was 203 per cent greater than in 1913, the cost of limestone at quarries 60 per cent greater, and of labor 54 per cent greater. About 1¾ tons of raw material and coal are required to produce one ton of cement. Freight rates on coal in February, 1922, were 107 per cent greater than in December, 1913, and on limestone 52 per cent greater. But the increase in selling price of this company at this time as compared with 1913 is only 48½ per cent.

When these facts are considered those of us who have held to a view that current cement prices are high may revise our ideas. It may help us to read what the War Industries Board said in an official bulletin in 1919:

"The remarkable lowering of the prices of Portland cement from $3 a barrel in 1880, while the prices of its chief competitors, lumber, brick and stone, advanced from 20 to 75 per cent, is one of the reasons why Portland cement has gained new uses at the expense of its rivals. The decline in cement prices from 1913 to 1914 and 1915 was the result of sharp competition between cement mills with productive capacity over 50 per cent in excess of the output. The subsequent rise in the price of cement from 1916 to 1918 was due to rapidly increasing wages and fuel costs. On the whole, however, cement prices did not rise as rapidly as the prices of other building materials."

Cement a Standardized Product

Cement is so widely used that users themselves have standardized it. Today every cement maker, regardless of his brand, meets the specifications set jointly by the U. S. Government and the country's leading engineering societies. The different brands of cement, therefore, are all alike.

Because of this, the prices of various brands of cement in any given market usually are the same. The reason for this puzzles many. But the answer is simply and well stated by W. Stanley Jevons, M.A., F.R.S., in his standard work, "The Theory of Political Economy," which says:

"If in selling a quantity of perfectly equal and uniform barrels of flour, a merchant arbitrarily fixed different prices on them, a purchaser would, of course, select the cheaper ones; and where there was absolutely no difference in the things purchased, even an excess of a penny in the price of anything worth a thousand pounds would be a valid ground for choice. Hence follows what is undoubtedly true * * * *, that in the same open market, at any one moment, there cannot be two prices for the same article."

Applying Jevons' economic law, a simple illustration of cement competition may be cited thus: A, B and C are cement makers. Each seeks business at M, a town with a 50-cent freight rate from A, 60 cents from B and 70 cents from C. This gives A a 10-cent advantage over B and 20 cents over C. A figures he can sell at say, a mill price of $2.00, so adds the 50 cents freight and quotes $2.50 at M. Then if B and C want to do business at M they must meet A's price, requiring B to go 10 cents below A in his mill price and C to go 20 cents below A in his mill price. Unless B and C can make the mill price sacrifices required by the market at M as made by A's $2.50 price, then A will monopolize the market at M up to his capacity to supply that market.

Similar principles apply to other materials. Prices are not arbitrarily made. They are based upon competition, supply and demand and upon the cost of transportation, raw materials and labor. Supply of labor and materials now is plentiful. We cannot afford longer to delay needed building improvements. This is particularly true because building is so entwined with the nation's prosperity that a full revival of building will hasten a revival of other lines of business.

239

WALTER W. AHLSCHLAGER

W. W. AHLSCHLAGER, noted architect, was born in Chicago. July 20, 1887; s. of John and Louise Ahlschlager; ed. in Lewis, Armour and Art Institutes. Married Jennie Wiik, Chicago, 1914. Children: Walter W., Jr., Marcella, Charlotte. Practicing in Chicago since 1911. In 1921, business was incorporated under firm name of Walter W. Ahlschlager, Inc. Some of the buildings he has designed are: Sheridan Plaza Hotel, Senate Theatre, Union Liberty Office Bldg., Evanston Golf Club; Wagner Baking Co., Detroit. He is also pres. of The Realty Trust, North Shore Development Co. Mem. of Masons, Elks. Clubs: Evanston Golf, Ill. Athletic. Home: 3400 Sheridan Road. Office: 65 E. Huron St.

FRANK E. DAVIDSON

FRANK E. DAVIDSON, architect and engineer, was born in Hillsborough, Ia., June 7, 1867; s. of Mary Louis (De Sollar) and Robert Davidson; ed. in Iowa State Coll., Ames, 1887-90. Married Emilie H. Hardie, Chicago, Sept. 20, 1896. Mem. of bd. of local improvements and supt. dept. of sewers, Chicago, 1898-9; structural eng., Ill. Steel Co., 1899-1904; architect and eng. of construction for Western Elect. Co., 1905-08; mem. firm of Davidson & Weiss, architects, and Patterson & Davidson, engineers, since 1909. Dem. nominee for alderman of thirty-fourth ward, 1897; mem. of bd. of Park and Bldg. Advisers of Ill., 1917. Mem. of Am. Inst. of Architects, Ill. Soc. of Architects, N. F. P. A., Am. Specif. Inst., Am. Soc. C. E., W. E. S. Mason (Shriner). Mr. Davidson is serving fifth year as president of Ill. Soc. of Architects and seventh year as editor of society's publications. Home: 7436 Kimbark av. Office: 1448 Monadnock Block.

HENRY NEWGARD & COMPANY

H IS aversion to farm work and his penchant for delving into the intricacies of electrical machines gave Henry Newgard the reason for leaving his father's farm in Norway. Incidentally, it gave the United States Henry Newgard & Company, the oldest electrical contracting house in Chicago, which, in its half century of existence, has acquired a wide reputation for developing new electrical appliances.

Henry Newgard was born in Norway, May 10, 1858. His education was obtained in a rural school, after which family custom demanded that he till the land. This was not to his liking and at the age of 16 he left for Christiania. Through some of his acquaintances, he obtained a position as an apprentice in a locksmith shop and served his five years' apprenticeship.

Then to his ears wafted stories of the great opportunities to be found in America and he sailed May 6, 1879, landing in Chicago just fifteen days later. But he found conditions the reverse of what he had expected. Work was scarce and, when his money gave out, he was forced to take a position as helper in a furniture factory at $5 per week. He clung to this until several of his friends, working in the Northwestern R. R. shops, aided him in securing a place with the railroad. He was in the employ of the Northwestern R. R. for eight months, leaving to become assistant for E. T. Orne, locksmith and bell hanger, who had a small shop at 120 E. Randolph st. Here he worked for three years, utilizing every bit of leisure time in studying electricity and experimenting with batteries, bells, gas lighting and burglar alarms.

In 1882, he opened a locksmith shop in a basement at 167 Madison st., which he conducted for a decade. He sold out and started a strictly electrical contracting business at 88 La Salle st. Through careful and conscientious business methods, his clientele increased almost tenfold and he obtained larger offices in various places in the loop.

In 1898, he gave his brother, Martin, a half-interest in the firm. In 1902, he incorporated, under the name of Henry Newgard & Company, with Mr. Newgard as president and treasurer; Mr. Martin Newgard, vice-president and Mr. Charles Edward Browne, secretary. These same officers control the company's destinies today.

Because of the rapid strides taken by the business, the company found larger quarters a necessity and it moved its offices and shops to its present location at Washington blvd. and Morgan st. Here it improved its facilities for manufacturing switch boards, panel boards, steel cutout cabinets, Newgard waterproof receptacles and globes and motor and dynamo repairing and rewinding.

In the past thirty years, the company has installed lighting plants and wiring in many of America's leading structures.

Some of the Chicago office buildings the company has equipped are the Old Colony Life; Chicago, Burlington and Quincy; City Hall Square; Garland; Consumers. Some of the residences are those of Harold F. McCormick at Lake Forest, Ill., and Lake Shore Drive; E. V. Price, Highland Park, Ill.; George A. McKinlock, Lake Forest, and Mr. Clows, Lake Forest.

The company is a member of several associations, including the following: Electrical Contractors' Association of Chicago; National Electrical Contractors' Association; The Manufacturers and Dealers Association of Chicago; the Building Construction Employers' Association of Chicago.

ROBERT ISHAM RANDOLPH

ROBERT ISHAM RANDOLPH, consulting engineer, was born in Chicago, April, 14, 1883; s. of Mary H. (Taylor) and Isham Randolph; ed. in Virginia Military Inst., Cornell Univ., and Armour Inst. of Tech. Employed by Sanitary Dist. of Chicago, 1904-7; secy. of Int. Imp. Comm. of Ill., 1908-11; eng.-secy. of Rivers and Lakes Comm. of Ill., 1911-13; partner in firm of Isham Randolph & Co., 1913-21; in 1921 he incorporated the Randolph-Perkins Eng. Co. of which he is now secy. He married Martha Mac-Lean, Oct. 17, 1912, Chicago. He served with U. S. Army in Mexican border in 1917 and in France from 1918 to 1919. Mem. Am. Soc. of Civil Eng., ex-pres. Chicago Chapter of Am. Assn. of Eng.; pres. Ill. Soc. of Eng.; mem. Western Soc. of Eng. Vice comm. of Riverside Post Am. Legion. Clubs: University, Engineers, Riverside Golf. Office: 38 S. Dearborn St. Home: Riverside, Ill.

JOACHIM G. GIAVER

JOACHIM G. GIAVER, civil engineer, was born in Norway, Aug. 15, 1856; s. Jens H. and Hanna Birgitte (Holmbae) Giaver; C. E. Throndhjems Technical Coll., Throndhjem, Norway, 1881; came to America, 1882. Married Louise C. Schmedling, Throndhjem, Sept. 3, 1885. Children: Astrid (Mrs. Ralph Holmbae), Birgit (Mrs. A. C. Bull), Erling, Finn J., Einar. Draughtsman bridge dept. N. P. R. R., St. Paul, Minn., 1882-83; draughtsman, 1883-85, chief engr., 1885-90, Shiffler Bridge Co., Pittsburgh; asst. chief engr., World's Columbian Expn., Chicago, 1892-93; gen. cont., 1893 96; bridge designer for Sanitary Dist. of Chicago, 1896-98; chief engr., D. H. Burnham & Co., Chicago, 1898-1915; consulting engr., Chicago, since 1915; mem. Giaver & Dinkelberg, architects and engrs., since 1916. Chicago bldgs. for which he designed steel structure and foundations are: First Nat. Bank Building, Continental & Commercial

National Bank Building, Peoples Gas Building, Railway Exchange, Heyworth Building, Field Building, Conway Building; Equitable Building, N. Y.; Wanamaker Building, Philadelphia; Trustee Tabitha Hosp. Mem. Am. Soc. C. E., Structural Engr. Assn. of Ill. (pres. 1916-17), Western Soc. Engrs. Clubs: Chicago Athletic, Chicago Norske Klub, Svenska Klubben, Chicago Yacht Club, Engineers'. Home: 4632 Beacon st. Office: 500 Wrigley Bldg.

JOHN GRIFFITHS & SON COMPANY

MUCH of the country's leading structural work is the result of the efforts of John Griffiths & Son, builders. Buildings the company has erected dot the nation from coast to coast.

The firm owes its inception to the energy, unremitting work, and perspicacity of John Griffiths. He was born on a farm near Woodstock, Ont., April 3, 1846, and at seventeen began a three-year apprenticeship in the mason trade. He worked as a mason in Canada until 1869 and in Chicago until 1873, when he set out for himself as a builder and contractor.

Some of the out-of-town buildings erected by the Griffiths company are the John Wanamaker retail store, New York; Land Title, Philadelphia; Atlanta Federal prison; Brown Marx, First National Bank and Woodward, all of Birmingham, Ala.; First National Bank, Cincinnati; and Columbus Savings and Trust, Columbus, O. The Chicago buildings include the Masonic Temple, Great Northern Hotel, Butler Brothers, National Biscuit Co., Boston Store, Hotel Sherman, Mandel Brothers Retail Store, Rothschild Co. Store, The Hub, Marshall Field Store, Cook County Hospital, Chicago Telephone, Cunard, Federal Reserve Bank, Union Station foundations.

John Griffiths is president of the company, George W. Griffiths, vice president, and Louis C. Joyer, secretary. Offices are at 1011 Merchants Loan & Trust Building.

WHITE CITY ELECTRIC COMPANY

SUPERIORITY of its work and pursuance of a progressive policy have won for the White City Electric company a high place among building firms of the country.

Although still an "infant" corporation, having been organized in 1905, the White City Electric company has installed electrical equipment in many leading structures, built in America in the past fifteen years.

Some of the Chicago buildings which have been equipped by the White City Electrical company are: Chicago Tribune, Morrison Hotel, Butler Brothers, Excelsior Motor Manufacturing Co., Albert Dickinson Seed Co., Chicago Beach Hotel, South Shore Country Club, Florsheim Shoe Co., Rand McNally, Gulbransen Dickinson Piano Co. It has also equipped the Portland Auditorium, Portland, Ore.; Sears Roebuck & Co., Seattle; Post Office, Grand Rapids, Mich.

At the time of its organization, the capital of the company was just $2,000. This was increased to $50,000 and the volume of business each year has grown from $80,000 to $700,000. During the war, the company was called upon to install electrical wiring in many government buildings.

L. D. Grey is the president, and L. E. Mayer, secretary and treasurer. General offices are at 14 North Franklin street.

NASH BROTHERS

HANDLING some of America's largest sewage construction jobs is the specialty of Nash Brothers, general contractors of 10 S. La Salle St. The members of the firm are P. A. Nash and R. J. Nash. In the thirty years of their business career they have done millions of dollars' worth of construction work. They are now completing work on a $1,000,000 sewage contract for the City of Detroit and an $800,000 job for Oak Park, Ill. Nash Brothers are building the Bubbly Creek sewer for the City of Chicago. This is the largest sewer ever undertaken here and its approximate cost is estimated at $2,000,000. Nash Brothers are building a twenty-five-foot sewer to take care of Bubbly Creek and it is then to be filled on top and the Thirty-ninth Street Boulevard built over where the creek used to be.

DIXON C. WILLIAMS

DIXON C. WILLIAMS, manufacturer and lecturer on economic and spiritual topics, was born in Arkansas, 1859; s. of Mattie (Dillon) and Dixon C. Williams; ed. in Julia Jones Private Sch. and Cumberland Univ. Married Sallie McKnight, Woodbury, Tenn., 1876. Children, J. Lester, Mai Fare Soriano. Mr. Williams left college to enter First National Bank, Lebanon, Tenn.; later, became teller for People's Bank. Established and edited Lebanon Register, weekly paper, for a number of years, during which time he also served in Lebanon city council. He then became interested in Y. M. C. A. work and for 12 years conducted union evangelistic work for Cumberland Presbyterian church. Throat trouble limited this work. Between church campaigns he built street railway at Anderson, Ind. Established Lester Seminary for Girls, Holden, Mo., being president for two years. Because of continued bad health, forcing him to cancel lectures, he accepted position in creamery machine house in Chicago. In 1910, he organized Chicago Nipple Manufacturing Co., of which he is now president and general manager. During President Wilson's first term, he was appointed Chicago postmaster, but appointment was not confirmed by Senate, on account of the senatorial courtesy request of Senator Lewis made nearly one year after the appointment. Mem. S. A. R.; Mason; Odd Fellow; K. of P. Clubs: Southern, Iroquois, One Hundred Year. Home: 414 Diversey Pkway. Office: 1966 Southport av.

THE CRAWFORD AVENUE BRIDGE

THE STRAUSS BASCULE BRIDGE CO.

THE $1,000,000 Crawford avenue bridge, which is herewith shown, is one of Chicago's newest Strauss Bascule bridges. Part of the Pershing road-lake-zoo project, the span and approaches extend from 36th street alo.'g Crawford avenue to 41st street, forming a short north and south section of Pershing road.

The bridge has a total length of 3,000 feet, including embankment approaches. The bridge proper is 1,800 feet. A Strauss double leaf trunnion bascule bridge, measuring 228 feet between pivots, spans the drainage canal. The roadway is thirty-eight feet wide, with two street car tracks and eight-foot sidewalks on either side. The bridge is designed so the roadway can be widened to 56 feet.

Together with two other Strauss bridges of similar d'mensions at Cicero and California avenues, it connects two great districts of Chicago, once separated by the canal, and with no passenger bridges for several miles.

One of the great testimonials for the Strauss Bascule bridge is the fact that the last thirteen bridges built or being built by the City of Chicago and the Sanitary District are of this type. By virtue of its many patents, the Strauss company is able to save its clients thousands of dollars over and above its charges for engineering services and royalty. Its movable bridges are in use in nearly every large city of the country.

Main offices of the Strauss company are at 225 North Michigan avenue. Branch offices are at 603 Albee Bldg., Washington, D. C.; 14 Windsor Hotel, Montreal, Que.; 906 London Bldg., Vancouver, B. C.

NEWBERY ELECTRIC COMPANY

THE Newbery Electric company, one of the largest electrical contracting firms in the country, has a long record of unfailing service. During the thirty years of its existence, it has fostered co-operation in the industry, encouraged enterprise and surrounded itself with an organization of executives and workmen which insures flawless work. As a result, many of the leading construction jobs undertaken in America in the past quarter of a century have been entrusted to the Newbery company and not once has the trust been violated. The company handled the wiring and installation of electrical equipment in the Municipal Pier, Edgewater Beach Hotel and the Federal Reserve Bank Building. The rapid increase in business has necessitated the establishment of branch offices in New Orleans, Kansas City, Dallas, Los Angeles and San Francisco. F. E. Newbery is the president; H. C. Newkirk, vice president, and Miss E. Meyer, secretary and treasurer. The general offices are located at 14 E. Jackson boulevard.

AVERY BRUNDAGE

THE NAME of Avery Brundage, general contractor and engineer, with offices at 110 S. Dearborn st., has appeared over a number of important jobs in the loop and throughout Chicago. Mr. Brundage is a member of the Chicago Athletic Association, Yacht club and the Engineers' club.

JOHN J. SLOAN

J. J. SLOAN, gen. mgr. of Wisconsin Granite Co., was born in Chicago, Sept. 28, 1867; s. of B. A. (Grogan) and Frank Sloan; ed. in priv. primary schs. and Armour Inst. Married Margaret Frederick, May 25, 1892, Chicago. Daughter, Loretta. Mr. Sloan was asst. Co. agent, 1892-94; chief clerk, dept. of pub. works, 1894-96; mining engineer, 1896-99; supt. of House of Correction, 1899-1905; mem. of Bridewell Bd., 1905-19. He is now gen. mgr. Wis. Granite Co., vice-pres of Midland Terra Cotta Co., treas. of Hedges Construction Co. Home: 2908 Warren Av. Office: 1013 Chamber of Commerce.

JAMES E. McSHANE

JAMES E. McSHANE, former assistant state's attorney for Cook Co., was born in Chicago; ed. in Cathedral Coll. and studied law in Loyola Univ. Admitted to Ill. bar in 1916. Appointed asst. state's atty. of Cook Co., by Maclay Hoyne, Sept. 1918 and assigned to trial dept. Reappointed in 1920 by Robert E. Crowe. Resigned in 1921 and engaged in general practice of law with J. William Brooks, under firm name of McShane and Brooks. He is married to Grace E. Finnegan and has one child. He was one of the eleven lawyers to be appointed by Robt. E. Crowe, state's atty. of Cook County, Ill., as a special prosecutor for the purpose of cleaning up crime in Chicago. Clubs: Illinois Athletic, Olympia Fields Country, Lawyers Assn. of Chicago and Illinois Bar Association.

ROY JOSEPH EGAN

ROY JOSEPH EGAN, attorney, was born in Chicago, May 18, 1897; s. of Margaret (Brown) and John Egan; grad. Sacred Heart Sch., 1911; St. Patrick's Commercial Acad., 1915; De Paul Univ., Coll. of Law, 1919; L. L. B. degree from De Paul in 1919. Appointed dep. Probate Court Clerk, 1919; appointed asst. U. S. Dist. Atty. by Pres. Wilson, in 1920. He was youngest man ever to hold that office and gained title of "boy prosecutor." Resigned, Oct, 1, 1921, to enter private law practice. Served in U. S. Navy. Democrat. Mem. of K. of C., Order of Alhambra. Home: 2129 So. Halsted St. Office: 1st National Bank Building.

SAMUEL EVANS

SAMUEL EVANS, manufacturer of ornamental glass, was born in Montgomeryshire, Wales; son of Mr. and Mrs. Edward Evans. He was educated in public schools and in private college and in 1880 came to the U. S., moving to Chicago in 1890. In 1882, he married Elizabeth Jones, Racine, Wis. Children: Anne (Mrs. S. M. Halsted), Wallace, Daisy (Mrs. Harry Hall), and Samuel, Jr. Mr. Evans organized the firm of Rawson and Evans, which continued until the death of Mr. Rawson in 1905, when the business was incorporated as the Rawson and Evans company, of which he is president and treasurer. Mr. Evans is inventor and patentee of most of the important processes of sandblasting ornamental glass, including the chipped glass signs used by leading banks. For this he was presented a medal at the World's Fair in Chicago. Mr. Evans is interested with his son, Wallace, in the largest game propagating farm in the world, at St. Charles, Ill. He is a member of the Chicago Association of Commerce and Illinois Manufacturers Association. Home: St. Charles. Office: 710 W. Washington street.

JOHN BERNARD DE VONEY

JOHN BERNARD DE VONEY, realtor and president of the realty company known as John B. De Voney Co., was born in New Orleans, June 11, 1882; the son of Terene (Lampias) and Anthony De Voney. When very young Mr. De Voney moved to Chicago where he received his education and, in a modest way, organized the John B. De Voney Co., real estate firm which has grown to be one of the largest in the city. He resides at the Drake hotel and his business address is 133 W. Washington st.

THE VITROLITE COMPANY

C LEANLINESS, to be a real advertisement, must be apparent. The Vitrolite Company, by the manufacture of pure white Vitrolite counters and table tops, wainscoting and ceilings, has made cleanliness profitable in restaurants, hospitals, homes and in many other capacities.

In the restaurant, the sparkling clean whiteness of Vitrolite counters and table tops is a standing invitation to tarry. Its delightfully cool surface is just the place to serve palatable drinks and dainties. It keeps clean—nothing stains it and it just wears and wears. Vitrolite eliminates use of expensive table coverings and the incidental cost of laundering and linen replacement. It is economical because it cuts overhead—profitable because it builds a better business for the owner.

Vitrolite has also been put to use in a number of the modern hospitals. The architect who specializes in the design of hospitals knows only too well the insistent demand for scientific sanitation in everything that enters into the construction and equipment of an operating, diet and utility room, as well as the laboratory. Vitrolite is aseptic and can be installed in large slabs so that seams and joints are reduced to a minimum, thus eliminating to a very considerable degree the space that is ideal for the germinating and propagating of bacteria. No chemicals can possibly stain or react with Vitrolite; it does not craze and can be sterilized without injury. Permanence is also an important feature of Vitrolite walls and ceilings.

Vitrolite is the product of the fusion at 3,000° Fahrenheit, of sand, feldspar, fluorspar, kryolith, and several other natural ingredients, which, in passing from a fluid state to that of a solid, becomes homogeneous in substance, impermeable to the absorption of foreign matter and acid-resisting. It is manufactured in the form of large slabs of various thicknesses, which are subjected to a thorough process of annealing, making them tough, with a tensile strength and surface wearing qualities that are said to exceed even those of marble.

Vitrolite may be called scientifically sanitary because it has a natural fire polished surface that is non-porous, therefore, non-absorbent. The surface of Vitrolite is said to possess greater abrasive resistance than marble. Vitrolite is of a uniform texture and its depth of rich white color gives it the appearance of wholesome cleanliness which completes its sanitary qualities. Organic acids have no effect on Vitrolite.

The Vitrolite Company was founded in 1907, with a capital of $125,000. Its present capitalization is $900,000. In its first year, the volume of business approximated $54,000. In 1922, it reached the figure of $1,500,000. G. R. Meyercord is president; D. S. Beebe, vice president and treasurer; J. W. Wiley, secretary and assistant treasurer. Directors are G. R. Meyercord, D. S. Beebe, James B. Day, James H. Furman, William H. Powell. The main offices are at 133 W. Washington street, Chicago.

The plant behind the Vitrolite product covers six acres of ground at Parkersburg, W. Va., and is capable of producing 5,000,000 square feet of material each year. To meet the foreign demand, there have been formed in the principal cities of the United States, in Cuba, England, China and Japan, separate organizations composed of thoroughly trained Vitrolite specialists who carry a stock of material and have the necessary machinery to work it and who are capable of making proper installation.

249

MICHAEL E. WHITE

FROM brakeman to one of the leading contractors of the country—thus reads the story of the life of Michael E. White. He was born in 1863 in Oak Creek, just outside of Milwaukee, the son of Elizabeth and Patrick White. His education was received in Oak Creek and Chicago public schools.

Mr. White started his career as a brakeman on the North Western Railroad. At the age of 19, he was made a conductor, which position he held until the age of 42, when he entered the railroad contracting business. Later, he handled his first contract for paving in the city of Milwaukee. This was soon followed by many contracts for bridge building for western railroads.

The steady increase in business induced him to move to Chicago, where he has handled many of the city's biggest paving jobs. Mr. White is president and treasurer of the White Construction Co., White Paving Co., Western Boarding and Supply Co., Fox River Sand & Gravel Co. and M. E. White Co. In 1883 he married Mathilda O'Brien, of Columbus, Wis. Children: Albert W., Alice, Francis L., Edward W., Marion, Michael E., Jr. Home: Milwaukee, Wis. Office: 130 N. Wells st.

HENRY PASCHEN

HENRY PASCHEN, member of Paschen Brothers, general contractors, was born in Chicago, Oct. 7, 1882; son of Theresa (Bonning) and Christian P. Paschen; educated in Chicago public schools and Lewis Institute. Married Lillian M. Field, Chicago, Jan. 23, 1918. Daughter, Marjorie Theresa. From the time of his graduation from college to the incorporation of Paschen Brothers in 1906, Mr. Paschen engaged in an intensive study of the rudiments of building. Paschen Brothers have constructed some of Chicago's leading edifices, including the Carter H. Harrison school, Municipal Pier, Chicago Theatre, Somerest Hotel and the Loop Office Building. The company is a member of the Chicago Assn. of Commerce, Builders and Traders Exchange, Carpenters and Building Assn., Building Employers' Assn. Mr. Paschen resides at 2144 Alice Place. Office: 111 W. Washington St.

T. J. FORSCHNER CONTRACTING CO.

THE above are various views of Chicago's great sewage treatment plant, which is being built by the T. J. Forschner Contracting Company for the Sanitary District of Chicago. Municipal authorities from all sections of the United States have come to Chicago to study the plant.

The sewage plant contract was awarded to the Forschner company because of its reasonable bids and its long experience in municipal work. The Forschner company, prior to beginning construction of the sewage system, had just completed a pumping station and power plant for the Sanitary District of Chicago at an approximate cost of a million dollars.

The company's officers are: T. J. Forschner, president; A. J. Forschner, secretary and treasurer, and W. P. Forschner, vice president. Main offices are in Chicago.

WILLIAM F. QUINLAN

WILLIAM F. QUINLAN, president of the Edgewater Coal Company, was born in Chicago in 1859; son of Catherine (Blackhall) and Michael Quinlan. He was educated in the public and parochial schools of Chicago. In 1888, in Chicago, he married Annie F. McMahon (deceased). Children: William J., J. Perry, Francis M., and Gertrude. Mr. Quinlan organized the Edgewater Coal Company in 1902 and, under his direction, it has developed into one of the biggest fuel firms in Chicago. Mr. Quinlan resides at 6350 Winthrop avenue. His office is at 5627 Broadway.

PATRICK HENRY MOYNIHAN

UNDER the leadership of Patrick Henry Moynihan, the Calumet Coal Company has become one of the greatest purveyors of fuel in Chicago. Despite the vagaries of the fuel situation, the Calumet Coal Company has won high esteem for the methods it employs in trading.

Mr. Moynihan was born in Chicago, the son of Celia (O'Donnell) and John Moynihan. His education was received in Chicago grammar and high schools. He is married and has four children. They are Harry, Leslie, Marie and Mildred. Following his marriage, Mr. Moynihan entered the coal business and his indefatigable energy soon placed him in the forefront of the local trade.

In addition to being vice-president of the Calumet Company, Mr. Moynihan is president of the Hiawatha Phonograph Company. He is also president of the South Chicago Business Men's Club. Mr. Moynihan resides at 2328 E. 92d Place. His office is at 9022 Commercial avenue.

CURTISS CANDY COMPANY

FIGURES tell the story of the Curtiss Candy Company. In 1917, the first year of its existence, the company's sales aggregated $92,623.46. For the year 1921, the sales totalled $1,091,020.65, representing more than a 1,000 per cent increase in the volume of business.

The growth becomes all the more remarkable when one considers that it came during a critical period in the nation's history, the war with Germany.

The Curtiss Company had its beginning at 3256 North Clark street, where it occupied a store room that measured 20 by 30 feet. The candy making force consisted of one man and at the time of leaving this location, the company employed one helper and four girls.

Offices were next transferred to 3222 North Halsted street, where the company had the use of the second floor, a space about 45 by 175 feet. Here it began with two men and four girls. As many as 120 men and women were employed at times.

On January 10, 1919, the company moved into its own building, The Curtiss building, at 750-758 Briar place. This structure has three floors and measures 100 by 125 feet, containing a total of 37,500 square feet. With the opening of its own building, the company increased its working force to 400 men and women, not including salesmen.

Having reached this far, the reader's query, no doubt, will be: "But what accounts for this rapid expansion?" And the answer is: Curtiss executives know not only candy but also the public's taste and it has been their aim ever to satisfy it; they have won the esteem and good will of their customers through an honorable policy of trading, and by surrounding their workers with the best of conditions and giving them a voice in the company's affairs, they have naturally heightened their employes' interest in their work, with the result that their candies are better. The element of hard work should not be overlooked, however.

Some of the delicacies for which the company is noted are the Mint Patty, Nougat, Kandy Kake, Orange Ice, Cream Cake, Sweet Mama, Dixie Flyer, Jolly Jacks, Listen Lester, Polar Bar, Ko-Ket, Swan-ee, Lightnin,' Baby Ruth, Zebra Suckers, and the Big Bite. The company's affairs are in the hands of the following officers: Otto Y. Schnering, president; William C. Bickle, vice president; William C. Moller, secretary; H. J. Krieger, assistant secretary; Julius Schnering, treasurer, and Karl F. Keefer, assistant treasurer. The directorate consists of Otto Y. Schnering, Julius Schnering, Lawrence H. Whiting, George Blossom, Jr., Milton M. Morse, F. H. Borneman, E. V. Zeddies, J. F. Kenfield, and K. F. Keefer.

Of the Curtiss candies, one customer has said, "Their taste is that of sunshine." The company is known as the "Chocolate Bar Goods House of America," as its line of bar goods is larger than that of any other manufacturer in the country. The firm sells only to jobbers.

253

DR. EDWARD GEORGE PATERA

DR. EDWARD G. PATERA, physician, was born in Chicago, May 26, 1875; s. of Caroline (Sladek) and Mathew Patera; educated in Chicago public schools; N. Western Univ. School of Pharmacy, 1894-5; Univ. of Ill. Med. School, 1903. Married Jane Florence Smyth, July 2, 1910, Chicago. Children: Edward Smyth, Jane Karoline. Dr. Patera served as interne at St. Mary's hospital, Chicago, from 1903-5; mem. surgical staff, St. Mary's hospital; asst. clinical surgery, Augustana hospital; associated with Dr. A. J. Orlisners Clune, 1917-18; attended European clinics in 1910 and 1913; awarded Fellowship degree, American Coll. of Surg., Philadelphia, 1921. Served during Spanish-American war as corporal in 2d Ill. Vol. Inf. Mem. Am. Med. Assn.; Ill., Chicago, Bohemian Med. Socs. Club: Chicago Athletic. Home: 2830 Sheridan rd. Office: 1809 Loomis st.

DR. HERMAN EARHART ALMES

DR. HERMAN EARHART ALMES, physician, was born at Long Rung, Pa., Dec. 28, 1867; s. Samuel A. and Mary (Hineman) Almes; ed. in pub. schs. at Elders Ridge, Pa. Academy; M. D. Univ of Wooster, Cleveland, O., July 4, 1889; M. D. Western Univ of Pa., March 27, 1890. Married Cora Carnahan, Dec. 30, 1891, Cochran Mills, Pa. Practiced medicine at Murraysville, Pa., for short time; at Cochran Mills, Pa., 1890-6; in Chicago since 1896. Mem. A. M. A., Ill. State Med. Soc., Chicago. Med. Soc., Life mem. Chicago Art Inst. Republican. Mason (32d degree Shriner), Elks. Clubs: Colonial, Chicago Press (life), Mystic Athletic. Home: 4226 Michigan av. Office: 4255 Indiana av.

WERNER W. SCHROEDER

WERNER W. SCHROEDER, counsel for Gov. Small in his trial at Waukegan, was born in Kankakee, Ill., Dec. 20, 1892; s. of Sophia (Steinmeyer) and Frederick Schroeder; ed. in Kankakee schools; Univ. of Mich., A.B., 1914; Juris. Doctor, 1916. Married Elizabeth Sinclair More, Milwaukee, Sept. 22, 1920. Mr. Schroeder was instructor in polit. economy, Univ. of Mich., 1914; mem. of law firm of Small, Bratton & Schroeder at Kankakee, 1916-18; gen. practice, 1918-21. In 1921, he was appointed secretary, Legislative Reference Bureau, Springfield, Ill., and in this position, 1,000 bills were drawn up under his direction for members of the legislature at the 52nd General Assembly. Successfully defended Gov. Small in the suits instituted last year. Home: Kankakee. Office: 38 S. Dearborn St., Chicago.

ELIE SHEETZ

IT WAS Elie Sheetz' sweet tooth, his wife's unfailing aid and a pawn shop that started Mr. Sheetz on the way to the head of the Martha Washington Candy stores, now located in more than 30 cities. Born in Berlin, Pa., in 1849, he quit his father's farm to become a candymaker. His first candy was made on his wife's cook stove and sold in Lancaster. Many times he was forced to pawn his watch to buy sugar. Undaunted, he kept plodding away until his inspiration came. He conceived the idea of calling his candy Martha Washington Candy. The name caught the public's fancy and it was not long before his quaint shops began springing up all over the country. In addition to his stores, he has eight factories. Here's Mr. Sheetz' recipe: "First find the thing that appeals to you most, and see that it will meet some need. Mix plenty of good hard work, great faith, and a desire to get ahead. Then add a pinch of intuition. And don't wait for Opportunity. Use what you have."

WILLIAMSON CANDY COMPANY

IN five years, the Williamson Candy Company, an Illinois corporation, has climbed to the top in the candy manufacturing business of America. Its specialty, the Oh Henry! chocolate nut bar, is enjoying a wide sale because in it the company has concentrated all its efforts and because its blend comes not only of knowing candy but also people.

The Williamson Candy Company was organized in 1917 in Chicago, with George H. Williamson, president and treasurer; May J. Williamson, vice president, and Charles H. Crocker, secretary. Today, its main offices and factories are located at 1038 N. Ashland av., Chicago, and 1674 Broadway, New York City, and its selling organization extends into every state.

When Mr. G. H. Williamson, the president, was asked to give the reason for the success of Oh Henry! candy, he replied: "It was a question of the good taste of the public and the good will of the trade."

This, in a .phrase, describes the policy dominating the Williamson organization; it embodies the right ideals of service—satisfaction to the public and loyalty to the trade.

From the first, the combination of flavors in Oh Henry! pleased the popular fancy. The blend is the result—not only of knowing candy, but of knowing people—their varied needs and tastes. Oh Henry! is the product of careful study and experience in what the majority of candy-lovers like.

And here comes in the old story of the responsibility of success—it is not enough to make the quality right in the first place; it must be uniform. It must be sustained by constant watchfulness—unremitting care, from materials to tissue wrapping. To provide, every month, over 5,000,000 bars of Oh Henry! each like the other and all as good as the original—this is a task which calls for concentrated attention.

And here is one fundamental of the logical success of Oh Henry!—concentration on the making of this one piece! Two factories, working with specialized, trained skill on this one famous confection!

"The good taste of the public and the good will of the trade"! This summing-up of the Williamson idea is assurance that a trade built on Oh Henry! is not only an asset for today but for tomorrow!

THE HARTMAN CORPORATION

THE Hartman Corporation is one of America's largest distributors of furniture and home furnishings by ₁mail. In addition, it operates retail stores in many of the leading cities of the middle west. The receipts for the first six months of 1922 approximated $6,500,000. Its mail order department is located at 3913 Wentworth avenue, Chicago. The retail stores serving the Chicago district are at 226-32 S. Wabash avenue, 2556 W. North avenue, 1327 Milwaukee avenue, 23 W. 63rd street. Other Hartman retail stores are in Omaha, Minneapolis, Milwaukee, Peoria and St. Joseph, Mo. The company was organized in 1891 and today has a capitalization of $12,000,000. The officers are Max Strauss, president; Irvin H. Hartman, vice president; Edward G. Selsenthal, secretary and treasurer, and Harry A. Cohen, assistant secretary and treasurer. The directors are Max Strauss, Chicago; Morris Wertheim, New York; Melvin Emerich, Chicago; Sidney H. Cohn, Chicago; Irvin H. Hartman, Chicago; and Stanley H. Hartman, Chicago.

DR. J. ELLIOT ROYER

DR. J. ELLIOT ROYER, through his work both here and abroad, has contributed much to the knowledge of nervous diseases. In 1909-1913, Dr. Royer was professor of neurology in the Kansas City Post-Graduate Medical college. In 1913 he was a member of the International Medical Congress in London. He took up post-graduate courses in the University of Berlin and the University of Munich, and when war was declared he went to London, where he gave over a year of special neurological service to the wounded in the base hospitals. Dr. Royer then returned to America to take up his work as professor of neurology in the College of Medicine of the University of Illinois, Chicago. Since his return, he has built up a large practice as a consulting nerve specialist and has also found time to be one of the organizers of the Lake Shore Athletic Association. Member of American Medical Association, Chicago Neurological Society, Alpha Kappa Kappa Club, University Club of Evanston. Office: 30 N. Michigan blvd. Home: Drake hotel.

DR. GEORGE J. HINN

GEORGE J. HINN, physician and surgeon, was born in Fond du Lac, Wis., Aug. 25, 1872; s. of Margaret (Weigel) and George Hinn; ed. in Fond du Lac pub. schs.; Wis. Univ.; Lewis Institute; Northwestern Bus. Coll.; Northwestern and Illinois Med. Colls., 1904. Married Anna Klingelhoefer, Chicago, April 3, 1907. Children: George J., Jr., Wilbur C. Dr. Hinn has practiced in Chicago since 1904, specializing in stomach and nervous diseases. He is examining physician for a number of insurance and fraternal organizations. Mem. of American Med. Assn., and Illinois and Chicago Med. Socs. Home: 919 Ridgewood Drive, Highland Park, Ill. Office: 30 N. Michigan Av.

HENRY TELLER ARCHIBALD

HENRY TELLER ARCHIBALD, owner of the Fannie May Candy Shops, was born in Washington, D. C., June 1, 1879; son of Kate Minor (Lemen) and Caleb Putnam Archibald. He was educated in Washington public schools and business high school. In 1901, he married Mildred Rose King in Chicago. Mr. Archibald was associated for many years in Washington with the late William E. Curtis, correspondent for the old Chicago Record and later the Record Herald. He served on the Washington staff at various times of the Chicago Record Herald, the Chicago Daily News, Scripps-McRae Press Association and the San Francisco Chronicle. In 1903, Mr. Archibald quit newspaper work to organize the Employers' Association of Hotel and Restaurant Men in Chicago and later organized the Wholesale Meat Dealers' Association; promoted the Western Packing and Provision Company, 39th and Morgan streets, and the Independent Pure Ice Company, of which he was secretary and treasurer. Mr. Archibald then engaged in real estate subdividing. In 1920, he opened his first Fannie May Candy Shop and in 1922 he had nine shops and was doing the largest retail candy business in Chicago.

I. B. BARTKOWSKI

I. B. BARTKOWSKI, president of Keg & Kettle Co., was born in Pennsylvania, March 20, 1881; s. of Dorothy (Bon Bronkff) and Anthony Bartkowski. He moved to Chicago with parents from Nanticoke, Pa., in 1890. He was ed. in pub. schs., Chicago. He entered confectionery business in 1912, opening a store at 114 S. Dearborn St. Three years later he opened another store at 240 S. State St. In 1919 he opened a new store at 40 S. Wabash Av., and in 1921 a store in the Randolph Hotel. In the same year he opened a candy manufacturing factory. He is also planning to open a store in Masonic Temple Bldg. Mem. of Assn. of Commerce, Director of Providers Life Insurance Co. Home: 19 Bellevue Place. Office: 114 S. Dearborn St.

JOHN J. CALLAHAN

JOHN J. CALLAHAN, noted sportsman and secretary of the Diamond Cab Company, was born in Chicago, Sept. 13, 1888; son of Helen (Condon) and James D. Callahan. He was educated in Chicago public schools and Lewis Institute. In 1908, he was wed to Mae Ethel Edmunds in Chicago. Children: Patricia Mae, John J., Jr. Mr. Callahan has been in the heating business for a number of years as a member of the L. J. Mueller Furnace company, Chicago. He was made secretary of the Diamond Cab company, when it was organized to take over the taxis operated by the Hotel Morrison. He is also a director of the Motor Car United Underwriters. Mr. Callahan has been one of the most prominent figures in semi-pro baseball in Chicago, the past 18 years. He is president and manager of the Logan Square Baseball Club. His residence is at 4706 N. St. Louis ave. Office: 2301 Clybourn ave.

AL TEARNEY

ALBERT R. TEARNEY, baseball president and well known Chicago business man, was born in Chicago in 1877. During the last few years Mr. Tearney has spent most of his time directing the affairs of the I. I. I. and Western Leagues of professional baseball clubs, being president of the I. I. I. League since 1909 and of the Western League since 1919. The I. I. I. League ("B" Classification) is as follows: Terre Haute, Ind., (John J. Cleary, Pres.); Evansville, Ind., (Wm. J. Asplan, Pres.); Bloomington, Ill., (Chas. P. Goelzer, Pres.); Peoria, Ill., (John C. Ryan, Pres.); Decatur, Ill., (Jake Hill, Pres.); Danville, Ill., (Bert Gibbons, Pres.); Moline, Ill., (W. C. Giles, Pres.); Rockford, Ill., (I. L. Bell, Pres.). The Western League, ("A" Classification) is as follows: Tulsa, Okla., (Jas. Crawford, Pres.); Oklahoma City, Okla., (John Holland, Pres.); Wichita, Kansas, (Frank Isbel, Pres.); Des Moines, Ia., (Tom Fair-

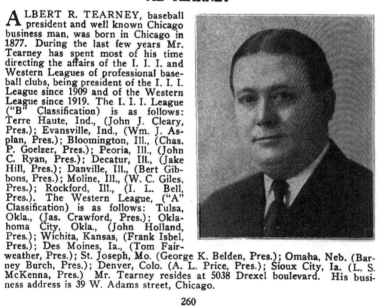

weather, Pres.); St. Joseph, Mo. (George K. Belden, Pres.); Omaha, Neb. (Barney Burch, Pres.); Denver, Colo. (A. L. Price, Pres.); Sioux City, Ia. (L. S. McKenna, Pres.) Mr. Tearney resides at 5038 Drexel boulevard. His business address is 39 W. Adams street, Chicago.

WALLACE M. ROGERSON

WALLACE M. ROGERSON, president of the Wallace Institute, has made "Get Thin to Music" a byword in America. Through the introduction of the Wallace records for talking machines, he has eliminated much of the discomfort attendant to taking off adipose weight.

Mr. Rogerson founded the Wallace Institute two decades ago. His weight reducing methods won favor and his clientele soon included many of the leading men and women of America. Early in his career he conceived the idea of teaching in "bulk," that is to say, teaching more than one individual at the same time, and a plan for instructions by mail followed soon after. This was continued until 1917, when Mr. Rogerson thought it might be a good idea to reach his clientele with his voice, rather than with his thoughts on paper. He began in a small way to give personal instructions to certain of his clientele by means of a dictating machine. This aroused so much interest that in a course of a year he set about to manufacture disc records.

When he found he was unable to obtain the support of any of the big phonograph firms, he determined to build his own recording and pressing plant. This he did. A plant was taken over in Newark, N. J. This plant has grown into quite a pretentious institution and the Wallace records have found their way into almost every other home in the nation. The Wallace Institute is located at 630 S. Wabash Ave., Chicago.

DR. FRANK J. PATERA

DR. FRANK J. PATERA, noted Chicago physician, was born in Prague, Bohemia, December 7, 1860, son of Karolina (Sladek) and Mathias Patera. Five years after his birth, he came with his parents to Chicago. He was educated in Foster Grammar School, Chicago High School, and was graduated from Rush Medical College in 1883. In June, 1888, he was married to Jennie M. Kolar, of Chicago. Dr. Patera, in the past thirty-five years, has built up a large clientele, which includes some of the leading men and women of Chicago. He resides at 151 North Mason avenue. His offices are at 1152 North Ashland avenue.

DR. ARNO MEYER

ARNO MEYER, physician, was born in Sauk City, Wis., 1879; s. of Emma (Boller) and Henry Meyer; ed. in Sauk City pub. schs.; studied pharmacy in 1900. He attended Spencerian Business College at Milwaukee in 1901. He married Lydia Hoffman, Chicago, Sept. 3, 1902. Son, Vernon. In 1902, Mr. Meyer took pharmacy examination in Chicago and went into the drug business at Belmont av. and Broadway. He graduated from College of Medicine and Surgery of Chicago in 1910. The same year he took charge of the drug store at Clark and Lake sts., and a year later went into active practice at that location. Mem. Am., Ill., Chicago Medical Socs. Mem. Chicago Motor Club. Home: 4529 Calumet av. Office: 189 N. Clark st.

POTTINGER-FLYNN COAL COMPANY

BACKED by nearly fifty years of experience, the Pottinger-Flynn Coal Company is one of the largest coal distributing agencies in Chicago or the Central West. It is the largest concern of its kind in the city that does not belong to a coal association or dealer combination and whose coal is independently priced.

It is Chicago built; Chicago owned; and Chicago operated. The main yard and executive office is at 2221 S. Ashland ave. Other branches of the company are the 16th st. yard, on the tracks of the Chicago, Burlington & Quincy R. R. at Blue Island av. and 16th st., and the 90th st. yard, at 9015 S. Halsted st. adjoining the tracks of the Rock Island Road.

The Company has nearly 3,000 feet of trackage and in two of the yards alone there is storage space of 145,000 square feet. The 16th street yard is unique in that it has no storage space and yet it is considered one of the most efficient coal handling yards in the United States. This is due to the fact that here has been installed an electric crane, the only one of its kind in the world, known as the National Simplex Crane. The inventors were members of the Pottinger-Flynn organization. So efficiently does this crane operate that it is able to transfer coal from the trains almost as fast as they can be shunted into the yard. This invention is in line with the policy of the company to install labor saving and cost saving mechanical equipment just as soon as such equipment has shown itself to be practical.

In the matter of service, there may be mentioned the fleet of nearly half a hundred of motor trucks, which have a capacity of 153 tons. These trucks can deliver approximately 200 tons of coal an hour within a radius of five miles. The yards of the company are so located that they can cover the entire city. The company is in a position to handle any contract, large or small, commercial or domestic, and the proof of this is that it has handled and is handling such contracts.

One of the main factors in its service to the public is the cost accounting department, which enables executives to compute cost to the consumer on an exact knowledge of the cost to the company. The consumer is not asked to shoulder the mistakes that a newer or less careful organization might make. This precaution extends also to the buying department, where men with years of experience are in charge of the wholesale purchase of coal for the company.

The personnel of the organization is composed of men who have spent their lives in this particular field, and the policy of the company, as maintained from the first, has been: a fair price to the consumer; quality in the coal itself; and real service. The officers of the company are: Mortimer B. Flynn, president and treasurer; J. D. Hanrahan, vice-president; J. R. Troutman, secretary.

ISHAM JONES

ISHAM JONES, one of the most famous orchestral directors in America, was born in Coalton, O., Jan. 31, 1894; the son of Alice (Coyer) and Richard Jones. His education was received in Ohio and Michigan schools and eight years ago he came to Chicago from Saginaw, Mich. Mr. Jones was married to Marguerite Kirkpatrick in Chicago, July 31, 1918. Since his entry into the Chicago musical domain, the fame of Mr. Jones as an orchestral leader has become nation-wide. Through the medium of his phonograph records, he has contributed to the pleasure of millions and has inculcated in the hearts of many a love for good music. Mr. Jones now plays exclusively for the Brunswick - Balke - Collender Phonograph company. He is almost as widely known for the songs he has written as he is for his orchestra. Mr. Jones is president of Tell Taylor, Inc. He resides at 1708 Arthur av. and his office is at 119 N. Clark st.

CHARLES WINFIELD VAIL

CHARLES WINFIELD VAIL, state supreme court clerk, was born on farm near Fairbury, Mar. 14, 1861; son John D. (St.) and Harriet A. (McNulty) Vail; Chicago, 1884; married Clara I. Barton, Evansville, Ind., Dec., 1896; children: Edna C., Charles Winfield, Jr., Marjorie. Entered Mortgage brokerage business, 1891; clerk Superior court of Cook Co., 1904 to 1912; clerk state supreme court since Dec., 1914. Formerly mem. Rep. State Central Com.; delegate Rep. Nat. Conv., 1912; Mason (K. T.), Oriental Consistory and Shrine, Odd Fellow, Moose, Woodman. Club: Hamilton, Home: Chicago. Office: Supreme Court Bldg., Springfield.

DAVID ROSE LEVY

DAVID R. LEVY, lawyer, was born in Kansas City, Mo., Apr. 27, 1867; s. Zadig and Rose (Benjamin) Levy; ed. pub. and high schs. Springfield, Ill. Married Sadie Salzenstein, Chicago, Aug. 5, 1908. Children: Stanley David, David R., Jr. Teacher in Springfield, Ill., 1885-86; in employ of Wabash R. R. and was successively in claim, engring. and trans. depts. 1887-93; admitted to bar of Ind., 1893; of Ill., 1896; asst. sec. Ill. R. R. and Warehouse Commn., 1893-95; sec. to Hon. John P. Altgeld, gov. of Ill., 1895-96; in practice of law in Chicago since 1896, making a specialty of corpn. law; partner firm of Prentiss, Gregg & Levy, 1896-98; asst. corpn. counsel of Chicago, 1902-6; Appellate and Supreme Court atty., City of Chicago, 1911-15; mem. Am., Ill. and Chicago Bar Assns., vice-pres. Lawyers' Assn. of Illinois. Democrat. Mason; mem. K. of P., Maccabees. Clubs: Idlewild Country, Covenant, Ambassador. Home: 5542 Blackstone av. Office: 7 S. Dearborn st.

MANN'S RAINBO GARDENS MAGNIFICENT

MANN'S RAINBO GARDENS MAGNIFICENT strikes a new note in American entertainment—bringing to Chicago the sumptuous, cultivated forms of gaiety heretofore found only in the capitals of the Continent. Located at Clark street and Lawrence avenue, near enough to Lake Michigan to have the pleasant lake breezes without the disadvantage of sudden climatic changes, Mann's Rainbo Gardens Magnificent achieves its every justification. Entering the outdoor gardens, one finds himself in a realm of exotic loveliness. In the afternoon sunlight, the green hedges stand out in sharp contrast to the shining expanse of the dancing floor, the brick walks and the gay massed flowers. The gardens are entered through broad French windows at the west end of the Rainbo room opening directly on a veranda. The stage opens on both the Rainbo Room and the Gardens and the entertainment is offered simultaneously. Below the stage is the wide dancing floor surrounded by low terraces and, at the far end, a rich and glowing grotto with trickling cascades, illuminated by colored lights, forms a rare background for the entire scene. Hedges cut up the Gardens into small areas for serving private parties and tiers of tables are ranged along the paths and at the sides of the dancing floor.

The story of how the Rainbo Gardens got its name is timely and interesting. After operating for a time under the name of Moulin Rouge, Mr. Fred Mann, the proprietor, determined in 1918 that the character of the Gardens demanded a name more appropriate to a city so essentially American as Chicago. At that time, his son, Alexander Mann, serving as a Signal Corps photographer with the A. E. F., wrote his father that he had been attached to the Rainbow Division during the Meuse-Argonne drive. Mr. Fred Mann, forthwith, gave the name Rainbo Gardens to the place.

The management holds a high ideal for the Rainbo Gardens. It is primarily for the pleasure and comfort of its patrons and nothing is spared to this end.

FRANCIS GRANT BLAIR

FRANCIS GRANT BLAIR, state superintendent of public instruction, was born in Nashville, Ill., in 1864; early life spent on farm in Jefferson Co. Educated in county schools and in Mt. Vernon high school. Instructor in public schools several years and principal at Malden, Bureau Co., three years, and also Le Roy, McLean Co. Then became principal of Franklin school, Buffalo, N. Y. Following appointment to fellowship in Columbia Univ., effective 1899, he was tendered position by Eastern Illinois State Normal school. For seven years he headed its training department. Mr. Blair is graduate of Ill. State Normal Univ. and Swarthmore college. Awarded LL.D. degree by Colgate Univ. in 1912 and by Illinois Wesleyan in 1916. Elected superintendent of public instruction on Republican ticket in 1906 and now serving fourth term.

CHAUNCEY H. JENKINS

CHAUNCEY H. JENKINS of Springfield, state director of public welfare, was born in Fulton County. He was educated at the University of Michigan. Practiced law in Springfield. Married April 27, 1911, to Miss Ella McRoberts. He served as probate judge of Sangamon County from 1910 to 1921. He was appointed director of public welfare Jan. 18, 1921.

266

CHECKER TAXI COMPANY

"FROM a frontier trading post to a city of three million inhabitants," tells in a single phrase the romantic story of Chicago's growth. The phrase at once brings up visions of stalwart pioneers, valorous and ever ready to sacrifice brain or brawn for Chicago, and then realization of their hope for a bigger and better city, with recognition everywhere.

A parallel record for progress and valor and sacrifices can be traced in the rise of the Checker Taxi Company, which a few years ago was among the city's infant organizations, operating only forty cars but invested with a determination to serve. In 1922, the Checker Taxi Company was a million-dollar corporation, maintaining a fleet of approximately one thousand taxicabs with stands and stations placed at appropriate intervals throughout the city.

A nation's backbone, some one has said, is its railroads; a city's is its conveyances and roads. The Checker Taxi Company has contributed a good share to expediting intra-Chicago transportation. Its rates are said to be the lowest in the world, thereby putting their service within the reach of everyone. Its cars are of the best and operated with the geometrical theorem in mind, that the nearest way to a certain point is by a straight line. Progress means moving forward and the Checker Taxi company is "Always One Move Ahead," as its slogan indicates.

To the continued good management and the energy and faithfulness of its officers does the company owe much of its success. These officers have been with the company since its organization: M. M. Sokoll, president; Philip Thomas, vice-president; A. Camozzi, treasurer, and Stanley Stupner, secretary.

JOHN RAKLIOS

JOHN RAKLIOS, restaurateur, found the road to success a hard one to travel. Business depressions, explosions and fires all conspired to work against him but these experiences left him unscarred and today he has caught that fleeting thing called success.

He is at the helm of a $500,000 restaurant business, which operates in every part of Chicago. He is also a director of the Atlas Exchange National Bank. Mr. Raklios was born in Greece, 1879; s. of Jenny (Johnson) and Hercules Raklios. He was educated in schools of Greece. In 1915, he married Mary Zydel, Chicago. Children: Helen, Hercules.

When Mr. Raklios set foot in the United States in 1900, he had just $10. His first venture was peddling fruit in Chicago loop office buildings. He then entered the flower business, but this proved disastrous and he opened a restaurant at 489 S. State st. Poor business forced him to sell out. With two partners, he opened a restaurant at State and Harrison sts. A gas explosion wiped out the business and left him $2,000 in debt.

By obtaining an extension from his creditors, he was able to start anew at 613 S. Kedzie av. Here he prospered, was able to wipe out all of his debts and build a nucleus for a $500,000 Raklios Restaurant Corporation. As he bought more restaurants, he established a commissary at 125 W. Ohio st., where also are located his offices. Mr. Raklios resides at 6326 Sheridan rd.

267

GEORGE HEBERT STARR

GEORGE HEBERT STARR, owner and manager of the Bissell Laundry, was born in Canada, Oct. 21, 1862; s. of Susan (Hawkins) and Joseph Herbert Starr; ed. in grammar schls. of Toronto. Married Stella R. Whiting, Oct. 10, 1896, at Chicago. Son, Herbert Whiting. In 1892, Mr. Starr came to Chicago and entered laundry business. After a series of struggles, he rose to the presidency of the Bissell Laundry, which today is unsurpassed in the handling of wet wash, dry wash, rough dry, and family finish. The Bissell Co. prides itself on the fact that its delivery system is second to none in Chicago. Mr. Starr resides at 7621 Saginaw Av. Office: 651 E. Pershing Rd.

ALBERT H. SEVERINGHAUS

ALBERT H. SEVERINGHAUS, president of the G. A. R. Laundry Company, located at 3118-20-22 Armitage ave., is a pioneer in the laundry industry of Chicago. Since his entry into the business, he has been identified with a majority of the progress movements and he stands ready to lend his strength at any time to any effort to place the industry on a more efficient basis. Through his amiability and the efficiency of his company, he has built up a large clientele.

KING JOY LO RESTAURANT COMPANY

THE KING JOY LO restaurant, the house of a thousand gastronomic delights, which nestles in the theatrical district of Chicago, has been the rendezvous of republic-makers. It is located at 57-59 W. Randolph street.

Over its blackwood tables and in the mystic enchantment of its exotic settings was born the movement which later was to release the shackles welded by a bureaucratic monarchy on the hundreds of million inhabitants of China. Thousands of miles removed in distance from Honkong or Shantung, the fortunes of this eating-place have been intertwined with those of China.

Although its settings, draperies and wood carvings inlaid with ivory are designed to have a restful effect, King Joy Lo is surcharged with an air of important activity. There is an association with adventure here. World-famous diplomats, merchants and artists, whenever they chanced to be in Chicago, always made King Joy Lo's their mecca, not only because of the likelihood of meeting cosmopolites and interesting characters, but also for the cuisine, which is unequalled by any of the Chinese restaurants of America.

King Joy Lo restaurant is the dream of Kang Yu Wei, come true. Kang Yu Wei, noted reformer, exiled because his teachings conflicted with the views of Chinese monarchy, founded King Joy Lo restaurant in 1906 for a dual purpose. The first was to obtain sufficient funds for a movement to supplant the harsh, highly centralized dynasty of China with a republican form of government, with direct representatives of the people sitting in the highest councils. The other was to finance the education in America of a number of Chinese students. In both purposes he succeeded.

During the tenure of his leadership, Kang Yu Wei installed in the restaurant numerous highly-prized Chinese paintings, statuary, scroll and wood carvings, which he brought with him following his exile and which, only by reason of the high esteem in which he was held, could he obtain. The value of these and other equipment that make up the restaurant are estimated at $200,000.

When Kang Yu Wei had accomplished the two things he had set out to do, a company was organized to take over control and Chin K. Shue was made president. The company has adhered to the same broad policy laid down by the founder. By furnishing them a means to make money during their spare moments, King Joy Lo restaurant has supported hundreds of Chinese students through school in the United States. The company also gave lavishly of money and food when the Chinese famine was at its height in 1920 and 1921 and thousands were dying daily.

King Joy Lo's is almost as widely known for its American dishes as for its Chinese. It has introduced a number of Oriental dishes to American epicures. Everything in food that is in season, whether fowl, fish or fruit, is at the beck of the diner. King Joy Lo's is popular with after-theater parties.

The company has also developed a large Chinese merchandise importing business, with warehouses and offices ranged along the Pacific Coast and in China. In addition to Chin K. Shue, the officers are Moy Wah June, vice president and manager; Charles P. Chan, treasurer; Howard S. Moy, secretary. Directors are Chin K. Shue, Charles P. Chan, Li Wah, Moy Tong Chow, Moy Wah June, Howard S. Moy, Chan Pak Sun.

269

CONSTANTINE NICHOLAS JOHNSON

CONSTANTINE NICHOLAS JOHNSON, president of C. N. Johnson, Inc., manufacturers of candy, was born in Sparta, Greece, 1880; s. of Susanna (Bootsoris) and Nicholas D. Johnson. He received his education in the public schools of Greece, and in 1897 he removed to Chicago with his parents. Married Tassia Stavru, Chicago, 1914. Children: Nicholas, Pyrro. Mr. Johnson started in the candy manufacturing business twenty-two years ago. Today his stores are spread all over the loop. Mem. of Shriners. Club: Hamilton. Home: 1321 Sherwin Av. Office: 229 N. State St.

JOSEPH TRINER

JOSEPH TRINER, manufacturing chemist, was born in Chicago, Oct. 19, 1894; s. of Catherine (Wecker) and Joseph Triner; ed. in Jefferson pub. sch., Harrison Tech. Sch., Columbian Univ. Married Mae Hajicek, Nov. 8, 1921, Chicago. He started in with Joseph Triner Co. as branch mgr. and is now pres. He served as sgt., U. S. A.; chief boatswain mate, U. S. Navy; military intelligence dept.; naval intelligence dept.; U. S. Dept. of Justice. Mem. of Art Institute, Historical Soc., Greater Chicago Lodge, 32nd degree Mason, Odd Fellows. Clubs: Ill. Athletic, Hamilton, Birchwood Country, D. K. E., Bohemia. Home: 931 Winona Av. Office: 1333 S. Ashland Av.

THE BEATRICE CREAMERY COMPANY

THE BEATRICE CREAMERY COMPANY whose general offices are located at 1526 South State street, Chicago, is reputed to be the largest creamery company in the world. This company takes its name from the town of Beatrice, Nebraska, which was its birthplace. It was founded in the year of 1897 and has been a big factor in establishing the dairy industry in the United States, particularly in the western states where dairying has proved to be the salvation of many farmers.

It has 16 manufacturing plants located throughout the region extending from the Ohio river to the Rocky Mountains and from the Dakotas to Oklahoma. It has numerous distributing branches, not only in the western territory, but also in a large number of eastern and southern states.

Its principal product is Meadow Gold Butter, which is probably the widest known brand of butter in this or any other country. The company also manufactures ice, ice cream, buttermilk products and cream separators; operates a number of large cold storage warehouses, and in addition to its own manufactures it distributes eggs, cheese, and dairy machinery, not only in the United States, but exports to foreign countries.

The men in charge of the affairs of the Beatrice Creamery Company are of wide and varied experience, and it is financially one of our strongest business institutions.

BRENNAN PACKING COMPANY

THE BRENNAN PACKING CO. is an Illinois corporation; its principal office and place of business is at 39th St. and Normal Av., Chicago. Incorporated in 1905, it has been in continuous operation since that time. Its principal business is the slaughter of hogs, and the preparation of edible and inedible products resulting therefrom. The edible products include fresh pork, cured pork and lard; the inedible such items as hog hair, grease, fertilizer materials, etc.

The business at first was entirely of a local nature, but gradually expanded, eventually covering most of the eastern and southern markets in this country. In 1907, an export business was opened. This also grew and expanded, until it covered all the Scandinavian countries (Finland, Norway, Sweden and Denmark), also in Continental Europe (Holland, Belgium, France, Switzerland, Italy and Spain), and the United Kingdom (England, Ireland and Scotland).

About 1918, on account of a very mild winter which interfered with the harvesting of natural ice, it was found necessary, to install a manufacturing plant to make artificial ice. That department, begun in a small way, has also grown, and it now includes facilities for the manufacture of 350 tons per day.

The organization, since its beginning, has been under the personal management of Mr. B. G. Brennan, president. Many of his present associates have been connected with this organization almost since its inception.

271

CHARLES MILLER JESSUP

CHARLES MILLER JESSUP, vice-president and general manager of Parisian Cleaners and Dyers, was born in Cleves, O., 1884; s. of Helen Mar (Cooper) and William Jessup; ed. in Cleves schs. and attended Sue Bennett Memorial Sch., London, Ky., for 4 years. He came to Chicago from Louisville to accept position as sales-man with the Eureka Coal and Dock Co. After 8 years with this firm, he became traveling salesman for White Oak Coal Co., later joining New River Coal Co. He then entered Lemmon & Co., which operates Parisian Dyers and Cleaners, and was gradually advanced to his present position. During the war he served as chairman for cleaners in the 19th Div. War Loan Org. ex-pres. and dir. of Illinois Assn. of Dyers and Cleaners; ex-secy. and dir. of Chicago Assn. Mem. West Madison Business Men's Assn.; West Side Kiwanis. Clubs: Town and Country, Birchwood Country. Home: 2243 Washington blvd. Office: 2324 W. Madison st.

FREDERICK AUGUSTUS GRITZNER

F. A. GRITZNER, laundryman, was born in Plainfield, Ill., Aug. 18, 1862; s. of Adelia Fannie (Pratt) and Charles F. Gritzner; ed. in pub. schs. of Chicago, Boston Sch. of Tech., 1890, and Univ. of Chicago. M. Shirley Willis Stevens, 1892, Chicago. Teacher in Dr. Mariner's Sch. of Assaying & Chemistry; chemist for 12 yrs. with Mariner & Hoskins; assayer for Philadelphia Mining & Milling Co. at Crestone, Col.; Rio Grande Mining Co., 1886; Tiger Mine, 1888; Chicago Smelting & Refining Co., 1886-7; chemist for W. K. Fairbank Co., 1888. Bought interest in Woodlawn Pk. Laundry in 1894, becoming sole owner, 1896. Incorporated in 1897 and sold part interest to J. N. Kimball, who served as manager from 1900 to 1917. Pres. of Clover Farm Co., Mich., vice-pres. of Windermere Press. Mem. of S. Side, Chicago, and National Laundry Owners' Assns.; mem. Laundrymen's Club, Ill. Mfg. Assn., Am. Inst. of Mining

Eng., Odd Fellows, and Knights Templar. Clubs: Woodlawn Business Men's, Kiwanis, City. Home: 1218 E. 62nd St. Office: 1221-23 E. 63rd St.

H. W. PELLAGE   B. O. LARSON   J. W. McLAUGHLIN

AMERICAN HOME SERVICE COMPANY

J. W. McLAUGHLIN, B. O. LARSON AND H. W. PELLAGE have given Uptown Chicago, in whose growth they have played leading parts, another great enterprise in the American Home Service Company.

The American Home Service Company consists of the Lincoln Hand, Paragon and Clark Street Wet Wash Laundries. The merger was effected in April, 1922, with Mr. McLaughlin, representing the Lincoln Hand Laundry, as president; Mr. Larson, of the Paragon Laundry, as treasurer; and Mr. Pellage, of the Clark Street Wet Wash Laundry, as secretary.

The plant of the new corporation will be a five-story edifice, costing $200,000, to be located on a site adjoining the Paragon Laundry at 3543 North Ashland avenue. The plant will be one of the largest laundry plants in the world and will contain all of the latest methods for improving and expediting the handling of wash. It will stand as a monument to the efforts of Messrs. McLaughlin, Larson and Pellage to enhance the industrial as well as residential and scenic possibilities of Chicago's North Side.

Of one thing, the American Home Service Company is already assured—a well-balanced management, backed by a definite policy and years of achievement in the laundry trade. Each of the three officers has been affiliated in one capacity or another with this business since he stepped out of the period of adolescence.

Mr. McLaughlin is among the North Side pioneers who had faith in the potentialities of his district. He began in the laundry business in an humble way, opening a tiny laundry at 1447 North Halsted street in 1893. Two years later, he moved to a store at 2007 North Halsted street, next to the Bismarck Gardens, opening the same week as this well-known resort.

When he began talking of moving to Broadway, then Evanston avenue, his friends presupposed that he was suffering from arterio-sclerosis but, nothing daunted, he built a three-story building at 1886 Evanston avenue, now 4539 Broadway, the first building in the block between Wilson and Sunnyside. The first floor was occupied by the Lincoln Hand Laundry and the upper floors were rented to families and for office purposes. Here the laundry was operated by five persons, including the proprietor, Mr. McLaughlin.

273

Plant to be erected by American Home Service Company at 3545 North Ashland Avenue

Ten years later, Mr. McLaughlin reached another turning point, with the erection of the first building of the group which is now known as one of the finest laundry properties in Uptown Chicago. The main laundry, the last section built, was added in 1913.

The wisdom of Mr. McLaughlin's move in locating on the North Side is attested to by the steady growth of his business.

Mr. McLaughlin organized the North Side Dyers and Cleaners in 1910 and served as president and manager for several years. He was president of the Chicago Laundrymen's Club in 1919 and 1920; member of the executive committee of the Chicago Laundry Owners' Association in 1920, president in 1921 and unanimously re-elected in 1921.

Mr. Larson, treasurer of the new concern, operated the Paragon Laundry, in partnership with Mrs. Amalia Threedy. For the past thirty-five years, the Paragon Laundry has confined its efforts to the North Side and, by dint of hard work and determination to treat its customers with the utmost consideration, has gained an enviable reputation. Mr. Larson was associated with Mr. McLaughlin in the organization of the North Side Cleaners and Dyers on Broadway, serving as treasurer for many years.

Mr. Pellage, the secretary, introduced the wet wash laundry to Chicago housewives. His departure so caught the fancy of housewives that no other designation was needed, it simply being known as the Wet Wash Laundry. Since then, the plan has been found so good that wet wash laundries have sprung up on all sides and Mr. Pellage has taken the name of the Clark Street Wet Wash Laundry. His plant is located at 4507-09-11 North Clark street.

GEORGE EDWARD MUNGER

GEORGE EDWARD MUNGER, president of Munger's Laundry Company, with branches in St. Louis, was born in Mercer, Pa., Dec. 25, 1880; son of Marcia Jane (Booth) and Orett Lyman Munger. In 1881, he removed to Chicago with his parents. He was educated in Chicago public schools; Hyde Park High School; and received B. S. degree from Princeton University, 1903. On Oct. 4, 1905, he married Bessie Entwistle Hinton, in Los Angeles. Children: Edward Entwistle, Orett Lyman, II. After graduating from Princeton, Mr. Munger became an employee of his father's in the laundry business. In 1907, he was manager of Munger's Drexel Laundry in Chicago; transferred to St. Louis in 1909 and the next year returned to take a place in the general offices in Chicago. He was made secretary and treasurer in 1913 and president in 1919, which position he still retains. He is also vice-president and director of the Westminster Laundry, St. Louis, and director of Cascade Laundry, Des Moines. Clubs: University, Midlothian Country. Home: 5805 Blackstone av. Office: 2412 Indiana av.

DAVID E. WALQUIST

DAVID E. Walquist, secretary and treasurer of Lindgren's Laundry company, was born in Chicago, Jan. 18, 1886; son of Matilda (Johnson) and Charles Gustav Walquist; educated in Chicago public schools; Kent College of Law and admitted to bar in 1915. Married Ada H. Anderson, Nov. 25, 1908, Chicago. Children: Lloyd Arnold, Robert Eugene, De Ett Elinor. Mr. Walquist served as bookkeeper for State Bank of Chicago, 1903; bookkeeper for Continental and Commercial National Bank, 1904-1907; collection man, credit man and later attorney for H. Channon Co., 1908-20. In 1920 Mr. Walquist assisted in the reorganization of Lindgren's Laundry and was made secretary and treasurer. Member of Chicago Bar Assn. Member of Lake Side Lodge No. 739, A. F. & A. M. Home: 7314 Crandon ave. Office: 858-60 N. Wells st.

JOHN LOSEY WILTSIE

JOHN L. WILTSIE, leader in the laundry industry of Chicago, was born in Chicago, Aug. 14, 1878; s. of Phoebe Elizabeth (Brower) and Thomas Morgan Wiltsie; ed. in pub. schs. of Chicago. He married Estelle Florsheim, in Chicago, Aug. 26, 1908. Mr. Wiltsie's connection with the Chicago laundry business began in 1896, shortly after he left school. He became an employe of the Goodhart laundry in 1905, rising to be president, a position which he now holds. His signal services on behalf of the laundry trade were recognized in his election as president of the Chicago Laundrymen's Club. Mem. Nat. Laundry Owners' Assn. Clubs: Bryn Mawr, Buena Shore. Home: 1262 Pratt blvd. Office: 2347 W. Harrison st.

275

JED LAKE JEWEL

JED L. JEWEL, president of the Jewel Laundry Co., was born in Brandon, Ia., Aug. 26, 1875; s. of Mahala (Rozelle) and James E. Jewel; ed. in Independence, Ia., pub. schs. and received Bachelor of Science degree from Northwestern Univ. In 1904, he married Nellie M. Root, Chicago. Children: Esther May, Eslee Marion, Mary Elizabeth, Jed L., Jr. Following his graduation from college, he purchased Rogers Park News Co., conducting it successfully for a number of years. He also handled the Nelson Brothers laundry agency. In 1912, he organized the Jewel Laundry Co. and built one of the finest laundry plants in the country. Treas. Rogers Park Methodist Church. Mem. Park Lodge, No. 843, A. F. & A. M.; Park Chapter, No. 213, Ill. Commandery, No. 72, Knights Templar; Odd Fellow; Woodmen. Home: 1852 Lunt av. Office: 1730 Greenleaf av.

CHARLES NIELSEN

CHARLES NIELSEN, president of the White Eagle Laundry, was born in Horsens, Denmark, March 13, 1880; son of Charlotte and Gregers Nielsen. In 1889, he removed with his parents to Chicago, where he received his early education. In 1906, he married Minnie A. Freeman, of Chicago. Children: Marian A., Charles F., Robert F. Mr. Nielsen's first enterprise was the White Eagle Laundry, which has grown into one of the largest on the north side. He was secretary and president at various times of the West North Avenue Business Men's Association and also the Chicago Laundrymen's Club. Member of Chicago, Illinois and National Laundryowner's Associations. Member of Ben Hur Lodge No. 818, A. F. & A. M., Palmer Square Chapter No. 259, R. A. M., Humboldt Park Commandery No. 79, Knights Templar; Medinah Temple; Humboldt Park Chapter, O. E. S., No. 472. Member of Dania Society and Logan Square Kiwanis Club. Mr. Nielsen was affiliated with the American Protective League in 1918 and 1919. Home: 2738 Logan boulevard. Office: 2719-23 Fullerton avenue.

ROBERT MATHEW BIRCK

ROBERT MATHEW BIRCK, leader in dyeing and cleaning industry of Chicago, was born in Chicago, Feb. 10, 1872; son of Pauline (Mathias) and Charles Birck Ed. in Pub. Schs. and in Am. Conservatory of Music. Entered employ of Marshall Field & Co. as cash buy in 1885. He rose to the position of asst. gen. salesman for wholesale dept., and resigned in 1901 to enter dyeing and cleaning business. Married Lillian Belle Hannan, Dec. 26, 1893, in Chicago. Children: Stanley McClean, Billie Jean. Mr. Birck is president of Birck-Fellinger Co., Robert M. Birck Co., Blackstone Petroleum Co. He also has extensive oil holdings. Mem. Chicago Assn. of Commerce; Am. Petroleum Institute; chmn. of bd. of directors, Chicago Master Cleaners and Dyers Assn. Clubs: South Shore Country, City Club of Chicago. Office: 506 E. 47th St. Home: 5700 S. Park Blvd.

DAVID WEBER

DYERS and cleaners of the Chicago district acknowledge David Weber as "the man who knows." This omniscience, plus years of undeviating work, has made him the recognized leader in the industry and has also developed a city-wide clientele for his own business. Mr. Weber became a dyer and cleaner in 1888. His general offices and factory are located at 3519-31 S. State st., where he has a large establishment consisting of five buildings and a big "family" of contented employes, who are very fond of their genial and indulgent employer, and some of whom have been with him many years.

Mr. Weber is not only a scientific dyer and cleaner, but he is a connoisseur of Chinese ceramics and jades and art work in general. He has a wonderful collection of porcelains and articles of vertu in his home and has some fine pieces about him in his office. He is a man of fine personality and refinement and a most interesting conversationalist. He is a member of the Chicago Athletic Club, a public spirited and progressive citizen, and a builder for the good of humanity in general. His establishment, with its many branches, is one of the largest in Chicago and is noted for the excellence of its work and business methods.

WILLIAM PHILLIP STROH

WILLIAM P. STROH, secretary and treasurer of Edgewater Laundry Co., was born in Chicago, May 1, 1874; s. of Elizabeth (Oswald) and John Phillip Stroh. He was educated in pub. schs. of Chicago. Married Emma Hild, June 8, 1898, Chicago. Son, Charles Phillip. Mr. Stroh, in addition to being an officer in Edgewater Laundry Co., is also treasurer of North Side Cleaners & Dyers Co. He served as inspector of laundry machinery and equipment in quartermaster's dept. from 1917 to 1918. Club: Hamilton. Home: 5410 Glenwood Av. Office: 5541 Broadway.

WHITE EAGLE LAUNDRY COMPANY

THE WHITE EAGLE LAUNDRY COMPANY, after passing through the various stages of laundry growth and development, today represents, in the highest sense, the modern power laundry, with all the latest methods and modern equipment in use.

The company dates back to 1894, when it was started as a hand laundry by Mr. and Mrs. Gregers Nielsen, under the name of the West North Avenue Laundry. In 1900, their son, Charles Nielsen, succeeded to the leadership and his first act was to change the name to the White Eagle Laundry. Under his direction, the receipts increased and the capital stock was raised from $10,000 to $30,000. Carl G. Swanson purchased a half-interest October 15, 1921, becoming secretary and treasurer of the company.

The annual volume of business has grown to $125,000. The trade is almost exclusively confined to the north and northwest districts of Chicago. The plant and offices are located at 2719-23 Fullerton avenue.

GREAT WESTERN LAUNDRY COMPANY

ORGANIZED seventeen years ago, the Great Western Laundry company plant is the cynosure of the entire laundry industry in America. Its plant represents all that is new and efficient in laundry equipment.

One of its big advantages is that it has a great water softening plant, by which it is able to filter and soften 500,000 gallons of water a day. Machinery alone did not make the company a success, however. A keen administrative board, plus unfailing service, also contributed. It is the company's boast that it spares no effort to live up to its motto "A Service to Every Housewife."

It caters to the whole city and Oak Park. The company's delivery equipment consists of 25 horse-drawn wagons and ten auto delivery trucks. Main offices and plant are located at 2125-2147 W. Madison st.

The company's heads and the men responsible for its meteoric rise are Lewis Levitetz, president; Samuel Levitetz, secretary-treasurer and general manager; Nathan Levitetz, vice-president and auditor and Charles Levitetz, superintendent.

WOUTERS' LAUNDRY

WOUTERS' LAUNDRY has twelve branch offices and more than 700 agencies in Chicago and its suburbs. Since its organization, 32 years ago, it has won favor with the public because of the prompt and excellent service it renders.

The laundry plant is located at 2529-2537 Wabash avenue and the dry cleaning plant at 4105-4107 State street.

Charles Wouters, the sole owner, was recently decorated by King Albert of Belgium in recognition of his work on behalf of the Belgian Relief Fund during the war. Mr. Wouters was born in Antwerp and educated at Louvain. He has summer homes at Grimsby, Ontario, and at Glendale, Calif. He is a member of the Flossmoor and South Shore Country Clubs of Chicago; Olympian Club, Los Angeles; and the Grimsby Country Club, Olympia Fields Country Club, Chicago.

Mrs. Wouters is a member of the well-known Hewitt family, being a niece of the late John Hewitt, founder of the Miehle Press & Manufacturing Company.

CHARLES FREDERIC BLISS

C. F. BLISS, president and treasurer of Peerless Steam Laundry Company, was born in Kalamazoo, Mich., May 7, 1868; s. of Helen M. (Boynton) and George W. Bliss; educated in Plainwell, Mich., schools. One of his ancestors, Robert Treat Payne, signed Declaration of Independence. Mr. Bliss married Louise Nagel, Chicago, April 8, 1901. Son, George Morgan. The first job Mr. Bliss had was as stock clerk in 1884; had charge of shipping department of Hibbard, Spencer, Bartlett & Co., 1886-1904, after which he entered laundry business. In 1909 he incorporated Peerless Company. He had charge of all laundry service at Camp Grant and at General Hospital, Ft. Sheridan, during the war. He was president of Illinois Laundrymen's Assn., 1920-21, and is now on execut. comm. Also on execut. comm. of Nat. and Chicago Laundryowners' Assns. Mason, mem. Blue Lodge, Cyrene Royal Arch Chapter, Hyde Park Council, Imperial Knights Templar, Englewod Command.; Shrine, Medinah Temple. Home: 6511 Yale av. Office: 4432 State st.

ARTHUR HENRY SCHULZE

ARTHUR HENRY SCHULZE, president and treasurer of the North Side Laundry Company, has had a varied career. Born in 1878 and educated in Chicago public schools, his first aim was to become a pharmacist. To satisfy this ambition, he took a course in the University of Illinois, graduating in 1901. For three years he was engaged in practice in Chicago. Then the real estate business beckoned him and he entered this field as a member of his father's company, T. H. Schulze & Co. In 1906, Mr. Schulze formed a laundry company, in partnership with his brother, Edward R. Schulze. Ten years later, he organized the North Side Laundry company. In 1904, he married Emma E. Schuess, of Chicago. Children: Dorothy Louise, Eleanor Emma, Adele Elisa, Arthur Henry, Jr. In addition to being president of the North Side Laundry, Mr. Schulze is secretary and treasurer of the Schulze Brothers' Laundry and a director of National Mutual Casualty Insurance Co. Member of Chicago Laundrymen's Club, Chicago Laundry Owners Assn.; Kiwanis; Logan Square Club. Home: 2439 Smalley court. Office: 3319-21 Fullerton av.

OTTO RICE

OTTO RICE, president of Quick Service Laundry Company, was born in Germany, Sept. 26, 1868; son of Jetta (Reizenstein) and David Rice. Educated in public schools and came to Chicago in 1885. Married Tillie Hoff, Chicago, in 1889. Daughter, Lottie. For six years he operated Rice Laundry Co., and for the past 24 years has been affiliated with Quick Service Laundry Co. As the result of his efforts, National Laundry Owners' Association is building an institute of laundering in Joliet. Mr. Rice is president of National Mutual Casualty Co., and director of Madison & Kedzie State Bank, Investors' Co., Little, Rice, O'Connell Co., Schriver Laundry Co. Member of Kiwanis, Iroquois and Motor clubs. Member of Chicago Laundrymen's club; Chicago, Illinois and National Laundryowners' Associations. Member of Union Park Lodge, A. F. & A. M. No. 610; York Chapter, R. A. M. No. 148; Syrian Council, R. & S. M. No. 78; Columbia Commandery No. 63, K. T.; Oriental Consistory, S. P. R. S., 32d degree; Medinah Temple, A. A. O. N. M. S.; Francisco Lodge, No. 562, K. P. Home: 3259 Washington blvd. Office: 319 S. Paulina st.

OLE ODEGARD

OLE ODEGARD, president of the Flat Iron Laundry Company, was born in Odegard Estate, Norway; s. of Ellen and Anders J. Odegard; educated in Trondhjem Military Academy, Norway. He married Josefa C. Landseth, in Chicago. Children: Arthur Edward, Evelyn Ruth, Dorothy Jeanne. Mr. Odegard came to Chicago from Norway in 1886 and engaged in furniture manufacturing. He later became connected with North and West Street Railway. In 1896 he founded the Flat Iron Laundry. The excellent work and good service of the Flat Iron Company gave it a steady growth and larger quarters became necessary. In 1911 the company built a modern plant at 3629-31 N. Halsted st. Mr. Odegard is a mem. of State and National Laundry Assn.; Employers' Assn. of Chicago; Ill. Mnfrs.' Assn.; Chicago Art Inst. Home: 3801 Rokeby st. Office: 3629-31 N. Halsted st.

JACOB A. BARKEY

JACOB A. BARKEY, sccy.-treas. of the Schriver Laundry Co., was born in Canada, 1865. He was educated in schools of Canada and Chicago. He is director of Madison-Kedzie State Bank, National Mutual Casualty Insurance Company, Dupage County Real Estate Improvement Corporation. Republican. Member of Masons, Elks, and Kiwanians. Clubs: Glen Oak Country and Town and Country. His office is at 3128 W. Lake St., and his residence in Glen Ellyn.

RODERICK ROBERTSON

RODERICK ROBERTSON, president of West Lake Laundry Co., was born in Scotland, Aug. 15, 1868; s. of Christina (Fraser) and Donald Robertson; ed. in Dornock, Scotland. He was married to Margaret Hayne, Nov. 19, 1902, in Chicago. Coming to Chicago from Denver, Col., in 1892, Mr. Robertson engaged in laundry business, rising to the presidency of West Lake Laundry Co., which specializes in railroad, hotel and restaurant work. Mem. of Keystone Lodge, Englewood Chapter, No. 176 R. A. M., Englewood Commandery No. 59 Knights Templar, Oriental Consistory S. P. R. S. 32nd degree, Medinah Temple, A. A. O. N. M. S. Clubs: South Shore Country, Chicago Equestrian Assn. Home: 5460 Hyde Park Blvd. Office: 3323-31 S. State St.

CHICAGO WET WASH LAUNDRY COMPANY

THE Chicago Wet Wash Company had for its place of nativity a tiny store in the northwest district of Chicago in 1913. The wet wash method was then comparatively new, but it struck a responsive chord among housewives because of its efficacy.

In 1914, the present officers of the Chicago Wet Wash Company became

interested in this modest enterprise and, after a series of negotiations, they purchased a controlling interest and incorporated the company for $6,000. They went out for new business after having added to the possibilities of rendering immediate and efficient service with new machinery. How admirably they succeeded can be judged from the fact that within a short space the capital rose to $400,000, a large, spacious plant and offices were erected, a subsidiary company formed and a fleet of automobiles and trucks organized for speeding deliveries. Today, the Chicago Wet Wash Company is the largest wet wash laundry in the world.

The Chicago New Way Service Company is a subsidiary of the Chicago Wet Wash Company and dates back to 1921. Its chief asset is a complete washing and ironing service,

LLOYD R. TORGERSON

which is offered to its patrons at a cost far below the regular rates charged both in Chicago and throughout the Middle West. This company was the first in Chicago to attempt to render such a pretentious service at so small a price and its success has been without parallel in the laundry business.

Every device known to the laundry business that will reduce the time required for washing and will leave a garment immaculate afterward is employed in the plants of the Chicago Wet Wash Company. These plants wash ninety tons of clothes per week and use 200,000 gallons of soft water every day. The business of the Wet Wash company and its subsidiary reached $600,000 in 1921, the highest figure in the history of the two enterprises, and receipts for the first half of 1922 indicated that even this mark would be passed.

Encouraged by the favorable impression their efforts to lift the laundry industry on a higher plane have met, the officers are already formulating plans for the erection of an-

JULIUS E. HOFFMANN

other plant. This, the officers say, will mark another era in the laundry business. While it is to be a model of efficiency and sanitation, it will also be one of the most beautiful laundry buildings, architecturally, in the whole country.

The spirit behind the Chicago Wet Wash Laundry Company and the Chicago New Way Service Company is best indicated by the slogan they have adopted: "We believe that we are engaged in the best business on earth, that of saving the health and strength of women, our nation's greatest asset."

The plants of the two companies adjoin each other at 2901-2911 Montrose avenue and are known as the home of soft water. The men who have brought the enterprises through their various stages of development and now to their high pinnacle are Lloyd R. Torgerson and Julius E. Hoffmann. Mr. Torgerson is president and Mr. Hoffmann secretary and treasurer.

The Plants of the Chicago Wet Wash Laundry Company and the New Way Service Company at 2901-2911 Montrose Av.

JULIUS C. BIRCK, INC.

THE introduction of the latest administrative methods and innovations for making its work better has put Julius C. Birck, Inc., on such a basis that it is today one of the leading cleaning and dyeing firms in Chicago.

Since the acquisition of the Birck firm by Frank J. Prasil and Ludwig W. Kaeuffl three years ago, the business has more than tripled. When ownership changed, the company's activities were confined to its neighborhood, but today, it is doing a city-wide trade and has eight branch stores, with the main office located at 4410-12 S. State street.

Mr. Prasil, the president, obtained his thorough knowledge of cleaning and dyeing through years spent in the tailoring business. In 1915, with only a small capital, he started his first tailoring shop and within four years he had acquired three other shops. In 1919, he bought the Julius C. Birck, Inc., and under his direction, it was the first in Chicago to introduce the Bowser Clarification System. Garments are insured against loss by theft or fire at the company's own expense. The firm is a member of the National, Illinois and Chicago Cleaners and Dyers Associations.

BROR OSCAR LARSON

B. O. LARSON, manager of Paragon Laundry, was born in Sweden, March 12, 1867; s. of Hedvig Charlotte (Tingwall) and Per Magnus Larson; ed. in Swedish schs. and Technological Institute of Norrkoping, Sweden. Married Lisa Hellquist, Chicago, 1893. Daughter, Margaret (Mrs. Knute A. Warner). Mr. Larson came to U. S. in 1892 and was appointed secretary to the World's Columbian Exposition for the Swedish government. In 1894, he entered laundry business in Chicago, and in 1900, with Amalia Threedy, he bought the Paragon Laundry. In forepart of 1922, the American Home Service Company was incorporated, absorbing several large laundries, and Mr. Larson was made secretary and treasurer of the new company, which has a capital stock of $600,000. He was president of Chicago Laundry Owners' Assn. two years. Director of Swedish club; mem. of Knights Templar, Illinois Commandery. Home: 119 Maple av., Wilmette, Ill. Office: 3543 N. Ashland av., Chicago.

JOSEPH C. WILSON

J. C. Wilson, president of the Excelsior Laundry company, was born in Westerly, R. I., March 28, 1862; son of Elinor and George Wilson. He was educated in the public schools of Rhode Island and Vermont and from Newport came to Chicago. He married Alice M. Wilcox in Chicago. Children: Joseph C. Jr., John W., Gertrude, George B. More than thirty years ago, Mr. Wilson established the Excelsior Laundry Company, of which he is now president and treasurer. He is also a director of the Employers' Indemnity Corporation and the South Central Association. Mr. Wilson served in the Illinois National Guard for twenty years, rising from private to colonel. During the Spanish-American war, he was a second lieutenant in the First Illinois Cavalry. Member of U. S. Cavalry Association, Illinois Commandery, Spanish-American War Veterans. Clubs: Illinois Athletic, La Grange Country. Home: 129 Sixth av., La Grange. Office: 64 and 66 E. 22nd st., Chicago.

MARVIN H. BEEBE

MARVIN H. BEEBE, president of the Chicago Laundry company, was born in Waverly, Ia., in 1863; son of Minerva (Case) and Hinkley Francis Beebe. He was educated in public schools of Kansas City. Married Alice Mathews, in Kansas City, in 1888. Daughter, Ruth M. In 1892, Mr. Beebe came to Chicago and by unremitting toil he achieved the presidency of the Chicago Laundry company. His other partners in this enterprise are his wife, who is secretary, and his daughter, who is treasurer. Mr. Beebe is a member of Chicago Laundrymen's club, Elks, Shriner (Medinah Temple Order of the Mystic Shrine). Home: 4204 Drexel blvd. Office: 4243 Cottage Grove av.

MARION S. ANDERSON

MARION S. Anderson, prominent Chicago laundryman, was born in Las Animas, Col., Oct. 14, 1898; son of Hilda C. (Sandquist) and Samuel John Anderson. He received his education in public schools of Colorado and in Lane Technical High School, Chicago. He married Ester E. Sodergren, Chicago, Sept., 1920. Daughter, Doris Emily. Following the reorganization of the Lindgren Laundry company in 1920, Mr. Anderson became vice president and general manager. He is a member of Lake Side Lodge No. 739, A. F. & A. M. Home: 7039 Wabash av. Office: 858-60 N. Wells st.

REPRESENTATIVE BUSINESS INTERESTS
OF CHICAGO

Adams and Pigott Co., 3141-45 S. Wabash avenue, have been engaged in the dry cleaning business since 1899, serving a clientele that reaches out all over Chicago. The company is capitalized at $50,000. The officers are Victor W. Adams, president; W. B. E. Pigott, vice-president; and Otis H. Adams, secretary.

The Akron Tire and Vulcanizing Co. is one of Chicago's leading retailers of automobile and solid truck tires. The company was incorporated in Illinois in 1909, with a capital of $50,000. A. J. Whisler is president and treasurer and S. Carl Whisler, secretary. Directors are A. J. Whisler, S. C. Whisler, S. S. Whisler and L. J. Brooks. Its general offices are located at 932-942 Jackson blvd.

The American Oven and Machine Co., manufacturing Patent "New Era" mixers as well as Patent "Simplex" Dough-Mixers for the baking industry, was founded in 1902 by Felix J. Notz and Jos. Baker & Sons, London, Eng. Later, Mr. Notz became sole owner. Today he is president and treasurer; Paul O. Diedrichs, vice-president; Ida K. Notz, secretary, and Dorothy Mc-Lay, assistant secretary. General offices are at 753-755 Conway Bldg. Factory at 1506-08 Fulton St.

O. T. Anderson & Co. Brokerage House, dealing in stocks, bonds and grain, has enjoyed a steady growth since its organization by Olaf T. Anderson in 1920. When the firm was established it had three employees; today it has twenty employees, and its branch offices are located at Pittsburgh and Aurora. It is a member of the Chicago Board of Trade. Its Chicago offices are at 166 Jackson blvd.

Anderson & Lind Manufacturing Company, 2127 Iowa street, has made its name synonymous with the best in mill work through seventeen years of service. Its dealings mainly have been with builders and contractors in the Chicago district. The Anderson & Lund company represents an investment of between $125,000 and $150,000. Officers are Lillit G. Anderson, president; George Sonne, vice president; and B. G. Anderson, secretary and treasurer.

The Blue Valley Creamery Co. is the largest exclusive manufacturer of pure pasteurized cream butter in the world. Organized in 1900 with an authorized capital of $4,000,000, it today has 17 factories in various parts of the country. By buying all creams on a direct shipment plan, the company has eliminated the middle man. The company is under control of Huston Wyeth, president; J. A. Walker, vice-president; L. C. Hamilton, treasurer and G. T. Guthrie, secretary and general manager.

The Brewster Laundry, established in 1896, is one of Chicago's leading laundries on the South Side, catering to high-grade service in all departments. William E. Brewster is president; J. N. Kimball, vice-president, and James L. Brewster, secretary and treasurer. Main offices and laundry are at 5915-31 Lowe Ave.

The Brock and Rankin, Inc., has established a wide reputation for the excellency of its book binding. The company was organized in 1892. Its offices are located at 619 S. La Salle St.

Brooks Laundry Company, with offices and plants at East avenue and North boulevard, Oak Park, and 315 W. Grand avenue, Chicago, is one of the finest equipped laundries in the country. The company is capitalized at $50,000. John Heist is president and Morris Jepson general manager.

MORRIS JEPSEN

MORRIS JEPSEN, general manager of the Brooks Laundry company, was born in Copenhagen, Denmark, in 1866; the son of Elizabeth (Sorensen) and John Jepsen. He received his education in Copenhagen public schools and in the University of Copenhagen and in 1883 he came to Chicago. In 1893 Mr. Jepsen married Jennie Robinson (deceased). Son, Ralph. Mr. Jepsen became affiliated with the Central Steam Laundry Co. upon its organization in 1893. Under his direction, it has built up a city-wide and suburban trade and today represents one of the finest equipped laundry organizations in the country. Mr. Jepsen is a member of the Chicago Motor Club. He resides at Oak Park. His office is at 315 W. Grand av.

CARL G. SWANSON

CARL G. SWANSON, secretary and treasurer of the White Eagle Laundry, was born in Sweden, April 15, 1868; son of Hedvig and Sven Swanson. He was educated in public schools of Sweden and came to the United States in 1888. He married Huldah Casperson, of Chicago, June 28, 1899. One daughter, Hildur Louise. Mr. Swanson established the Crystal Laundry at 1446 N. Clark street in 1894 and continued to operate it until 1921, when he sold out to purchase a half-interest in the White Eagle Laundry Co. He was a member of Co. M, Illinois National Guard from 1917 to 1919. Member of church council of Holy Trinity English Lutheran church. Member of Chicago, Illinois and National Laundryowners' Associations and Chicago Laundrymen's club. Clubs: Chicago Aviation, Swedish. Home: 911 Buena Terrace. Office: 2719 Fullerton avenue.

Brummel Brothers, insurance underwriters, located in the Insurance Exchange, Chicago, represent as managers ten leading American insurance companies. These men have been in the insurance business virtually all their lives. They have been doing business as Brummel Brothers for the past twenty-seven years.

Brunswick, O'Connell and Company, through its financing program, has given Chicago four of its leading hostelrys, the Chicago Beach, Webster, Parkway and Belden. The company deals exclusively in mortgage bonds and preferred stocks and has financed many enterprises in the Middle West. Ronald F. Brunswick and John E. O'Connell are the members of the firm, which has its offices at 110 S. Dearborn st.

P. W. Chapman & Co., Inc., engaged in the purchase and sale of investment securities, has built up a large clientele since its organization in 1912. Its field comprises all the territory centering in Chicago. The main office is at 116 S. La Salle street, Chicago. The eastern office is at 115 Broadway, New York.

The Chicago Dental Laboratory Co. (Reese & Wiedhofft) manufactures everything in mechanical dentistry, including plates, bridges and crowns. It was incorporated in 1905, and its staff of employees numbered three men. Today it has fifty employees and occupies 4,000 square feet of floor space at 215 N. Michigan ave. It supplies dentists in all parts of the country. Officers are Charles N. Reese, D. D. S., president and treasurer, and A. Wiedhofft, secretary.

The Chicago Railway Printing Co. specializes in railroad, catalogue and miscellaneous printing work of all kinds. The firm was incorporated in 1912 by James H. Walden. Its main offices and plant are situated at 720 S. Dearborn st.

Clifton Cleaners and Dyers, 5709-11 N. Clark street, has built up a large clientele on the North Side by giving its customers a highly systematized and efficient dyeing and cleaning service. The company was founded seventeen years ago by Joseph Krauss and Mrs. Anna M. Seymour, who still retain control.

Paul H. Davis & Co. have been dealing in investment securities for more than six years. They are members of the Chicago Stock Exchange and have offices located in the New York Life Building, 39 S. La Salle st.

The H. W. Elmore & Co., dealing in real estate investments of subdivision and brokerage, has enjoyed a remarkable growth since its organization in January, 1921. It specializes in Chicago subdivisions and business property. Its owner is H. W. Elmore. Offices are 348 National Life Building, 29 S. La Salle st.

The C. L. Frame Dental Supply Co. has been satisfying the needs of dentists of Chicago and surrounding territory for twenty-five years. It was organized with an authorized capital of $250,000. Its officers are C. L. Frame, president; W. L. Truesdell, vice-president; A. Jane Taylor, treasurer; A. D. Gray, secretary. Main offices are in the Mallers Building with branches at 63d and Halsted sts., Harrison and Wood sts. and Dearborn and Lake sts.

The French Hand Laundry Company, 2159-63 N. Clark street, has a thirty-year record of achievements in the laundry business of Chicago. Three years ago, the management of the company changed hands and F. R. Hicks became president and Mrs. Anna Hicks secretary. The company now caters to a high class trade on the north side.

The A. J. Gamble Co., specializing in direct mail advertising, has been in business for more than fifteen years. It numbers in its clientele some of the largest companies of the middle west. L. F. Mueller is president. General offices are located at 328 Federal st.

The Globe Laundry Co. prides itself on the fact that it has the best equipped laundry plant in Chicago. It is located at 222-26 S. Morgan st. The company has earned a reputation for prompt and reliable service.

WILLIAM HENRY HARRISON MILLER

WILLIAM HENRY HARRISON MILLER, state director of registration and education, was born in Upshur Co., W. Va., in 1866. Graduated from W. Va. Classical Normal and Austin Coll.; taught 8 years in pub. schs. of W. Va. and 18 years in Ill. Principal of Fairland Schs., 1892-6; principal of Hindsboro Schs., 1896-7; supt, of Bushnell Schs.. 1900-09; located in Champaign in 1909. Married to Cloah M. O'Bryan, March 19, 1892, in Champaign. Children: Garnet O'Bryan, Hazel Cloah Miller Fries. Director of Twin City Ice and Cold Storage Co. Mem. of 50th and 51st General Assemblies and cand. for Lt.-Gov. in 1920 Rep. Primary. Appointed director of registration and education by Gov. Small, Jan. 19, 1921. Mem. of M. E. Church, Elks, K. P., Odd Fellows, Modern Woodmen, Sons of Veterans, chmn. of supreme auditing com., Tribe of Ben Hur, Traveler's Protective Assn. Club: Hamilton (Chicago). Office: Capitol, Springfield. Home: Champaign, Ill.

EDWIN SCOTT DAVIS

EDWIN SCOTT DAVIS, president of the Chicago board of education, was born in Greenville, Pa., December 24, 1877; son of Mary Elizabeth (Templeton) and Abram R. Davis. In 1888, he moved with his parents to Chicago and was educated in the public schools here. He was married to Grace Brown, of Crown Point, Ind., October 20, 1903. Children: Edwin Clark, John Brown. Mr. Davis began as secretary and treasurer of the Lake Shore Sand Company; president of the Ideal Crushed Stone Company since 1916; also president of the Davis Electric Equipment Company since 1915. Republican. Mr. Davis was elected president of the board of education and re-elected at the following election. Club: Builders'. Home: 6740 Bennett avenue. Office: 650 S. Clark street.

Hong Kong Lo Restaurant, 73 W. Randolph street, is noted for its unexcelled cuisine that will tickle the palate of the most fastidious. A special menu is printed every day offering new dishes. A service for housewives is also maintained. The restaurant was established in 1897. George Der Wing is president and manager.

The Keeley Brewing Co. has been engaged in the brewing business since 1850 when it was organized by Michael Keeley. Upon his death in 1888, the management of the company devolved upon his sons, Thomas F. and Eugene M. Keeley. Mr. Thomas F. Keeley became president, following the death of his brother in 1920. The Keeley company has a large interest in the Dallas, Texas, Brewery, the Ryan hotel in St. Paul and valuable coal and iron lands in Utah. Officers are Thomas F. Keeley, president, and L. Henely, secretary and treasurer. Directors are T. F. Keeley, P. J. Lawler, Clara G. Lyon, Kate A. Lawler and L. Henely.

King Yen Lo Company, operating one of Chicago's oldest Chinese-American restaurants at 349 S. Clark street, has served the city's gastronomic needs faithfully for a quarter of a century. The restaurant abounds in the splendor and exotic flavor of Chinese objects of art and no expense was spared in bringing them to this country. The company makes a specialty of catering to private parties. Nu Tom Lak is the owner.

King's Model Laundry Company, 2213-19 W. Madison street, furnishes a laundry service that is designed to meet every requirement. That it does is evidenced in the growth of its trade, which now covers the west, north and northwest districts of the city. V. E. Adland is president; R. J. Elliott, secretary; and L. H. Kamper, secretary.

The Lakeview Laundry, 3018 N. Clark street, was founded in 1898 by Charles P. Jones. In 1912, Mr. Jones died and his daughter, Genevieve A. Jones, then attending Wellesley, left college and took charge of the business. On June 5, 1922, Miss Jones sold out to Mr. Joseph A. Hamstengel of the Rogers Palace Laundry Company.

George Lill Coal Co., wholesale and retail coal dealer, serves a vast territory in Chicago's north and northwest side districts. The Lill company was incorporated in 1882, with an authorized capital of $100,000. George Lill is president and William Lill vice-president and treasurer. Its main offices are situated at 1122-38 Berwyn av.

The Manz Engraving Co. introduced to the engraving industry the zinc process and the system of making half-tones. The company was founded in 1867 by Jacob Manz, a wood engraver. In 1880, Mr. Alfred Bersbach joined the firm and today is its president. Mr. F. D. Montgomery, one of the first to develop the halftone process, became a member in 1889. The Hollister Press was absorbed by the Manz company just before it moved to its present location at 4001-43 Ravenswood av. in 1908. From 500 to 600 men are employed at this plant.

F. H. McNulty & Co. has built up a nation-wide business in stocks and bonds. Today it has correspondents in every big city of the United States and a direct wire service from Chicago to New York. General offices are at 25 Broad st., New York City. Chicago offices are at 166 W. Jackson blvd.

The Meyercord Co. manufacturers decalcomania tranfers for industrial uses. In the 30 years of its existence the company has made great strides and today it has 40 branches throughout the universe. George Meyercord is president; J. C. Walker, vice-president; A. O. Johnson, vice-president. Main offices are at 133 W. Washington st.

The Midwest Hardware Co. furnishes quality finish hardware for buildings of all types. It is the distributor for Yale & Towne Manufacturing Co., Stamford, Conn., on Yale Builders' Hardware in Chicago. The company was formed in 1920, with George H. Hilgendorf, H. H. Walsh, L. W. Kent and W. D. Lewis each holding an equal share. Offices are located at 56 W. Randolph st.

The North Side Cleaners and Dyers Corporation, 5427 Broadway, was founded in 1910. Its branches are spread over Chicago and suburbs. Officers of the corporation are W. H. Fricke, president; W. C. Buhl, vice president; J. H. White, secretary; and W. P. Stroh, treasurer.

The Page Engineering Co. manufactures drag line machinery and excavating buckets. John W. Page is president and R. J. Barry secretary and treasurer. General offices are at 189 W. Madison st.

The Rathborne Hair & Ridgway Co. has been engaged in the manufacture of lumber and box and box shooks for forty years. Its territory is the middle west and east. B. F. Masters is the president. Its main offices and plant are located at 2279 S. Union st.

The W. C. Ritchie & Co., manufacturing paper boxes, fibre cans and mailing tubes, was formed in 1892, succeeding the Ritchie & Duck. The company has two factories in Chicago, 831 W. Van Buren st. and 89th st. and Baltimore av. R. C. Ritchie, son of the company's founder, W. H. Ritchie, who died in 1917, is president. Other officers are T. W. Ritchie, vice-president; K. H. Beattie, treasurer; C. T. Simpson, secretary. The board of directors is comprised of R. H. Ritchie, T. W. Ritchie, K. H. Beattie, C. T. Simpson and J. A. Stock.

Rogers Palace Laundry Company, 4856 Broadway, is known for the quality of work in all its departments. On June 5, 1922, the Rogers Palace Laundry took over the business of the Lakeview Laundry, formerly at 3018 N. Clark street. Joseph A. Hamstengel is the sole proprietor of both companies.

Mrs. Ora Snyder has achieved a national reputation in candy. Her chocolate delicacies are known in every city of the United States. Her first confectionery was made on a gas stove in the kitchen of her home. Today her stores are spread all over the loop. Mrs. Snyder's offices are at 121 N. Wabash ave. She is now preparing to open a seven-story building on Wabash ave. The whole building will be devoted exclusively to the sale and manufacture of candy.

Standard Glass Co., with general offices at 2533 Cottage Grove ave., manufactures glass for automobiles and furniture. The company was incorporated in 1900 and has enjoyed a steady growth. W. L. Eaton is president and E. G. Eaton is secretary and treasurer.

The Sumner Sollitt Co., contractors, was organized in 1899, succeeding the Ralph & Sumner Sollit Co. The company established a record in the war by building 86 buildings in eight days at Fort Sheridan. Officers of the company are Sumner Sollitt, president and treasurer; Grace Shannon Sollitt, vice-president; Oscar S. Johnson, assistant treasurer and secretary. Directors are Sumner Sollitt, Grace Shannon Sollitt, Oscar S. Johnson and Edward P. Strain. The company has general offices at 225 N. Michigan av.

The White-Home Laundry Company, with offices and plant at 4892 N. Clark st., represents a merger of all that was best of two leading laundry firms, each more than 20 years old. The consolidation was effected in 1918. Although the capital is fixed at $125,000, the company has $250,000 invested. Two

The Wieland Dairy Co. was founded in 1890 and incorporated in 1908, with an authorized capital of $500,000. Its business, which is confined to Chicago and Evanston, aggregates two million dollars a year. George C. Wieland is president, Charles J. Wieland, secretary and Fred A. Wieland, treasurer. Directors are George C. Wieland, Charles J. Wieland, Fred A. Wieland, Robert A. Wieland, William Wieland, Christopher H. Wieland. General Offices are at 3640-44 Broadway.

INDEX

295

www.ingramcontent.com/pod-product-compliance
Lightning Source LLC
LaVergne TN
LVHW011941060326
832903LV00045B/126